A DABHAND GUIDE

Ability & Ability Plus

GEOFF COX

The
Integrated
Power Tool
For the PC

DABS
PRESS

Ability & Ability Plus : A Dabhand Guide

To Edna Maud and William Henry Albert Cox

in their Golden Year

Written by Geoff Cox

© Dabs Press 1992

ISBN 1-870336-51-8

First Edition, first printing, May 1992

Edited by Robin Burton

Production by Janice Horrocks

Typeset by Andrew Wygladala. Cover design by David Wilson.

Set in 10 on 11 point Palatino

Published by Dabs Press, P O BOX 48, Prestwich, Manchester M25 7HF. Telephone 061-773 8632. Fax 061-773 8290.

Printed and bound in the UK by BPCC Wheaton, Exeter, EX2 8RP

Contents

11 : Advanced Database

12 : Built-in Functions

H : Spreadsheet Facilities 359

1: What Is Ability?

Ability combines wordprocessor, spreadsheet, database and communications software into a single, integrated software package. With Ability you can merge figures from a spreadsheet into a document and then use the database facilities to send it to selected people. If you wish, you can send graphs or documents over the telephone lines to other Ability users, or you can send telexes and electronic mail all over the world. You can use Ability with a mouse to make your computer more user friendly.

While it is an extremely powerful tool for both business and home, Ability is very easy to learn to use, even for those who have never used a computer before. This book will describe the features of Ability and show you how to get the best from the software. All of the examples have been chosen to illustrate real usage and to provide a basis for your own designs. The appendices cover basic computer operations together with the installation of Ability for your system and a brief review of the features of each application.

Ability and Ability Plus

Ability is available as two products, Ability and Ability Plus. While the two share many features there are some differences and Ability Plus has a number of additional capabilities. These are listed in Table 1.1 below. Throughout this book any differences will be highlighted by preceding each relevant section with a symbol indicating the product to which it applies.The symbol [A] indicates Ability, and the [A+] symbol indicates Ability Plus

Any features not so marked apply to both products.

There now follows a list of the additional features of Ability Plus module by module.

WRITE   Spelling Checker
Decimal Tabs
Super and Subscript
Double and Triple Line Spacing
Triple Line Headers
Set Top and Bottom Margins

Set Page Breaks
Create or Edit Printer drivers

DATABASE Virtual Joins
Multiple Relational Links
Links to other Modules
Database Size restricted only by disc space
Set
Picture
Mandatory Field Types

COMMUNICATE
XMODEM File Transfer

SCREEN EGA supported in addition to CGA
Horizontal or Vertical Windowing
View more than one file simultaneously

MACROS More powerful macro facilities

Table 1.1. Major Additional Features of Ability Plus

Versions

Software writers update products occasionally to include new features or to take advantage of new technology and this is true for Ability. Major features generally will remain unchanged but some details may be different from those given in this book or in the software manual. This book was written using Ability versions 1.2 and 1.2E and Ability Plus version 1.0. You will find additional information on your version of Ability in a WRITE file called READ_ME, and in the Help screens.

We'll now take a brief look at the main modules provided in Ability.

Wordprocessing

The major difference between typewriting and wordprocessing is that a typewriter prints onto paper, whereas a wordprocessor "prints" initially on a screen. This gives the advantage that you can correct the document before you commit it to paper. The principal disadvantage is that very short documents will take slightly longer to complete due to the separate typing and printing processes.

WYSIWYG and PTF

Wordprocessors are essentially one of two types, WYSIWYG (or What You See Is What You Get), or Print Time Formatted. WYSIWYG wordprocessors, like Ability, try to show on screen, as far as possible, what the printed page will look like. Print enhancements such as underline, boldface and italics are clearly seen on Graphics screens (See Appendix D). Text screens show print enhancements with a colour highlight.

Print Time Formatted wordprocessors may show a limited number of features on the screen and insert most effects and formats only when printing the document.

WRITE

WRITE is a WYSIWYG wordprocessor which allows you to include data from spreadsheets or database files to produce standard letters and to insert graphs in a document. You can also "import" text from other wordprocessors or even from other computers!

All of the printing facilities you would find on an expensive electronic typewriter are available to you. For example, you can embolden, underline, change typeface, auto-centre, indent and justify. Margins, tabs and page size can be set at variable positions and you can define headers and footers to be printed on each page automatically.

WRITE has facilities for moving, copying or deleting blocks of text.

[A+]
In addition, Ability Plus provides a spelling checker.

Ability Spreadsheet

Spreadsheets often seem to be surrounded by an air of difficulty, but far from being esoteric or complex, we all use them everyday. Railway timetables, price lists, job estimates and Income Tax forms are all examples of spreadsheets. If you can use a calculator you can use a spreadsheet and you will soon wonder how you ever managed without it!

The Ability spreadsheet provides a wide range of arithmetic and logical functions to allow quick and easy construction of sheets for many applications. In addition to the usual financial functions, mathematics and science are also well catered for.

[A+]
Ability Plus allows spreadsheets to be linked. This means that a change on one spreadsheet will be reflected through all related spreadsheets. For example, if you change the manufacturing cost of a part, the price of all items containing that part can be changed automatically in other, linked, spreadsheets.

[A+]
Ability Plus allows two spreadsheets to be viewed on screen at the same time by using the Window facility.

Ability DATABASE

A database is simply an organised collection of data, like a card index, Filofax, or a telephone directory. The major advantage of a computerised database is not the speed with which you can retrieve information, it may be quicker to consult a written list but that you can sort and correlate data quickly. If you need to store telephone numbers for a couple of hundred customers, use an address book! If you need to locate all companies employing less than 30 people in the West of England who are involved in concrete testing, you need a computerised database.

The Ability DATABASE lets you enter and store data in customised formats. The data can be searched, sorted or used to produce various reports. When used with WRITE the DATABASE is an extremely powerful marketing and organising tool, as it allows you to select the recipients of personalised mail based on many and variable conditions.

Ability COMMUNICATE

Has it ever seemed strange that in this world of satellite communications we still write to each other? Of course, we need a record of what was said but, if we look at the process, it is most inefficient.

1. Office A prepares a document with its wordprocessor.

2. Office A prints the document and posts it.

3. The postal authority puts the document through a number of sorting operations to ensure that it reaches Office B in due course (hopefully).

4. Office B reads the document.

If Office B needs to modify and send on the document, it must be retyped and follow steps 1 to 4 again.

Ability lets you dispense with steps 2 and 3 by sending the document from computer to computer directly along the normal telephone lines.

COMMUNICATE also allows you to exchange any other data with other computers. Some of these computers are designed for public access and contain useful information which you can obtain for a small fee. You can also acquire software or exchange messages with other users on some computers, while other systems provide telex and electronic mail facilities.

Ability PRESENTATION

PRESENTATION allows you to make screen copies of all or part of your Ability work. You can then, for example, assemble these "snapshots" and add pieces of music to produce computerised "Slide Shows". Very useful for meetings, presentations and exhibitions!

Getting Started

In the next chapter we will start to use Ability in earnest. If you haven't yet installed Ability on your computer, appendices A to E contain details on installing and setting up Ability for your system.

2 : The Library Screen

The Library screen is the heart of Ability. All Ability applications and files can be selected from the Library screen. You can also use the Library to delete, rename or copy files and to change directories or disc drives.

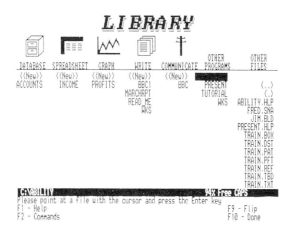

Figure 2.1 The Ability Library Screen

[A+]

If you have Ability Plus the Library screen is a little different:

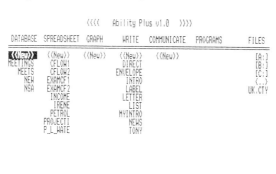

Figure 2.2. Ability Plus Library Screen

Starting Ability

To start Ability from a floppy disc system you should use a system disc with an AUTOEXEC.BAT file, as described in Appendix C. Press CTRL-ALT-DEL with the configured disc in Drive A:. After a pause you will see the Library screen.

If you have a hard disc wait till you get the:

    C>

prompt, then type:

    ABILITY

and then press the RETURN key. From now on, I will not mention the RETURN key. It should of course be pressed after typing in any command (other than single letter/number selections from lists and menus).

Changing Discs

If you have a floppy disc based system you will notice that Ability is spread over several discs. This means that you will need to change discs from time to time but Ability will prompt you when this is necessary. Disc changes vary with disc type and software version, so they will not be specified in this book.

Help

Ability has a comprehensive help system which is accessed by pressing F1. (F1 means function key 1 — one of the group of ten function keys on your PC, either at the left hand side or across the top of the keyboard). Help is context sensitive: in other words, the help you get refers to the menu and the application you are using. You always exit help by pressing ESC.

Applications

The Library screen is divided into seven columns across the screen. Five of these are headed by the names of the Ability applications:

    DATABASE

SPREADSHEET
GRAPH
WRITE
COMMUNICATE

The other two are headed PROGRAMS and FILES.

The PROGRAMS column contains programs that can be run independently of Ability.

The FILES column contains names of document or data files that were not prepared using Ability. Many of these could be imported to Ability, although some will be associated with the programs in the PROGRAM column.

Under each application column heading is a list of names, representing the files belonging to that particular application.

Files

At this point it is worth clarifying the term "file". If you write a letter and store it on disc, the contents of that letter become a file. In order to store the letter you must give it a name, the filename. This name is then used to read and write the file between disc and memory. Ability filenames can be up to eight characters long. Files and filenames are fully explained in Appendix A.

The Cursor

The Ability screen cursor appears as a large rectangle in the screen's foreground colour. To work on a file or run a program, position the cursor over the file or program name by using the mouse or cursor keys.

Status Line

Four lines above the bottom of the screen is a band of foreground colour, the Status Line. This displays, in the Library screen, the current drive and directory on the left and the amount of system memory free on the right. Further to the right on the Status Line is the Keyboard Status area. This shows whether CAPS LOCK or NUM LOCK is currently selected.

Command Area

Below the `Status Line` is the Command area. The top line of this usually carries either a brief instruction on what to do next, or a request for more information. The next two lines of the command area show the function keys currently available.

Keyboard Keys

As much of this book will describe pressing keys on the keyboard we could easily confuse instructions and keypresses. For example, `F10` could mean type F-1-0 or press function key ten. To save confusion, any keyboard key with a "name" rather than representing just a single letter is always denoted in capitals, in a slightly smaller typeface ie, `ESC, RETURN, ALT` and so on.

Other keys will be indicated by either the legend engraved on the key or by the meaning, whichever is clearest. Keyboards do differ a little from machine to machine, so the text may not exactly reflect the engraving on your key. The meaning should be obvious but a few equivalents are listed below.

```
ESC              ESCAPE
INS              INSERT
DEL              DELETE
RET              RETURN
Broad up arrow   SHIFT
```

Simultaneous Keypresses

Occasionally, it will be necessary to press two or more keys simultaneously. In this case, the keys to be pressed will be linked by a hyphen:

> `CTRL-E` means press `CTRL` and E together

> `ALT-F2` means press `ALT` and F2 together

Duplicate Keys

There are some key duplications in Ability. Most noticeable are:

> `*,+,-,1,2,3,4,5,6,7,8,9,0`

Numbers can be obtained from the right-hand group of keys by pressing NUM LOCK, or holding down one of the two SHIFT keys while pressing the appropriate key, by using the typewriter keyboard. In most cases it is the character represented by the key that is important, not the actual key pressed to obtain it. The one exception is the + key on the extreme right of the keyboard. This can only be used as a normal key when the snapshot facility is not in use.

The more useful duplicated keys are:

Editing Keys	Mouse equivalent	Control & Letter
CURSOR LEFT	move mouse left	CTRL-S
CURSOR RIGHT	move mouse right	CTRL-D
CURSOR UP	move mouse up	CTRL-E
CURSOR DOWN	move mouse down	CTRL-X
RETURN	left mouse button	
ESC	right mouse button	
ENTER		RETURN
PgUp		CTRL-R
PgDn		CTRL-C
CTRL-left arrow		CTRL-A
CTRL-right arrow		CTRL-F

Table 2.1. Cursor Key Equivalents.

Function Keys

Ability uses all ten function keys, although not all are used in each application. The Command area shows which keys are currently available. Where a function key is used in more than one application it performs the same, or a similar, purpose in each. Some function keys carry sub-menus which may change with the application.

The meaning of each of the ten function keys is shown below.

Key	Meaning	Key	Meaning
F1	Help	F2	Commands
F3	Goto	F4	Edit Field
F5	Pick Up	F6	Put Down
F7	Shade	F8	Calc/Draw
F9	Flip	F10	Done

F1

Gives help, if the ABILITY.HLP file is installed either on a hard disc or on the current path (in the current directory or one listed in the MS-DOS PATH directive). If you are running Ability on a floppy disc system, to use the Help you may need to swap discs or to perform the special installation described in Appendix C.

ESCAPE returns you to the Library screen from the Help system. The following two sections describe specific differences between Ability and Ability Plus.

Ability Specifics

F2 [A]

Gives a menu of commands:

Put-away	Remove a file from memory
Active-drive	Change the disc drive
Directory	Create, erase, or change
Erase	Erase the current file
Rename	Rename the current file
Copy	Copy the current file
File-stats	Check the size of a file and the time written
Other	More commands, as shown below:
Print	Print a file
Snapshot	Create a snapshot library
Macros	View/change keyboard macros
Devices	Set up printer, plotter or screen
Run	Run a program
Use Dos	Escape to Dos

Type EXIT to return to Ability

Macros will be covered in detail in a later chapter and the Devices screen is detailed in Appendix D. Two of the "other" sub-commands also carry further sub menus. These are:

Directory

Other (Print option)

The `Directory` sub menu covers directory handling, allowing you to change directories.

The `Print` sub menu allows you to set up the print format for your document, as follows:

Go	Print now
To-File	Make an ASCII file or send to the printer
First-Page	First page to print
Cpi	Set character spacing
Range	Select whole file or a range of pages
Paper	Single sheet or continuous paper
Sideways	Print sideways or upright
	(NB. Sideways print is available only on a dot-matrix printer)

Positioning the cursor on a command causes a brief command description to appear on the bottom line of the command area.

Pressing ESCAPE cancels the command.

Pressing RETURN accepts the command.

F9 [A]

If you press this key the screen "flips", changes colour and the word FLIP appears on the right-hand end of the status line. F9 provides a convenient way to flip between different Ability applications or files. Pressing F9 a second time returns you to the original screen.

F10 [A]

Lets you return permanently to DOS, ending the Ability session.

[A+] Ability Plus Specifics
Ability Plus allows a few additional commands from the Library, listed below. If you have Ability, skip ahead to the [A] [A+] symbol.

F2 [A+]

Has a menu of commands:

Ability	Support features
Print	Print a file
Snapshot	Create a snapshot library
Dos	Use DOS or other programs
File	File utilities
Quit	Return to Dos

Four of the commands, Ability, Print, DOS and File, produce additional sub-menus, as follows:

Ability Sub Menu

Three functions are available:

Macros	View/change keyboard macros
Devices	Set up printer, plotter or screen
Library	Change Library screen settings

We will deal with Macros in a later chapter and the Devices screen is detailed in Appendix D.

The Library screen allows you to change the title and to specify the types of files you can import and export. Importing of files is automatic. Ability Plus detects the file types shown below and translates them accordingly.

You can translate Ability Plus Files into files for other software. Select the required application with the cursor and press RETURN to choose one of the options.

When you have made your selections, press F10 to return to the library.

DATABASE dBase II
            dBase III (and dBaseIII Plus)
            PFS
            Enable
            Comma separated ASCII list

SPREADSHEET
            DIF

Lotus 1-2-3 v1A

WRITE   Wordstar
PeachText
Multimate
ASCII (Wordstar non-document)

Release 1.0 also allows you to define Country settings and Field formats, as shown below.

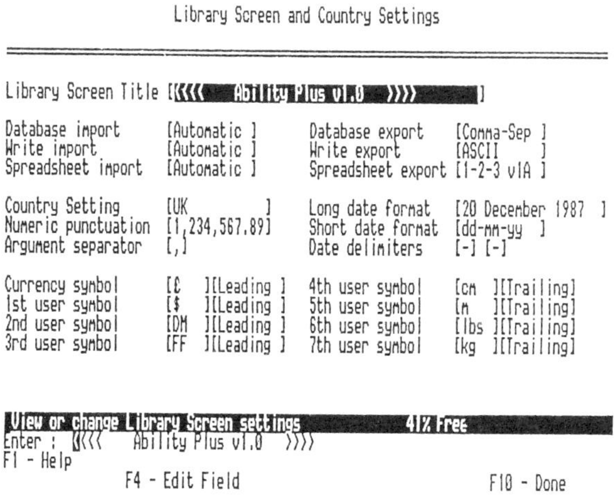

```
                   Library Screen and Country Settings

═══════════════════════════════════════════════════════════
───────────────────────────────────────────────────────────

Library Screen Title [((((   Ability Plus v1.0   ))))        ]

Database import      [Automatic ]   Database export    [Comma-Sep ]
Write import         [Automatic ]   Write export       [ASCII     ]
Spreadsheet import   [Automatic ]   Spreadsheet export [1-2-3 v1A ]

Country Setting      [UK        ]   Long date format   [20 December 1987 ]
Numeric punctuation  [1,234,567.89]  Short date format [dd-mm-yy  ]
Argument separator   [,]             Date delimiters   [-] [-]

Currency symbol   [£  ][Leading ]  4th user symbol   [cm ][Trailing]
1st user symbol   [$  ][Leading ]  5th user symbol   [n  ][Trailing]
2nd user symbol   [DM ][Leading ]  6th user symbol   [lbs][Trailing]
3rd user symbol   [FF ][Leading ]  7th user symbol   [kg ][Trailing]


View or change Library Screen settings         41% Free
Enter : [(((   Ability Plus v1.0   ))))
F1 - Help
              F4 - Edit Field                        F10 - Done
```
Figure 2.3. Library and Country Screen

The Numeric punctuation field determines how a number is displayed. Three formats are available:

```
123.456.789,00
123 456 789,00
123,456,789.00
```

The third option is the one most often used in English. Pressing RETURN chooses one of the three.

The argument separator is automatically set by Ability Plus.

The Date Format fields toggle between a number of options. The Long Date Format prints the month and year in full. The Short Date Format selects an all figure date using the delimiter specified

35

by the `Date Delimiter` field. Once again RETURN chooses between the options.

The `Currency Symbol` field allows you to enter a single character. This will be used on the screen where $ is shown in the Format menus. Note that the $ sign in the menus will not change, whatever the currency setting.

The remaining user fields are used for user `Symbol Formats`. Define the characters, then toggle between leading or trailing for the positioning of them.

File sub menu

`Put-away`	Remove a file from memory
`Active-drive`	Change the disc drive
`Directory`	Create, erase, or change
`Erase`	Erase the current file
`Rename`	Rename the current file
`Copy`	Copy the current file
`Stats`	Check the size of a file and the time written

Print sub menu

`Go`	Print now
`To-File`	Make an ASCII file or send to the printer
`New-Page`	Send a form feed
`Line`	Send a line feed
`First-Page`	First page to print
`Cpi`	Set character spacing
`Range`	Select whole file or a range of pages
`Paper`	Single sheet or continuous paper
`Sideways`	Print sideways or upright

Quality	Draft or Final quality

Dos sub menu

Run	Run a program
Use-Dos	Escape to Dos temporarily
	Type EXIT RETURN to return to Ability Plus

F3

This key allows you to find a file in a particular column. Type the name of the file you want and Ability Plus will find it. You must be exact with spellings and wildcards aren't allowed.

F5

This used in conjunction with F6 to import or export files. This process is dealt with in a later chapter.

F9

This key "flips" the screen between Ability applications. The screen colour changes and the word FLIP appears on the status line. The two flip screens are independent and files can be opened in either or both.

F10

Done. Offers you the opportunity to return permanently to DOS, ending the Ability session.

[A] [A+]

Selecting a Command from a Menu

The cursor can be positioned on a command by:

> Using the mouse
> Using the cursor keys
> Typing the initial letter of the command

The last of these is much faster once you have mastered the basics of Ability.

Pressing the appropriate function key displays a menu in the Command area. You can select from this menu by positioning the cursor. If you make a mistake, press the ESC key to cancel.

Let's try temporarily returning to DOS.

[A]

```
F2 OU
```

[A+]
```
F2 DU
```

You should now see the standard DOS prompt. Type DIR and you should see a list of files in the current directory. Type EXIT to return to the Library. Note that you can either use the cursor keys or the initial letter to select command options.

Moving Around the Library

The cursor may be moved to any part of the screen above the Status Line. There are two methods of moving the cursor, the cursor movement keys or a mouse. When using the cursor keys the ENTER or RETURN key selects a file or a program, the ESCAPE key cancels some functions and most commands.

The Amstrad mouse works very well but its movement is a little coarse. Setting the X and Y scaling parameters to 20 using the NVR program is recommended. If you use the mouse the left-hand (or finger) button is "SELECT" and the right-hand "CANCEL".

Selecting an Application

You will notice that the Library screen is arranged as a series of columns, one for each application. You select an application by positioning the cursor over a filename in the correct column and pressing RETURN or the left-hand mouse button. If you need to create a new file, simply select NEW in the appropriate column.

In order to demonstrate this, we will take a look at a WRITE file and learn a little more about your version of Ability into the bargain. Move the cursor to the WRITE column and look for a file called READ_ME.

Select this file by pressing RETURN (or ENTER or the left-hand mouse button). The screen will change and you will see something like this:

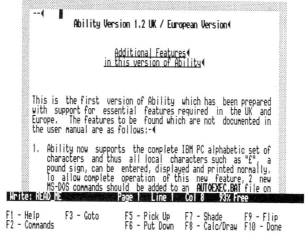

Figure 2.4. READ_ME FILE

Now you can use the cursor arrow keys, with Pg Dn, Pg Up, Home and End to move through and read the file. This document normally contains the latest information on your version of Ability, so it is worth spending a few minutes reading through it.

When you have finished, press F10 to return to the Library.

Files in Memory

If you look at the WRITE column you will notice that the file READ_ME is now marked with an asterisk. This denotes that the file is now in memory. These files are read much faster than files on disc. On a hard disc machine file reading time is reduced by 50% or more.

When a file has been loaded, the Status Line will show the figure for remaining free memory, to reflect the space used by the file stored in memory.

3: WRITE

Perhaps the most important thing you will want to do with Ability is to transfer text, whether a letter, a report, or even a book, to paper. The Ability application module that does this is called WRITE.

The best way to learn about WRITE is to use it, so if you are not sitting in front of your keyboard with the Library screen in front of you, adjourn to the computer, start Ability, and get to the Library screen.

Starting a Document

Move the cursor to New under the WRITE column and press RETURN. When you see the prompt:

        Please enter the name of the new file

enter:

        MYFILE

Now type the following but do NOT press RETURN:

        Thank you for your enquiry, enclosed please find
        details of our complete range of pressure testing
        equipment

The screen should now look like this:

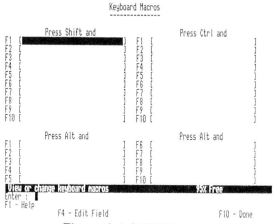

Figure 3.1. WRITE screen

Notice that, although you didn't press RETURN, the line is split between "our" and "complete". This is called word-wrap and it means that you don't have to worry about pressing RETURN or fitting words into the line as Ability does it all for you.

We will now extend the document by adding two new paragraphs. Move the cursor to the end of the document by pressing CTRL–END, then press RETURN twice and type the following. Press the appropriate key wherever you see RETURN in the text.

```
As requested we are enclosing a quotation for our
Supertest system.RETURN-RETURNWe hope that the
quotation meets with your approval and look
forward toreceiving yourformal purchase order in
the near future.RETURN-RETURNYours
faithfullyRETURN-RETURN-RETURNFred Bloggs.RETURN
```

You should now have a screen that looks like this:

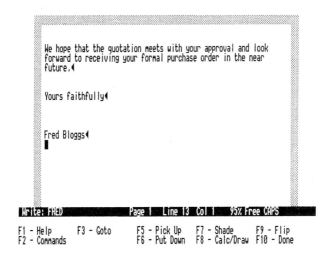

Figure 3.2. Extended Letter

Characters

Now we have entered some text the time has come to look at a little theory.

We all know the alphanumeric characters A-Z, a-z and 0-9, and we've all used punctuation marks, brackets etc. These are all known as characters. In fact your computer can handle 256 different characters. Half of this number includes all the letters, punctuation and numbers you use in typing; the other half consists of special characters seldom used in wordprocessing, so we can ignore them.

Computers represent all characters internally, on disc or in memory, as numbers. It greatly simplifies matters if the number your computer recognises as capital A is the same as that recognised by any other computer and is the same number your printer uses when it prints an A. The American Standard Code for Information Interchange (ASCII) is the standard most often used by micro-computers. Of the first 128 ASCII characters, 95 are "printable" characters: these are the letters, figures and punctuation. There are also 32 "control" characters, which control the screen and cursor. These can often be invoked by pressing a key with the CTRL key held down at the same time.

The control characters most used in wordprocessing are:

> CURSOR KEYS
> INSERT
> DELETE LEFT
> TAB
> CARRIAGE RETURN

These are represented by special keys on the keyboard and can also be obtained with CTRL-KEY combinations. DELETE is also a control character but it can't be obtained using CTRL-KEY.

It is important to remember that all characters used in wordprocessing can be deleted. If you delete a Carriage Return, all the text below it in the document moves up one line. Similarly, if you insert a RETURN, all the text below moves down one line.

The word RETURN is a bit misleading. In theory all a Carriage Return does is to move the cursor back to the beginning of the current line. To move the cursor down a line you need a Line Feed (LF) character. In common with most wordprocessors, Ability interprets a RETURN as two commands, Carriage Return (CR) and Line Feed (LF). The way this is done varies between different wordprocessors and is one of the reasons why special import and export programs are needed to convert between formats.

Spaces and Returns

There are two types of `Carriage Return` in wordprocessing. These are hard `Carriage Returns`, which are typed in by the writer, and soft carriage returns, such as the one between "our" and "complete", which are inserted by the wordprocessor. The latter will be changed if you alter the page width, the former won't. Spaces will be inserted by the wordprocessor if you request a straight right margin. These spaces are called soft spaces and they too will change if you alter the length of a line. Spaces you insert using the space bar are called hard spaces. They never change unless you delete them.

Return Marker

It is useful to see where you have put in a carriage return and where the wordprocessor has added one. Ability marks a hard `Carriage Return` with a little triangle on the screen. There is always a hard carriage return at the end of the document.

Page Boundary

The shaded area you can see on the screen marks the limits of the printed page. Think of it as a border round a sheet of paper. If you go over the edge, you either need a bigger "sheet" or another page. We will deal with this further in Chapter Seven.

The Status Line

The status line shows, from the left, the application name, in this case WRITE, the Filename, the Page, Line and Column number. Next is the amount of free memory, `CAPS LOCK, NUM LOCK` and `FLIP`.

Moving Around

There are two levels of cursor movement. Smallest are those obtained by using the cursor keys alone, while amplified movements are obtained by using the `CTRL` key with a cursor key. Cursor movements are as follows:

> The four arrow keys move the cursor one character or one line at a time in the direction of the arrow.

The left and right arrow keys move one word when used with the CTRL key. The up and down arrow keys have no effect with CTRL.

HOME and END move the cursor to the beginning and end of the current line. When used with the CTRL key the movement is to the beginning or end of the current document.

PgUp and PgDn move the cursor up or down one screenful (about 21 lines). When used with the CTRL key the cursor is moved up or down to the top of the nearest page. In this case the page is the printer page, not a screenful.

Over-typing

Let's change the word "equipment" to "instrumentation". There are a number of ways to do this: we will use the simplest.

Move the cursor to the first e of equipment and type:

```
instrumentation
```

Insert

We'll add a couple of words to the above sentence. Move the cursor to e of enquiry and press INS. The screen should now look like this:

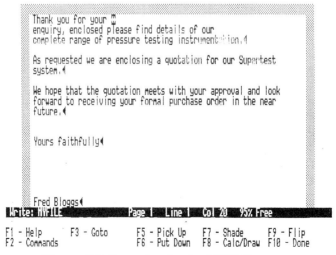

Figure 3.3. Inserting in the WRITE screen

Add the words:

```
recent enquiry which was received from 'Stress
Weekly'
```

Now press INS again to close up the text. Ability is intelligent enough to realise that you normally wouldn't want to move through the text whilst inserting so, if you press any cursor key, the text will close up automatically.

Delete

You will see that this has left us with a superfluous word that we must delete. Move the cursor to the comma following the second "enquiry". Press the DEL left arrow key once (if you hold the key down the keyboard will treat this as a series of keypresses). The "y" should vanish and the text will close up. You can obviously delete the whole word this way but there is a better method. Move the cursor to the e of enquiry and press DEL. As you can see, we have two methods of deleting:

DEL   Deletes the letter under the cursor

DEL LEFT   Deletes the character to the left of the cursor

If you need to delete a word or two hold the DEL or DEL LEFT key down. For larger blocks of text there is a third method of deleting which is a lot quicker.

Shading — Block Operations

If you look at the Command line you will see that F7 is the SHADE key. This is used to mark a part of the text for a subsequent move, delete or copy. To illustrate this, move the cursor to the first e of "enclosed" on the second line. Press F7 and move the cursor to the space at the end of the word.

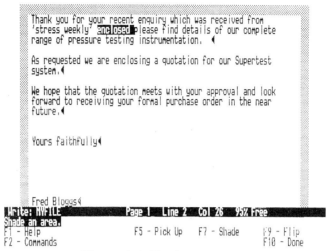

Figure 3.4. Shading a word

Press DEL, the word will disappear and the text closes up.

Obviously you can delete any shaded area and the shaded area can be as long or short as you wish. The cursor movement keys are used to move to the start and then the end of the block to be marked.

Moving Text

Move the cursor to the d of "details" on the second line. Press F6 and the deleted word is inserted again. This process is known as undeleting and is the method used to move text. Note, however, that you can only move the last deleted text.

You can undelete a single character by pressing F6 to re-instate the last deleted character if only one character was deleted.

Copying

A variation of this process allows you to copy text. Shade a block of text but instead of pressing DEL, press F5-Pick Up. The shaded area remains but if you move the cursor to a new location and press F6 a second copy of the shaded block will be made, leaving the original in place.

Load and Save

One of the nice things about wordprocessing is that you can write a number of paragraphs to suit common situations, then merge them together to make a complete document. These paragraphs, called `Boiler Plates`, can be called into any document by the `Load` command, available via the `F2` key.

When completed, the new document can be saved to another file, if required, by using the `Save` command from the `F2 Files` menu.

[A+]
A shaded block of text can be saved to a file using the Ability Plus `Block Save` command, which is found on the `F2 Files` menu.

`Load` may also be used to import ASCII files into WRITE.

Saving the Document

Once you have finished editing you must save the document to disc. If you don't do this all your hard work will disappear when you turn off the power! To avoid this, press `F10`. The document will be saved and you will return to the `Library` screen.

Help Yourself

You now know all the basics of the WRITE wordprocessor. You can enter and edit text, move, delete, copy, load and save. Now is the time for you to review these operations using our test file. Tidy it up, correct the punctuation, capitalise the magazine name and generally practise the things you have learnt until you are quite familiar with them.

When you have finished, press `F10`. This will exit WRITE and also automatically save the document in a single operation.

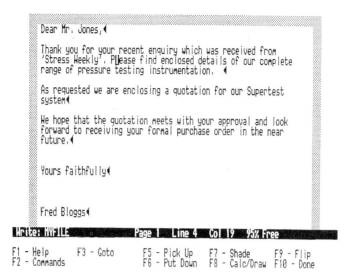

Figure 3.5. Completed WRITE document

4 : WRITE More

In the last chapter we examined the basics of wordprocessing using WRITE. In this chapter we will take a look at some more useful functions.

Search and Replace

We previously edited the `MYFILE` document by inserting and over-typing. This is fine for a short document, but what about those twenty page reports where you find you have spelt a name incorrectly? Forget the correcting fluid and photocopier. This is wordprocessing: you can correct your text directly.

To practise editing, first get the MYFILE document on the screen.

Press `F3-Goto`. You are given a choice:

```
Find Pattern
Page
```

In this case select `Find Pattern`. You will be offered another choice:

```
Search
Replace
```

Select `Replace` and type in the text to search for:

```
faithfully
```

Now you are asked for replacement text, so type in:

```
sincerely
```

The cursor will move to the first occurrence of the word "faithfully" and you will be given a choice:

`Fix`	Change this occurrence and move onto the next
`Skip`	Ignore this and go to the next occurrence
`Remainder`	Replace this and all remaining occurrences

[A+]

Ability Plus does not have the `Skip` option. This has been replaced with the `Next` option which is identical in meaning.

This time we select `Fix`. The word will be changed and a message will be displayed saying that Ability can find no more occurrences of the search text.

Press `ESC` to exit the `Search` and `Replace`.

Let's try a little experiment. Follow the procedure outlined above and try to replace the letters **re** with **nz**.

Did it work — do words like received now read nzceived? No!

This teaches us an important lesson. Ability searches for whole words only. Plurals and words with suffixes or prefixes are ignored in the search. Remember this when changing documents that may contain these extensions or variations to the search argument supplied.

Experiment a little more and you will find the following rules apply:

- Ability searches for whole words only

- If the search pattern is all in lower case letters, all patterns will be found; if one or more capital letters are included in the search pattern, only those patterns with capitals in the same places will be recognised.

- Ability searches from the current cursor position forwards to the end of the text. Patterns above the cursor are ignored.

- No matter how you experiment you cannot damage the machine!

Search

You may wish to find a specific word or group of words without doing a replacement. To do this press `PgUp` followed by `F3`. Once again you are given a choice:

```
Find Pattern
Page
```

In this case select `Find Pattern` and you will get another choice:

```
Search
Replace
```

Choose `Search` and you will be asked for the pattern to search for. Type:

```
your
```

The `Command` line will show:

```
Next            Previous
```

Select `Next` and the cursor will move to the first occurrence of "your". The command line will ask if you want to continue the search with the next or previous occurrence. Select `Next` again: the cursor moves to the next occurrence. For a change now select `Previous`: the cursor moves back to the previous find.

Press `ESC` to exit search and press `PgDn` to get to the end of the document. Press:

```
F3 RETURN RETURN RETURN
```

to return to the search from the end of the file. This time selecting `Next` causes a beep and the message:

```
No more occurrences searching forward
```

Try selecting `Previous`: the cursor moves to the last occurrence of "your" in the document.

Press `ESC` to end the search.

Wildcards

You may need to search for a number of similar words or, perhaps, words with spellings you are unsure of. Ability to the rescue again! You can insert a `Wildcard` in the search pattern. Ability will match all patterns with the `Wildcard`. You are very strongly advised not to use this facility in `Find` and `Replace` when using the `Replace Remainder` option. You could get some very odd replacements! Ability recognises the same wildcards as MS-DOS, PC-DOS, CP/M, DOS+ and BBC DOS:

> ?   replaces a single unspecified character

    *   replaces zero or more unspecified characters

Let's try it out on MYFILE.

Press PgUp to get to the top of the file then press F3. Select Find Pattern and Search, and type in the following:

    re*

From the menu select Next and the cursor will move to "recent". Next again takes the cursor to "received" and so on.

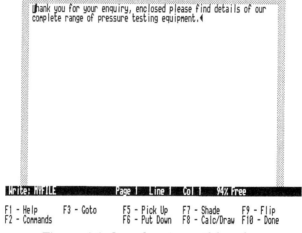

Figure 4.1. Search using wildcard

Try pressing PgUp to get back to the top of the document and searching first for th? then for th*. Do you see the difference? * matches any number of characters, but ? only matches a single character in the specified position.

Search for a Page

To find a page simply press F3 and select Page. You will be prompted to enter a page number. Enter any number and either the cursor will move to the top of that page or the computer will beep to tell you that the page number is too high.

The maximum page number depends on a number of factors like the page length and quantity of text so, in practice, this maximum will depend on the file you are working on.

We looked at the process of shading using F7 in the previous chapter. We will now look at its use in conjunction with F9 — the Flip key.

Press F9 and the screen will change colour. You will see the Library screen and the word "Flip" on the right of the Status Line.

Select another file in the WRITE column. I will use READ_ME but don't worry if your file is different.

Figure 4.2 Flip Screen

When you have the selected document on your screen shade the first paragraph.

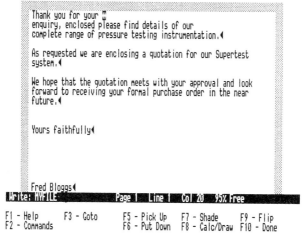

Figure 4.3. Shading Part of Flip Document

Press F5 to Pick-Up the first paragraph of the Flip document, then press F9 again to Flip back to MYFILE.

Move the cursor to the end of the document and press F6 to Put-Down the text.

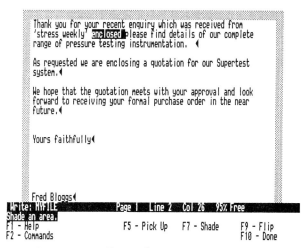

Figure 4.4. Copied Text in MYFILE

You can use this to "steal" parts of one file to use in another or you can prepare a file of standard paragraphs and copy the appropriate ones to make a new document.

Delete the paragraph you have just copied.

[A+]

Windows

Ability Plus users have a bonus — Windows. Using Windows it is possible to have two documents on the screen at the same time.

To demonstrate the use of Windows go to the WRITE column and select MYFILE again. Press F9 to Flip the screen and select another file. Once again I'll use READ_ME. Press F9 to return to the original screen and press F2, select WRITE and Window. You should now have the following menu:

```
Vertical
Horizontal
Sync
```

```
Unsync
Clear
```

Select Horizontal. A horizontal bar will appear across the centre of the screen. Move this to a convenient point using the cursor keys and press RETURN. You should now see the following:

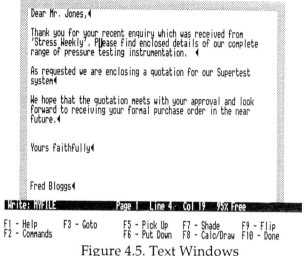

Figure 4.5. Text Windows

You can work on either document simply by pressing F9 to move the cursor into the appropriate window. Ability Plus treats each Window as a separate Flip state, so all functions are available for each Window.

To restore to one Window select the Clear option from the Windows menu. The currently selected Flip state will then become the single Window.

If you select a Vertical split for the windows you can synchronise the scrolling of the two windows by using the Sync option from the Windows menu. Unsync reverses this. It does not seem to be possible to synchronise scrolling in horizontal windows in the current software release.

Importing Data

You can just as easily add data from a spreadsheet by using F9 to Flip the screen and opening the appropriate spreadsheet. Shade the area of the sheet that you want to copy and press F5 to Pick-up. Flip the screen again and position the cursor where you want the data to go, then press F6 to put it into the document. This method copies the information as text, so you can then edit it as you wish.

An alternative method copies a part of a spreadsheet to the document. If you change either the spreadsheet or the part you copied to the document, the other version will also change.

To perform this minor miracle press:

[A]

> F2-S

[A+]

> F2-IS

and enter the name of the spreadsheet you want to use. If you want a new spreadsheet area simply type in a new name or use the one provided by Ability.

You will be asked to Shade part of the spreadsheet or to select the whole sheet. When you have done this, and made any adjustments you wish, press F10 to enter the data into the document. You will see that the page border changes colour to indicate an imported area from a different application.

Graphs may be entered in a similar fashion from the same menu. In this case, only the whole graph can be copied.

Data may also be obtained by WRITE from a database. This is explained in detail in Chapter Six.

[A+]

Exporting Files

Ability allows you to export files to other software. Exported files are placed in the Files column of the Library screen. To export files you must set up the translation parameter in the Library menu. You have a choice of formats as follows:

```
ASCII or Wordstar non-document files
Peachtree document files
Multimate document files
```

Exporting files is simply a matter of positioning the cursor over the appropriate WRITE file and pressing:

```
F5
```

The name of the file will appear in the command area. Now move the cursor to the Files column and press:

```
F6
```

You may put the file down on any drive, the current directory or the root directory.

Putting down the file automatically translates it.

[A+]

Importing Files

Import file translation is automatic. All you do is to position the cursor over the filename in the Library files column. Press:

```
F5
```

then move to the appropriate application and press:

```
F6
```

to import and translate the file.

If you attempt to import a file into an unsuitable location, Ability will produce an error message.

Fields

A powerful feature of Ability is the use of Fields. Fields are defined areas that can contain data, formulas, text or references to spreadsheets, or database fields.

Many wordprocesors allow you to add columns of figures or merge names or other data from files. WRITE, as part of Ability, allows you to use data from other Ability applications in your documents. You can use `Fields` to generate specialist mail containing financial or marketing information. You can perform mathematical operations on numeric data to produce technical reports or financial summaries.

We dealt very briefly with SPREADSHEET and DATABASE earlier. Some of the fields you may want to use can contain or refer to data from either or both of these applications. If you are not familiar with these applications please be patient: all will be revealed later!

To illustrate the use of `Fields,` return to the `Library` screen and open a new file called FIELDS.

With the cursor on the first line of the new document, start a field by typing the following, using command initial letters as before:

[A]

        F2-F

[A+]

        F2-IF

Now we need to define the `Field` contents. We will start with the date and to do this we use the built in function `TODAY()`.

Type +TODAY(), press RETURN and you will see a number appear in the field. This is the number of days since 31st December 1899! Not a very useful facility you may think, but the date can be presented in a number of different formats. You are seeing the default format, which is the way Ability stores dates. Although this may seem a little odd, it does allow the date to be treated in the same way as any other number in a database. You may search for records on a date basis and can use the date in formulas. You can define dates to be displayed in text form in long or short formats.

[A]

Ability allows the following formats:

        American (03/25/87)
        European (25-03-87)
        Metric (87-03-25)

Long (March 25, 1987)

[A+]

Ability Plus allows two formats — Long and Short. These are defined using the Library screen. The Long Date format prints the month and year in full. The Short Date format selects an all figure date using the delimiter specified by the Date Delimiter field in the Library screen. Once again RETURN chooses between the various options.

To illustrate these functions, let's return to the Fields document.

With the cursor on the field containing the TODAY function, press F4 and select Date. From this menu select Long and press RETURN. Press ESC to eventually return you to the edit screen.

Move the cursor down two spaces and open a new Field. Enter:

    100

as the contents.

This time press F4 and select Name to name the field. Enter the name as:

    FIRST

Move the cursor down two spaces and open a new Field. Enter:

    200

as the contents.

Press F4 and select Name. Enter the name as:

    SECOND

Move the cursor down two spaces and open a new Field. Enter:

    +FIRST+SECOND

as the contents.

Press F4 and name the field TOTAL. You should see an error message telling you that TOTAL is the name of a function. Insert an underline in front of the name and all should be well. The Field `TOTAL` now contains the sum of the contents of `FIRST` and `SECOND`.

`Total` is a built in function and Ability does not allow you to use function names as fieldnames. The above example, adding an underline, illustrates a useful method of avoiding name conflicts.

There are a large number of built in functions in both Ability and Ability Plus. These functions can be used in fields in any application. To avoid repetition, I have detailed them all in Chapter 11.

Field Contents

You can perform arithmetic on fields, both in the way shown above or by using a mixture of field references, built in functions and numbers. For example, if you need to calculate a discount of, say, 11%, you can start a `Field` called `DISCOUNT` and enter `11/100*TOTAL`. Alternatively, you can use built in function and enter `11%*TOTAL` in the field. Both of these produce the same result.

Commas

Commas have a special meaning in Ability and Ability Plus as they define items in a list. If you use a comma when entering a number you will get an error:

```
[.........]
```
To correct this, you should retype the number without the comma.

Spreadsheet Fields

`Fields` can also contain references to data in Ability spreadsheets. If you have a field called `PRICE` in a spreadsheet called `MATERIALS` then you can refer to it in a field in the WRITE document by entering `+MATERIALS\FIELD`. Now if the value in the spreadsheet changes, so will the value in your document. What can you use this for? Suppose you produce a price list using a spreadsheet (the best way). You can then produce a series of standard quotations, or even standard part quotations, using WRITE. Field references to the price list can be included and you can do all the mathematics in the spreadsheet document. When you update the spreadsheet price list, all your WRITE quotations are automatically updated.

Fieldnames

Fieldnames can be up to 13 characters long but the first three characters must be either letters or underscore characters ("_"). You cannot assign the same name to more than one field nor, as we've seen, can function names be used. Ability ignores the case of letters so "fred" and "FRED" will be regarded as identical.

5: Getting it on Paper

We have spent the last two chapters looking at some of the features of the Ability Wordprocessor, WRITE. You should now be able to enter a simple document onto the screen and then save it to disc. You can send the text over the telephone lines, copy it onto a blank disc and post it or, as there are still a few old-fashioned people in the world, print it on paper. The first step you need to take before printing is to make sure that Ability knows about the type of printer you have, and that its driver is correctly installed for Ability. If you are unsure of how to do this, check in Appendices D and E.

You can print a document from either the `Library` screen or the WRITE screen. In either case the procedure is the same. If you choose to print from the `Library` screen the document you want will be loaded into memory prior to printing.

Print Options

Ability has a number of print options. To see them:

[A]
Select `Print` from the `F2 Other` menu.

[A+]
Select `Print` from the `F2` menu.

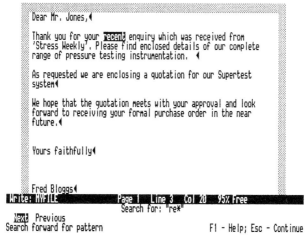

Figure 5.1. Printing menu

You will see a menu with a number of options:

Go	Start Printing now
To-File	Print destination menu
Printer	Print file on Printer.
File	This will produce an ASCII file on disc that you can send to people who don't have Ability. You will have to supply a name for the ASCII file.
First-page	Enter the number of the first page to be printed.
Cpi	Select the character size menu.
Pica	10 characters per inch
Elite	12 characters per inch
Condensed	Condensed print size
Range	Pages or whole file menu
Pages	Enter the numbers of the first and last pages to print.
All	Print whole file
Paper	Select paper type
Continuous	Fan fold paper
Single	Single sheet paper
Sideways	Print file upright or sideways
Sideways	Print file sideways
Upright	Print file upright

Printing to a file is a good way of overcoming the incompatibilities of various wordprocessors. All wordprocessors that I am familiar with can accept ASCII files.

Sideways printing is very useful for very wide files like spreadsheets and charts. The file is printed sideways down the paper. This option is not suitable for daisy-wheel printers because of the way they work. If you use this option on a dot-matrix printer, you will find that printing is much slower than normal. This is because sideways printing uses the graphics mode of the printer.

If you print a long document, only to find that you have a mistake on one page, you need not re-print the whole document. The Ability Range option lets you print one, several or all pages from the document. When part of the file is printed Ability keeps the page numbers correctly in sequence.

Selecting the number of the first page to print by using the First-page option also allows you to print long documents in sections. If you write a book remember that new chapters always start on odd numbered pages.

[A+]
Ability Plus has three additional options:

New-Page	Moves the paper to the top of the next page. This is done by sending a form feed command to the printer. If the paper does not feed to the top of the next sheet, check that the form length is set properly by the printer Dip switches and that the printer was at the top of a page when you began. Adjust the paper manually, if necessary, to the correct position.
Line	Move paper up one line only.
Quality	Quality Menu
Final	Best quality the printer can do.
Draft	Print as fast as possible.

Quality only applies to dot-matrix printers with NLQ or LQ facilities. If the printer does not have NLQ, Ability may send the Double-Strike command to improve print quality. This prints each line, then backspaces and rolls the paper up a small amount, equal to half a dot, and prints again. This effectively fills in the spaces between dots and produces better looking text. It does, however, reduce printing speed by around 70% (depending on the printer).

Printing

To start printing, set the options you want and select Go from the Print menu.

As an example of a print command sequence, to print MYFILE in Elite on continuous paper select the file with the cursor and press:

[A]

```
F2OPCEPCG
```

[A+]

```
F2PCEPCG
```

As usual, these are the command initial letters. Carefully check through them and work out what they mean.

Mail Merging

One very convenient and powerful facility in Ability allows you to send the same, or a similar letter, to a number of people. To do this you need to import data from database fields into the print stream sent out by WRITE. You have to use both WRITE and DATABASE facilities for this, so we will look at the WRITE part now.

Return to MYFILE in WRITE.

Delete the "Mr. Jones" on the top line, move the cursor to the comma after "Dear"

[A]

Press F2 and select Field

[A+]

Press F2, select Include then select Field.

Type:

```
SALUTE=
```

to name the field. This inserts a database field in the letter.

Move the cursor to the D of Dear, press Ins, press RETURN eight times then press Ins again to create some space. Go to the top of the document and add the following fields, not forgetting to put an = after each name:

```
NAME=
TITLE=
COMPANY=
ADDRESS=
SUBURB=
```

```
TOWN=
COUNTY= POSTCODE=
```

Note the space between COUNTY and POSTCODE.

Move the cursor down one more line and then along to column 50. Open another field, but this time, instead of a name, type:

```
+TODAY()
```

You will see a number. This is the number of days so far this century. To convert it to a readable date type:

```
F4FDL
```

This date is printed as the current date every time you print the letter.

Now move the cursor to point at the word Supertest, delete it and add a field called PRODUCT, again remember the = sign.

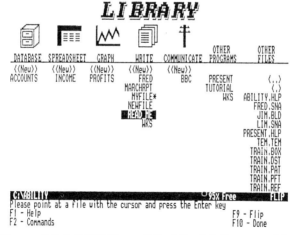

Figure 5.2. MYFILE modified for Mail-merge [A+]

All we need to do now is to write a database which includes the above fields. When we print the letter the fields will be filled in from our database and everybody gets a customised letter!

Labels

It's all very well having all these personalised letters, but we don't want to type a heap of envelopes, do we? If you have a clever sheet feed system you can get your computer to print the envelopes. If you don't have a sheet feeder suitable for envelopes you could feed each envelope into the printer by hand or, alternatively, you can print continuous labels. We'll take a brief look at setting up an appropriate label format, but we'll leave the printing until we get to the DATABASE chapters.

Open a new WRITE file called LABELS containing just the following fields:

```
NAME
COMPANY
ADDRESS
SUBURB
TOWN
COUNTY POSTCODE
```

Now you have to get out the rule. Measure the distance from the top of one label to the top of the next: call this H inches. Measure the width of the label and call it W inches.

[A]

Press F2OPR

Then enter a number equal to 10 x W. This is the new right margin.

Then select the Left-Margin and set this to 5.

Select Page-Length and set this to 6 x H

Press ESC to exit the Commands menu and F10 to finish editing.

[A+]

Press F10WMR

Then enter a number equal to 10 x W, this is the new right margin.

Then select the Left-Margin by pressing ML and set this to 5.

If 6 x H is greater than 6 you could add a Top-Margin by typing MT of half the difference between 6 and the 6 x H.

Press ESC-P

Set page length to 6 x H.

Press ESC-ESC to exit the Commands menu and F10 to finish editing.

To Be Continued

Having got this far it seems a shame not to go on and demonstrate how to write the DATABASE file. However, I'll resist the temptation and refer those who can't wait to Chapter Eight.

6 : Macros

Macros can be defined to contain phrases or sentences that you can "type" at the press of two keys. The function keys are used with ALT, CTRL or SHIFT to call up, or expand, keyboard macros. Ability Plus uses the same keys as Ability but also has a much wider range of advanced macro commands.

If you find this chapter a little difficult, don't worry. You can successfully use Ability and Ability Plus without using macros, if you prefer.

Keyboard Macros

Selecting the Macros option from the Library screen allows you to "record" frequently used functions or text. The recorded item can then be "played back" by simply pressing two keys together. Ability allows 30 such "recordings" with up to 250 characters in each one.

To record a macro press F2 and select the Macros option.

[A]
In Ability this is from the Other option.

[A+]
In Ability Plus this is from the Ability option.

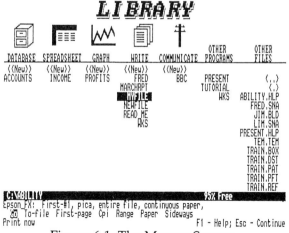

Figure 6.1. The Macros Screen

To define a macro, say, to end a letter, we select a key combination and type in the text. As an example we will define SHIFT-F1.

Position the cursor to the 'Press Shift and' column and select row F1. Type in the following, as one line. Be careful to copy the text exactly:

/ENT/ENTWe hope that the quotation meets with your approval and look forward to receiving your formal purchase order in the near future./ENT/ENT/ENTYours faithfully/ENTFred BloggsRETURN

Remember RETURN means press the RETURN key: don't type in the word.

Now press F10 to save the macro and return to the Library.

Move the cursor to the WRITE column and the New row. Press RETURN and type:

    MACRO

Now press SHIFT-F1 and you will see the following on the screen.

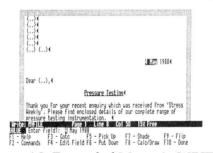

Figure 6.2. Expanded Macro in WRITE

Notice how the text has been expanded and formatted to fit the document.

Special Characters in Macros

You will have noticed that the macro you typed contained some entries preceded by a /. You probably also noticed that these /ENT entries have not been expanded as text but have now become carriage returns. Ability allows 32 such special characters. These are listed below:

Keyboard	Character	Macro Code
Back Tab	SHIFT-TAB	/BT
Backspace		/BS
Ctrl-End		/CE
Ctrl-Home		/CH
Ctrl Left arrow		/CL
Ctrl Right arrow		/CR
Del		/X
Down Arrow		/D
End		/END
RETURN		/ET
Enter		/END
Esc		/ESC
F1		/F1
F2		/F2
F3		/F3
F4		/F4
F5		/F5
F6		/F6
F7		/F7
F8		/F8
F9		/F9
F10		/F10
Home		/H
Ins		/I
Left arrow		/L
Pg Dn		/PD
Pg Up		/PR
Right arrow		/R
Slash </>		//
TAB		/T
Up arrow		/U
Ctrl-PgDn		/CPD
Ctrl-PgUp		/CPU

Table 6.1. Macro Key Codes

As you can see, you can use macros to write quite complex commands.

[A+]

Ability Plus lets you define a macro when you invoke the program. Simply type:

```
Ability shf1 d:
```

The first group after the program name is a representation of the keypresses needed to expand the macro, in this case SHIFT-F1. This can be followed by the default drive.

[A+]

Advanced Macros

Ability Plus has a range of advanced macros which can be set up in any application. Advanced macros are invoked either with the ALT key or with a function key, in a similar manner to keyboard macros. If you wish to use ALT to invoke the macro the underline character (_) is used to signify the ALT key.

There are two ways of writing macros - Learn Mode and Text Mode.

Learn Mode

Learn Mode is probably the easier method. Open a file in WRITE, SPREADSHEET or DATABASE and press the following keys:

WRITE   `F2,I,F,F4,N,_`

SPREADSHEET   `F4,N,_`

DATABASE   `F2,D,_`

The commas are to separate the items on the page and should not be typed! Now enter a keyboard character, say:

```
D RETURN
```

This has named our field _D and has marked it as being a macro invoked with ALT-D.

Now type:

```
ALT-= ALT-D
```

(or whatever your selected keyboard character was). If you look at the extreme left of the status line you will see a + sign. Ability Plus will now record all the keypresses you make until you again press ALT-D, which completes the macro definition and ends recording.

For example, if you typed:

```
+(TODAY() RETURN
```

in learn mode, each subsequent press of ALT-D would enter the date in the current field.

Text Mode

To use Text Mode open a file and press the following keys:

WRITE   `F2,I,F,F4,N,_`

SPREADSHEET   `F4,N,_`

DATABASE   `F2,D,_`

exactly as for Learn Mode. Next enter a keyboard character, say:

```
D RETURN
```

You can now type in your macro text. As an example:

```
[COMM]IF[EDIT]NTDAY#
```

opens a field in Write called TDAY.

Autoexec Macros

If you call a macro _Auto it will be automatically executed the first time the file is opened.

Some characters have special meaning in advanced macros:

CHARACTER   KEY

#	RETURN
!	F2

[   ]   surrounds a non printing character,
                         eg, ALT, ESC, etc.
If you need to enter any of the following characters, precede the
character by a slash:

    # ! { }

You can type text into the macro in the normal way. If you need a non
printable character use square brackets to surround it.

Character	Description	Keyboard equivalent
[HELP]	Help key	F1
[COMM]	Command key	F2
[Goto]	Goto key	F3
[Edit]	Edit key	F4
[PkUp]	Pick up key	F5
[PtDn]	Put down key	F6
[Shade]	Shade key	F7
[Calc]	Calc key	F8
[Flip]	Flip key	F9
[Done]	Done key	F10
[ESC]	Escape Key	ESC
[Home]	Cursor Home	Home
[Right]	Cursor right	→
[Left]	Cursor left	←
[End]	End key	End
[PgUp]	Page up	PgUp
[PgDn]	Page down	PgDn
[Up]	Cursor up	↑
[Down]	Cursor down	↓
[Enter]	Enter or Return	RETURN
[BS]	Backspace/delete	← Del
[Del]	Delete	Del
[Ins]	Insert	Ins
[Tab]	Tab key	TAB

Table 6.2. Macro equivalents

The following codes modify the effect of the code following, as if two keys had been pressed simultaneously.

    ALT CTRL SHIFT

For example:

    [Ctrl]H is equivalent to pressing CTRL-H

You can write macros to specify Ability formulas. If you use a spreadsheet, Ability will assume that any named row and column references are in the current spreadsheet file. You can specify the references to be in any other file by supplying a filename or fieldname as normal, or by using !d to set the default file for [!c], [!g], [!u], [!m] or @<target>. If you want to reference the current cell in a spreadsheet, use A0 in the formula.

These options can become quite complex, so we'll now look at how they can be used.

[A+]

Advanced Macro Input commands

You can ask for user input in a number of ways. Some input commands have optional parameters. Where this is the case, the parameter is shown enclosed in angle brackets <>. Required parameters are surrounded by spaces, which must not be used in the macro.

[?] Get input terminated by RETURN

[??<prompt>]
    Get a yes/no (or Y/N) response from the user. Enters 1 as a yes response and 0 as a no response.

[?$<prompt>#<min>#<max>]
    Get a number in the indicated range from the user. Commas and £ signs are stripped out.

[?d<prompt>#<year>]
    Get a date from the user. The date is converted into a number code. The optional year entry defines a default century.

`[?i<prompt>#<min>#<max>]`
>   Get an integer in the indicated range from the user.

`[?l<prompt>#<length]`
>   Get a counted label from the user. The result is preceded by an apostrophe to ensure that the label is defined as a label rather than a formula.

`[?p<prompt>#<length]`
>   Get a counted string from the user

`[?x<prompt>#<min>#<max>]`
>   Get a real number in the indicated range from the user.

`[@ target ?n ...]`
>   Get conditional input as described by the n command, which can be any of the above, and put it in the field indicated by the target. If the target is @ the result is put in the current field.

You can use macros to call other macros so, with the autoexec option, you can write limited programs.

[A+]

Macro control commands

These commands control macro expansion. This facility allows recursion and macro nesting and decision making steps can be implemented based on user input.

`[!b]` Beep
`[!c name]`
>   Call as a macro the field called name, which may be a field or a spreadsheet cell. Macros can be nested using this command. After the called macro has finished, execution returns to the calling macro at the instruction after the call.

`[!d file]`

Use file as the source for the cells specified in the !c,!g and !m macros and as the destination in the !u and [@target?...] input macros. @ indicates the current file is to be used.

[!e<line1><line2>]
Produce error message for the user. Esc allows the macro to continue or directs Ability to a macro defined by an !oe command.

[!f] Freeze, inhibits the updating of the screen.

[!g name]
Goto: similar to !c above but execution does not return to the calling macro.

[!i formula]{keys}
If the result of the given formula is not zero execute the keystrokes contained in {}. If the first character following the] is not {, the remainder of the field is skipped.

[!n formula]{keys}
Identical to !i command, but keys are executed only if result is a number.

[!l formula]{keys}
As the !i command but the keys are executed only if the result of the formula is a label.

[!m field]
Displays a menu with hints. When the user makes a selection the relevant macro is executed. When the called macro ends or is terminated when Esc is pressed, execution returns to the calling macro at the first character after the].

The menu is laid out as follows in a two dimensional array:

Option 1	Option 2	Option 3	0
Help 1	Help 2	Help 3	

Macro 1   Macro 2   Macro 3

The final 0 is used by Ability Plus to record the last choice made by the user. This choice is then highlighted next time the macro is called. Up to ten choices are allowed per menu.

The spreadsheet file EMACS contains an example of this type of macro.

`[!ob name]`
On beep call named routine. If `!ob` command exists computer will not beep when executing macros.

`[!oi name]`
Similar to `!ob` command but name is called when `Esc` is pressed to get out of an input macro. If no `!oi` macro handler exists the user cannot exit an input macro by using `Esc`.

`[!oe name]`
Similar to on beep command, but name is called when any message requiring an `Esc` to recover is issued (ie, an error). Note that the called macro must start with an `[ESC]` call.

`[!p pattern# formula]{keys}`
Pattern is a formula that results in a string to search for in formula. If the pattern is found, execute the keystrokes contained in {}.

If the first character following the] is not {, the remainder of the field is skipped.

Wildcards * and ? are allowed in pattern

`[!q]`   Quit execution of all macros

`[!r]`   Return from macro to caller or user

`[!sc dest # src]`

dest and src are names of fields, both must contain strings. The strings are joined. The new string will be truncated if it exceeds 250 characters.

[!sf dest # src# pattern]

dest and src are names of fields. Both must contain strings. Pattern is a formula whose result is a string or label. If this string is found within src, dest is set to point to the index of the first character in pattern otherwise it is set to zero.
Wildcards are not allowed.

[!s dest # src]

The length of the string in field src is put in field dest.

[!sm dest # src # start # len]

Field src must contain a string or label. start and len are formulas whose results are integers. len characters of src starting from start are put in dest.

[!ss]

Single step through macro waiting for a keypress between keystrokes. Used for testing macros.

[!stl dest]

Set string in dest to lower case only.

[!str dest]

Remove trailing blanks from the string in field dest.

[!stu dest]

Set string in dest to upper case only.

[!t]   Unfreeze (thaw) screen

[!u target # formula]

Update the target cell with the value calculated by the formula in field formula.

If either field is @ then the value of the current field is used.

[!v message]
> Display the message in inverse video on the formula line in the command area.

[!w delay]
> Wait for delay/10 seconds

[!x formula #<displayformat>]
> Insert the text result of formula into the input stream. <displayformat> is an option that indicates the formatting to use on the text.

> If the field is not present then the default format is used.

> If formula is a date <displayformat> can be:

> | | |
> |---|---|
> | Dymd | for metric format dates |
> | Ddmy | for European formats |
> | Dmdy | for American formats |
> | Dlmdy | for long format dates |

> If formula does not contain a date it can contain one or more of the following:

> | | |
> |---|---|
> | $ | Include a floating $ |
> | (| put negative numbers in brackets |
> | , | separate thousands by commas |
> | % | display numbers as percentages |
> | l | left justify (no effect in !x) |
> | e | use scientific notation |
> | . | floating decimal (default) |

> A number in the range 0-12 can be added to the above descriptors to define the number of decimal places.

[!y] This macro allows the user to press CTRL-C or CTRL-BREAK to exit from a macro. This is the default condition.

[!z]   After this macro is used CTRL-BREAK or CTRL-C will not stop a
        macro.

If you are feeling bemused by all this, you can gradually work your
way into the macros or, if you wish, simply ignore them altogether.

7 : Making it Look Good

We have now learned how to compose and edit documents, to produce documents to merge data from a database, to include spreadsheets and to print the document. You will be pleased to learn that Ability can do yet more. To illustrate this we will add a centred, underlined and boldfaced heading to our letter. Get the MYFILE document back on the screen and move the cursor to the beginning of the line after the salutation (Dear ..). Press Ins and add the following text:

```
RETURN-Pressure Testing-RETURN
```

This will be the heading. Unfortunately it is on the left of the page, and is in plain text. Let's rectify the situation and start with underlining. Like many Ability functions, we have to use the block marking system you learned about earlier.

Underlining

Press HOME followed by F7 and End. This will shade the text you have just entered. Press F2 commands and select typestyle.

You should see the following menu:

Bold	Boldface shaded text
Italics	Italicise shaded text
Solid-underline	Underline shaded text and spaces
Word-underline	Underline words only of shaded text
Plain	Remove any Typestyle enhancements

[A+]
Ability Plus users have two additional choices:

Raise Superscript the shaded text
eg, X[SUPER]2[SUPER]

Lower Subscript the shaded text
eg, H[SUB]2[SUB]SO[SUB]4[SUB]

Select `Solid-underline` to underline the text. If you have a graphics screen, you will see both the words and the spaces underlined.

If you just want the words underlined and the spaces left blank, select `Word-underline`. In this case you will see only words underlined on your graphics screen.

Reshading

We now have to boldface the text. Again there are two ways of doing this: a hard way and an easy way. The hard way is to go to the start of the text, press `F7`, move the cursor to the end of the text and press `F7` again. The easy way is to use the fact that Ability remembers the last block of text that you shaded. To recall it just press `F7-F7`. It doesn't matter what you do before reshading; every time you press `F7` twice you will reshade the last block.

Boldfacing

Boldfacing depends very much on your printer. Generally daisy-wheel and dot-matrix printers print a character, then move the head a fraction of an inch to print again. Many dot-matrix printers also have a double strike capability. In this case the paper is moved vertically fractionally and the letter reprinted. The effect of this is to fill in the gaps between some of the vertical dots thus giving a higher quality. Daisy-wheel printers double strike by printing each character twice.

To return to the subject of boldfacing. Reshade the text and press `F2` to select `Commands` then select `Typestyle`. From the menu, select `Bold` and you will see, if you have a graphics screen, the characters brighten to indicate that they will be printed in bold.

Centring

All we need to do to our heading now is to centre it. You could do this by counting the number of words on the line you want to centre, subtract this from the number of characters possible between the margins and divide the result by two. Insert this number of spaces to the left of the line and the text will be centred. Of course there is an easier way, but Ability and Ability Plus do things slightly differently:

[A]

Ability has a centre command, spelt **Center**, on the F2 Commands menu. To centre the line on which the cursor rests press:

    F2-C

You do not have to shade the text in this case.

[A+]

Ability Plus has an additional menu called Adjust-text. This has a number of other facilities which we will discuss later in this chapter. For now, select Center (sic) to centre the line on which the cursor rests. The sequence of keypresses is therefore:

    F2-AC

One point to remember is that if you subsequently change the page width, centred lines will not be re-adjusted. The moral is to set page widths before you start. Page width is set by adjusting the left and right margins.

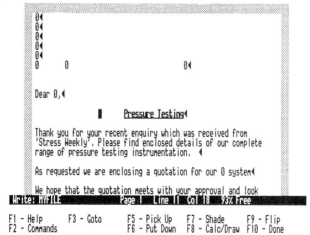

Figure 7.1. Underline, centre, and boldfaced text

Margins

If you look at a typewritten page you will see that it has two dimensions and four margins. The dimensions are length and width, the wordprocessor must know about these, otherwise the printer might print off the paper! The margins are used to make the printed page look neat and tidy. The margins are:

> Left
> Right
> Top
> Bottom

Page Width

The difference between left and right margins define the page width in characters. If you are using Pica there are 10 characters per inch (cpi), Elite has 12 cpi, and Condensed 15 or 18 cpi. An A4 page, therefore, can have 82 Pica, 99 Elite or up to 148 Condensed characters across the page. You can also imagine a printed page as a series of characters printed in columns across the page. The A4 page could therefore be referred to as 82,99 or 148 Columns wide. As you want the typed page to form a neat block on the paper, you can set the maximum and minimum column in which the printer will print. Ability and Ability Plus do things slightly differently, so we will look at them in turn.

Setting margins [A]

The margin setting is on the F2 Other Commands menu. So press:

    F2-O

to get to the sub menu. Select Page-Format, to get to the Page-Format menu. The first three options are the ones we are most interested in at this stage.

Page Length [A]

A4 paper is 11.675" long and a standard line height is 1/6". There are, therefore, 70 lines on an A4 sheet. To leave a one-inch margin at the top and the bottom of the page you would set a page length of 58 lines. If you are using a letter-head you must also allow for space taken by this in your calculations of page length.

To set the page length, select Page-length from the menu and type in the new length you want (in lines) followed by RETURN. The shaded margin box will get larger or smaller in length to match your setting.

To see this, set `Page-length` to a figure less than the screen height. The minimum page length is three lines and the maximum is 30,000.

Left Margin [A]

The left margin is the offset from the left edge of the page to the start of text. Its size depends on the character size you use, and the setting of the `Left-margin` parameter. A one inch margin is usual, but you may wish to change this for your own layout. If you desire a one inch margin, set the `Left-margin` parameter to 10 for Pica, 12 for Elite and 15 or 18 for Condensed text.

Right Margin [A]

The `Right-margin` setting method is similar to the `Left-margin` setting. If you are using A4 paper, the right-hand edge of the paper is at column 82 (Pica), 99 (Elite) or up to 148 (Condensed). If you are using A4 paper and Pica text, a setting of 76 will give you a 3/4 inch right-hand margin. The maximum setting is 250 and the minimum is a few characters more than the current `Left-margin` setting.

Setting margins [A+]

The margin setting is on the `F2 WRITE` Commands menu. So press:

    F2-W

to get to the sub menu.

Page Length [A+]

A4 paper is 11.675" long and a standard line height is 1/6". There are, therefore, 70 lines on an A4 sheet. To leave a one-inch margin at the top and the bottom of a page, you would set a page length of 58 lines. Ability Plus has top and bottom margin settings, and changing these will change the page length setting automatically. It is probably best, therefore, to set the page length to the size of the typing area you require, and then set the top and bottom margins for headers and footers if needed.

To set the page length, select `Page-length` from the menu and type in the new length you want followed by RETURN. The shaded box will get larger or smaller in length to match your setting. If you want to see this, set `Page-length` to a figure less than the screen height. The minimum page length is three lines and the maximum is 30,000.

Left Margin [A+]

Margins are set using the `Margins` option from the `F2 WRITE` menu. The `Left-margin` is the offset from the left edge of the page to the start of text. Its size depends on the character size you use, and the setting of the `Left-margin` parameter. A one-inch margin is usual, but you may wish to change this for your own layout. If you desire a one-inch margin, set the `Left-margin` parameter to 10 for Pica, 12 for Elite and 15 or 18 for Condensed text.

Right Margin [A+]

The `Right-margin` setting method is similar to the `Left-margin` setting. If you are using A4 paper the right hand edge of the paper is at column 82 (Pica), 99 (Elite) or up to 148 (Condensed). With A4 paper and Pica text a setting of 76 will give you a 3/4" right-hand margin.

Top and Bottom Margins

The top margin is set using the `Top-margin` option, the bottom margin is set with the `Bottom-margin` option. Both of these parameters affect the page length, so I tend to set them to 0, set the page length, then set the top and bottom margins. Settings are in lines or sixths of an inch. The shaded border illustrating the page boundaries on the screen will not show top and bottom margins as these fall outside the text.

Border

As you change the margins you will see the shaded border change on screen to match your settings, and the text rearranges itself to fit the margins. This is called automatic reformatting and is very useful. Watch out if you have any centred lines as these will not be re-centred.

Justification

No, this is not a list of reasons for using a wordprocessor, but the way the right margin of your document looks. If you look at a newspaper, you will see that the rightmost character on each line (except the last line of each paragraph) is in the same column.

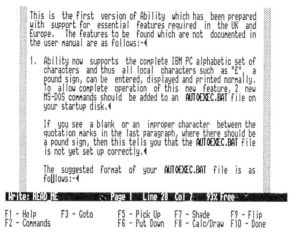

Figure 7.2. Right Justified Text

The margin you see in this book is an example of justified text.

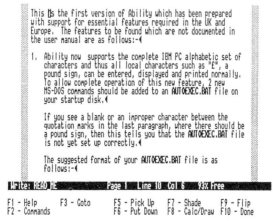

Figure 7.3. Non-Justified Text

[A]

To change the justification of your document, you need the `Page-Format` menu so press:

```
F2-OPJ
```

to get to the justification menu, then select Yes or No for right justification as required.

[A+]
To change the justification of your document, you need the Adjust-text menu so press:

```
F2-AJ
```

to get to the justification menu, then select Yes or No for right justification as required.

Here's an interesting historical note. Some time ago, when wordprocessors were new and expensive, people used right justification frequently on letters, only to show that they had the new technology. Today, people try to disguise computer written letters and strive for the personal touch. Right justification is definitely out of fashion. However, for reports and similar documents, right justification helps the presentation enormously.

Indenting

Figures 7.2 and 7.3 show examples of indented paragraphs. Ability always indents to the end of the paragraph, that is until you press RETURN. To indent text as you type, move the cursor to the column at which you want the indent, and select Indent from the menu. Ability will word-wrap to the indented left margin until you press RETURN.

If you have already typed the paragraph, don't worry, you can indent it just as easily. Move the cursor to the point where you want the indent to start and select Indent from the appropriate menu.

If you want to be clever and number or annotate the indented paragraphs, as in the example in Figure 7.2, move the cursor to the left of the indent until you reach the position for the first character of the number or margin note, then simply type it in.

[A]

To select `Indent` using Ability, move the cursor to the column at which you want the indent, using cursor keys, `TAB` or `Spacebar`, then type:

```
F2-I
```

If you number the indented paragraphs and make a mistake, overtype it with the `Spacebar` or the correct character. Do not try to delete or insert, as the automatic reformatting process will move the margin text into the indented paragraph. You can correct this easily, but it is a nuisance.

[A+]

To select `Indent` using Ability Plus, move the cursor to the column at which you want the indent, using cursor keys, `TAB` or `Spacebar` then type:

```
F2-AI
```

If you number paragraphs you can edit them in the normal way. Ability Plus does not automatically reformat margin text into the indent.

Tabs

We have mentioned the TAB key without saying too much about its function. TAB is named after the mechanical tabulation stops that typists had to physically set on the typewriter carriage. These "stops" arrested the mechanical movement of the carriage and allowed easy typing of aligned tables and the like. Ability's tabs are, of course, electronic but the idea is just the same. Pressing TAB moves the cursor to the next "stop" on the line; pressing SHIFT-TAB moves the cursor left to the previous "stop".

Ability sets TABS every eight columns by default when you create a new document, but you can change these to your own settings as you wish.

Figure 7.4. Tab ruler in Ability

To change tab stops you must select Tabs from the menu. You will see a ruler across the bottom of screen. The cursor will move along the ruler in response to the normal cursor keys and the TAB key. To set a tab, press S; to clear one press E. Should you wish to clear all the tabs in one go, press C.

[A+]

If you have Ability Plus you can set decimal tabs by pressing D. These are useful for typing quotations and the like, because when you type numbers at a decimal tab, they move left and the cursor remains in place until you press . for a decimal point, or until the first number typed collides with either previous typing or the left margin. This allows you to type columns of figures with the decimal points aligned.

To Set Tabs

[A]

Tabs setting is from the Page-format menu so type:

    F2-OPT

[A+]

Tabs setting is part of the WRITE menu so type:

    F2-WT

Headers and Footers

Probably not all the wordprocessing you do will be simple letters. You may want to write reports, manuals, proposals or even books. In these cases it is convenient to have pages numbered and perhaps a title on each page. The author's name, the date and a section or chapter title may also be required on each page. It is fairly easy to type these each time, but if you change the page format you have to do it all again! Ability to the rescue! You can define messages once only, which will then automatically be printed on each page. Those printed at the top of the page, above the text, are called HEADERS, and those at the bottom of the page, FOOTERS.

Headers and footers can be defined in three sections, all three fitting into the space between left and right margins. If any header or footer text is too long it will overwrite anything else on the header or footer line. If the text is longer than the line it will be truncated.

[A]

To enter a header or footer, select either `Header` or `Footer` from the `Page-format` menu by typing:

```
F2-OPH or F2-OPF
```

You will then be presented with a new menu:

`First page`	Is header or footer to appear on page 1?
`Left`	Left justify header or footer
`Right`	Right justify header or footer
`Centre`	Centred header or footer

Any of these can be used to produce a full width header and, of course, you can use all three in the same header or footer provided that they are short enough.

[A+] Ability Plus Headers and Footers

Ability Plus allows you to have a three line header and a single line footer. To define a header or footer, select either `Header` or `Footer` from the `WRITE` menu by typing:

```
F2-WH or F2-WF
```

You will then be presented with one of two new menus:

```
Header Menu
First page       Is header to appear on page 1?
1st Line         Define first line of Header
2nd Line         Define second line of Header
3rd Line         Define third line of Header
```

Any of the last three options will produce an additional menu:

```
First page       Is header to appear on page 1?
Left             Left justify header
Right            Right justify header
Centre           Centred header
```

```
Footer Menu
First page       Is footer to appear on page 1?
Left             Left justify header or footer
Right            Right justify header or footer
Centre           Centred header or footer
```

Any of these can be used to produce a full width footer or header, and of course you can use all three in the same header or footer provided that they are short enough.

Header and Footer contents

We have seen how to set up headers and footers, now what can we put in them? If you select either Left, Center or Right from the Header or Footer menus, you will get yet another menu:

```
Text             To type in text
Page-number      To enter the page number
Date             To enter the date
```

Only one of these options can be chosen for each part of either headers or footers.

Text

Text may be entered in free typing up to the length of the line. If you exceed the line length the text will be truncated.

Text mode can also be used to define new page number or date formats if you do not like the formats supplied by Ability.

Date

Selecting the Date option gives you another menu which allows you to select the date format you like. Dates are expressed as M Y D for Month Year and Day:

```
-American M/D/Y (e.g. 4/27/88)
-European D-M-Y (e.g. 27-4-88)
-Metric Y-M-D (e.g. 88-4-27)
-Long eg, April 27, 1988
```

If you do not like any of these, you can define your own format. Press # followed by a code to set a date anywhere you wish in the header text. This allows you to make the date part of the text header or footer if you wish. You can do things like:

```
Conditions of Sale   Issue date 4th February 1988
```

in which the date is an integral part of the header or footer. Every time you update the document the date will change. Useful, isn't it?

The following Date codes are available:

Month

#mm	Month shown as a two digit number
#mmm	Month shown as a three letter abbreviation, eg, Apr
#mmmm	Month spelt out in full, eg, April

Day

#dd	Day shown as a two digit number
#ddd	Day shown as a three letter abbreviation, eg, Fri
#dddd	Day spelt out it full, eg, Friday

If you want day and date use:

```
#dddd #dd
```
Year

`#yy`	Year shown as a two digit number, eg, 88
`#yyyy`	Year in full, eg, 1988

Page Number

If you select Page-number from the menu you are offered additional choices:

```
-Alone      4
-Hyphens    -4-
-Page    Page 4
```

Like the Date format, you can also define your own page number format from the text menu.

```
#pp           Puts current page number into the header
```

This may seem a little limiting at first glance but remember, it is part of text. You can use this to define a footer for a book or article, for example:

Page #pp of 27

Each page will be printed with the same footer but in each case the current page number will be printed.

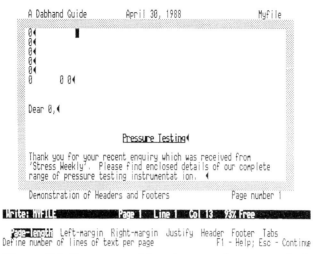

Figure 7.5. Footers and headers on short page [A]

You cannot redefine a footer or header part way through a document. If you need a different footer for the end of the document, you may have to resort to scissors, glue and a photocopier!

Deleting Headers and Footers

To delete part of a header or footer select the part to delete, and enter blank text by pressing RETURN. For example, to delete the centre part of a header, select the Header option from the appropriate menu. Select Center followed by Text and press RETURN without typing anything else.

[A+]

Ability Plus users can optionally select the Remove option instead of the Text option.

Page Breaks

Often a document will require several pages. Ability will automatically move to a new page when one is needed. You may find that an automatic page break occurs at an inopportune place. If this is the case, simply insert a few carriage returns to shift the page break to a better place. Alternatively, you can use the cursor keys to move to the top of the next page when you wish.

If you go back to insert text later, remember that you will need to adjust page breaks throughout the document below the insertion, if you had previously modified them manually.

[A+]
Ability Plus users have a `Page-break` command which is found on the `Adjust-text` menu. To force text below a given point onto a new page, move the cursor to the appropriate point then type:

```
F2-AB
```

This has the effect of inserting enough carriage returns into the document to start a new page. If you subsequently insert text above this point, you will have to re-adjust the page breaks below the insertion.

If you have Ability, we have now finished exploring the additional facilities of WRITE. If you have Ability Plus, read on!

[A+]

Linespace
If you are doing work for editing, perhaps a press release or similar, you will need to use multiple linespace. Double spacing, or even triple spacing, allows handwritten corrections and amendments, and editors love these! To set linespace, shade the area you wish to space using `F7` and select `Linespace` from the `Adjust-text` menu. Type:

```
F2-AL
```

This gives you a new menu for double, triple or single linespacing.

Spelling Checker
Ability Plus has a built in spelling checker. This has a disc based dictionary which Ability Plus uses to compare with words in the file. Any word not found will be listed as misspelt. To use the spelling checker, move the cursor to the start of the file and type:

```
F2-S
```

A new menu will appear:

Check	Search forward for misspelt words
Suggest	Suggest a replacement spelling
Enter	Type a correction
Ignore	Ignore the word throughout the text
Add	Add the word to the dictionary

Start the check by pressing C. When a word is not found the menu reappears:

Check	Search forward for misspelt words and take no action on the current word. This is different from the ignore option as any forward occurrence of the word will be found and queried again.
Suggest	Suggest a replacement spelling for the word. If one of the suggestions is acceptable, you can select it using the cursor keys and press RETURN. Ability Plus does not automatically replace all forward misspellings.
Enter	Type a correction. This will replace the misspelt word and reformat the text when you press RETURN. Ability Plus does not automatically replace all forward misspellings.
Ignore	Ignore the word throughout the text
Add	Add the word to the dictionary

Add should be used with discretion. The temptation is to add every word you find that is not already present to the dictionary. If you do this, you will quickly find that the effectiveness of the spelling checker is drastically reduced. The reason for this is that the checker cannot check for context. If you include a product name, say, ADE in the dictionary, if you subsequently erroneously type ade instead of add, the checker will ignore the error. The rule is, add only those words you will use frequently.

103

8 : Database

In Chapter One we discovered that a database is simply a collection of data, like a Telephone Directory or an Address Book. The computer database is a little more limited than a paper database, in that you have to plan what you need to put in it. There is no point in entering 5000 names and addresses only to find later that you need an extra space for a postcode!

This chapter will deal with the basics of using a database. We will not examine anything in great detail, but will set up a fictitious database to use with the `Mailmerge` letter we produced in an earlier chapter.

What is it Used For?

Small scale databases like Ability are seldom, if ever, used for simply looking up names and addresses. Paper is a much better medium for both storing and retrieving very simple data. If you have less than a thousand contacts, a good address book is probably the best database you can use. Computer databases do, however, come into their own when you need to correlate information. For example, most databases, if supplied with the correct information, could make short work of identifying all the Analytical Chemists in Kent who own their own home and have two children. Ability could even write a personalised letter to each of them! Databases are superb marketing tools. You can easily target selected customers and direct promotional material accurately to those targets.

You would also use a database to maintain lists of club members, and identify those whose subscriptions are due or overdue. In fact, any job where conditional selection from a list of similar information is required is a likely application.

You can, of course, sort the database into alphabetical or numerical order and browse through the records.

Ability's DATABASE can also include spreadsheet fields and fields containing formulas. This means that you could, for example, write a payroll system for a hundred or so employees and produce individual pay-slips for each. Needless to say, we will not be writing a payroll database at this point.

Finally, you can use DATABASE with a wordprocessor to produce personalised mail for enquirers.

Legal Status

U.K. readers should note that if they maintain names and addresses of individuals on a computer database they will almost certainly have to register under the Data Protection Act. There are exemptions and the user should ascertain whether or not these apply to his or her usage.

Fields

Data is entered into a database in fields. A field is like a box on a printed form. Its length is limited to the size set by the original form designer.

A single set of all the fields in a database is a form.

Records

A completed *form*, full of data, is called a *record*.

It is important to distinguish between fields and records. Perhaps the easiest way to think of a database is as an electronic card index. Each "card" is a record and each data box on the card is a field.

Designing a Master Form

In order to set up a database we must first decide what is going to be put into it. This involves designing a master form which will be used as the pattern for all the records in the database. To illustrate this we will design a purely fictitious master form. If you recognise a name or address, it will be coincidence.

One important thing to remember is that you should not include fields for things that are not easy to discover, likely to change, or offend the data subject. An example of this is the INCOME field below. I have included this field as an example of a numerical field and to illustrate what you can do with fields of this type, but unless you need a Personnel record or Payroll system, don't use it. Remember that you have both a moral and a legal duty to keep the information correct!

To start your database select New in the DATABASE column. When asked for the new filename type:

    MYBASE

the Status Line should read:

    DB MYBASE;Make a form Page 1 Line 1 Col 1

DB tells you it is a database, MYFILE is the name and Make a form is the activity in which you are currently engaged.

Form Heading

We should label the form so that we recognise it by name next time we look at it. Type:

    Mailing List

You can boldface, underline and centre the heading in the same way as you do for a WRITE document. The command structures are identical.

Now fill in the field identifiers, labels that define the position of fields on the form, and their contents.

We will start with the fields of the MYFILE WRITE document.

Use the cursor keys to move to line three and type NAME. This is the field identifier, not to be confused with the fieldname. Use the Spacebar to move to column 15. Press:

[A]

    F2-F

[A+]

    F2-D

When asked for the fieldname type:

    NAME

Fieldnames

A field name can be virtually any combination of up to 13 characters, but the first three characters must be letters or underline characters (_). You must of course use a different name for each field on the form. Underline characters are very useful for changing fieldnames. Name and _Name, for example, are different fieldnames. Numbers can be appended to distinguish between similar fieldnames (eg, ADDRESS1 ADDRESS2).

You cannot use spaces in a fieldname but you can use an underline character (eg, TOTAL_EXPENSE).

Finally, you cannot use the name of a built in function as a fieldname.

[A+]

In addition to the name rules for Ability, you can use a relation as a fieldname. This will be covered under "Conditional Joining" later in the book.

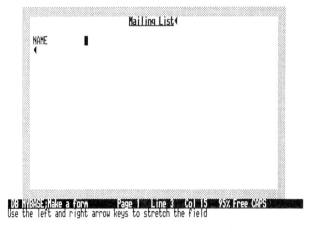

Figure 8.1. Setting up a Field.

Setting Field Width

You next need to set the width of the field. If we go back to our printed form analogy, this is the size of the answer box. The depth of the box is always one line, but you may set the width as you wish. If you watch the Column Number display in the Status Line this will help you to set the width. I make it a rule to start the field in a particular column, in this case 15, because it makes it easy to set the field width and it gives a neat appearance to the finished form. You should take care with field widths. If they are too long you will waste a lot of space in the database, too short and you will have problems fitting all the information in. In this case we will make the Name field 20 characters long. Ability and Ability Plus differ in the method used for this.

[A]
Press and hold down the Right arrow key until the field stretches to column 35. Press RETURN.

[A+]
You will see another menu:

```
Set                Enter the width of the field
Increase-by-1
Decrease-by-1
```

[A][A+]
Once you have successfully entered the field, enter the following:

Identifier	Name	Width
TITLE	TITLE	25
COMPANY	COMPANY	30
ADDRESS	ADDRESS	35
SUBURB	SUBURB	20
TOWN	TOWN	20
COUNTY	COUNTY	15

Move the cursor to column 32, using the Spacebar, to enter POSTCODE then start the field at column 45:

```
POSTCODE   POSTCODE   7
```

Telephone and telex fields can also be on the same line. Start the Telephone field at column 15, the Telex identifier at column 32 and the field at 40:

```
TELEPHONE  TELEPHONE  12
TELEX      TELEX       9
```

Move the cursor to the start of line 12 for the next field:

```
Dear  …       SALUTE      20
```

to the start of line 14 for the next field:

```
INCOME        INCOME      12
```

to the start of line 16 for the next field:

```
PRODUCT       PRODUCT     25
```

and to the start of line 18 for the last field:

```
DATE          DTE         20
```

We now need to amend a couple of fields to meet special needs. Move the cursor to the INCOME field and press F4 to edit the field. Select Format from the menu and then select Money followed by Standard. The complete key sequence is:

```
F4-FMS-ESC-ESC
```

Now move the cursor to the DTE field which will contain the date and again press F4. Select Format, Date and Long. The complete sequence of keypresses is:

```
F4-FDL-ESC-ESC
```

When you have completed this, press F10 to save the master form.

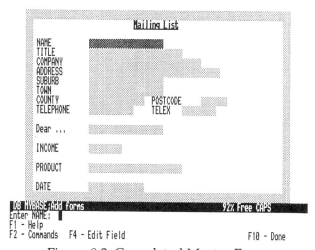

Figure 8.2. Completed Master Form

Add-Forms

You will now find yourself in the `Add-forms` screen. This is where you enter the data to be stored in the database. Data is entered into the form you designed in the master form. For this exercise, copy the following six names and addresses into the fields of the database. These names and addresses, by the way, are totally fictitious. At the end of each form, press `F10` to move on to the next form.

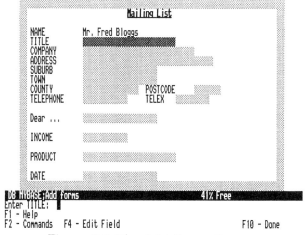

Figure 8.3. The Add Forms Screen

```
NAME            Mr. Fred Bloggs
TITLE           Managing Director
COMPANY         Bloggs Stationery Ltd.
ADDRESS         123 Letsby Avenue
SUBURB          Newtown
TOWN            Anyburg
COUNTY          Suffolk
POSTCODE        MB7 4RT
TELEPHONE       0012 345 667
TELEX           98654
DEAR            Fred
INCOME          20,000.00
PRODUCT         Pressure Meters
DATE            May 23, 1988

NAME            Mr. John Smith
TITLE           Sales Manager
COMPANY         Sow Bacon Company PLC
ADDRESS         Abattoir Buildings
SUBURB          Swineton
TOWN            Porkville
COUNTY          Kent
POSTCODE        PNZ23 1
TELEPHONE       09-876-53221
TELEX           56789
DEAR            Mr. Smith
INCOME          12,000.00
PRODUCT         Temperature Gauges
DATE            May 23, 1988

NAME            Mr. J Smith
TITLE           Sales Representative
COMPANY         Honey Hams Ltd.
ADDRESS         268 Smokehouse Road
SUBURB          Westborough
TOWN            Porksmouth
COUNTY          Hamshire
POSTCODE        PR7 QLN
```

```
TELEPHONE      098-709-1245
TELEX          975317
DEAR           Sir
INCOME         8,000.00
PRODUCT        Temperature Gauges
DATE           January 25, 1986

NAME           Mrs Lydia Binn
TITLE          Technical Manager
COMPANY        Bloggs Stationery Ltd.
ADDRESS        123 Letsby Avenue
SUBURB         Newtown
TOWN           Anyburg
COUNTY         Suffolk
POSTCODE       MB7 4RT
TELEPHONE      0012-345-667
TELEX          987654
DEAR           Lydia
INCOME         12,000.00
PRODUCT        Pressure Switches
DATE           May 23, 1987

NAME           Mr J Smithe
TITLE          Sales Manager
COMPANY        Sow Bacon Company PLC
ADDRESS        Abattoir Buildings
SUBURB         Swineton
TOWN           Porkville
COUNTY         Kent
POSTCODE
TELEPHONE      09-876-53221
TELEX          56789
DEAR           John
INCOME         12,000.00
PRODUCT        Pressure Gauges
DATE           May 20, 1988

NAME           Mr M O'Carte
```

```
TITLE          Buyer
COMPANY        Bloggs Stationery Ltd.
ADDRESS        123 Letsby Avenue
SUBURB         Anytown
TOWN           Anyburg
COUNTY
POSTCODE       MB7 4RT
TELEPHONE      0012-345-667
TELEX          987654
DEAR           Mike
INCOME         14,000.00
PRODUCT        Pressure Gauges
DATE           March 15, 1987
```

Notice that, like all real databases, some fields have not been filled in. Obviously, this limits the versatility of the database, as you cannot search on fields which contain no data.

Just to make things interesting, we will include a couple of real people on the database.

```
NAME           Mr D Atherton
TITLE          Proprietor
COMPANY        Dabs Press
ADDRESS        P O Box 48
SUBURB         Prestwich
TOWN           Manchester
COUNTY
POSTCODE       M25 7HF
TELEPHONE      061-773 8632
TELEX
DEAR           Dave
INCOME
PRODUCT
DATE           May 23, 1988

NAME           Mr B Smith
TITLE          Proprietor
```

```
COMPANY       Bruce Smith Books
ADDRESS       27 Hammers Gate
SUBURB        Chiswell Green
TOWN          St. Albans
COUNTY        Hertfordshire
POSTCODE      AL2 3DZ
TELEPHONE     0727 41243
TELEX
DEAR          Bruce
INCOME
PRODUCT
DATE          May 23, 1988
```

Now we have the data entered, we can work with our database. Press F10 a second time, after the last entry, to enter the Browse screen.

Should you wish to add additional forms to the database for any reason, press:

[A]

F2-A

[A+]

F2-DA

to get back to the Add-Forms screen.

Press F2-RM to select Mailmerge Report. When asked for the name of the mailmerge letter type:

MYFILE

You will see the MYFILE letter we prepared earlier on the screen, make any changes you feel necessary and either press F2-V to view the database form, or press F10 immediately. You will now see the normal printing menu. You can now commit your pearls to paper!

Notice that missing fields leave blanks in the text: an illustration of the importance of ensuring that as many fields as possible are filled.

Browsing

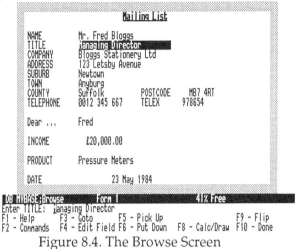

Figure 8.4. The Browse Screen

The first thing you can do with your new database is to browse through it. If you enter the database from the `Library` screen you will be in the `Browse` screen. Pressing `F10-F10` from the `Add-Forms` screen will also take you to the Browse screen. Pressing `PgUp` and `PgDn` will enable you to browse through the forms and you can make any corrections or additions you wish. You can move the cursor to any field you wish using the `CTRL-HOME`, `CTRL-END`, `Left Arrow` and `Right Arrow` keys. `CTRL-PgUp` and `CTRL-PgDn` will take you to the first and last forms on the database respectively.

Deleting

You can delete a form by pressing `Del` and answering `Yes` to the question:

```
OK to delete this form?
```

You can delete fields by positioning the cursor on the field and pressing `F4` to edit the field. You can now delete all or as many characters as you wish.

Sorting the Database

The database can be sorted in a number of ways. The simplest in our case is to sort by geographical area. To do this simply press:

F2-S

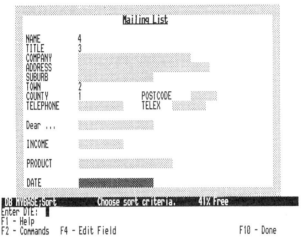

Figure 8.5. The Sort Screen

Now move the cursor to the COUNTY field and type 1. It would be useful to arrange the database in town order within counties, and in company and name order within towns. To do this we put 2 in the TOWN field, 3 in the COMPANY field and 4 in the NAME field. You can use any number of sort fields but, the more you use, the longer the sort will take. On a very small database like our fictitious mailing list the number of fields has little effect on the sort time but, on a database containing a large number of forms, the sort time can be significant. After entering the sort data, press F10, Ability will ask for a filename to hold the sorted data — enter a suitable name and press RETURN. Note that, although data is put into a file, this is not a new database, the file only contains pointers to the MYBASE file. If you erase the MYBASE file, you will lose the database!

Although this was an ascending sort, so the order was from A to Z, it is possible to sort in descending order. All you need to do is type a d after the number in the field you want in descending order. You can also sort on dates and, contrary to the information in the manual, Ability does appear to sort dates correctly.

Common Errors

If you browse through the database, you will see that the first form is for Bloggs Stationery, as is form eight.

Not a very good sort, was it?

If you look more closely, you will see that the COUNTY field on form one is empty. Ability has therefore put it at the beginning of the file. Another useful lesson: make sure that fields you sort all contain data.

Try sorting on names only. Notice that Mr O'Carte is first, because we omitted the full stop after Mr. All the others are in alphabetical order. This is our deliberate mistake! It is much better to split names into three parts: Title, Initials, Surname if you want to sort on names.

If you sort using either the TITLE or the COMPANY field, you will see that the Sow Bacon Company has two Sales Managers, Mr. J. Smithe and Mr. John Smith. This could be coincidence, as the entries were made a year or so apart but it is worth checking. If you look at the entry for Honey Hams Ltd., you will see an earlier entry lists a Mr. J Smith as a Sales Representative. So we have three people with similar names in similar occupations, quite a coincidence! In this case I know, because I made up the names, that John Smith left Honey Hams in February 1987 for a better job nearer home, at Sow Bacon. He telephoned in May 1988, but the line was bad and the person taking the enquiry added an e to his name. His enquiry a year later resulted in a third, and now correct, entry.

This illustrates a serious problem with all database mailing lists, they get out of date. There is no perfect solution to this problem, except weeding out everybody who you haven't been in contact with for a reasonable period, say a couple of years, and periodically checking lists.

Search

One of the things you will certainly wish to do is to check if somebody is on the database or quickly check their details if they are. While it is very useful to be able to `Browse` through a database, if you have a thousand or more forms it can be more than a little time consuming. Luckily, `DATABASE` has a solution to the time problem, `Search`. Press `F3` and you will see a new menu:

```
Form
Search
```

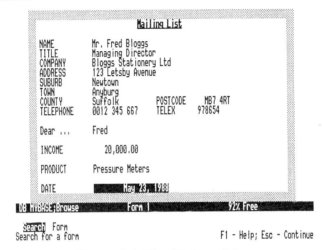

Figure 8.6. The F3 Goto Menu

`Form` allows you to go directly to a numbered form simply by entering the number of the form and pressing `RETURN`. To demonstrate this, select `Form` and enter 1 when asked for the form number to go to. `Form 1` should appear on the screen.

`Search` produces a blank form identical to the `Sort` form. You use this to define the criteria for the `search`. Search in `DATABASE` is very similar to the `Search` facility in `WRITE`. You can `Search` for forms in which one or more patterns are matched in designated fields. There are two basic types of pattern, `Text` and `Numeric`.

Text Searches

`Text` patterns can be either wholly defined or wildcards may be used. We can demonstrate this by searching our database for customers in Kent. Use `CTRL-Pg` up to move to `Select Search` and move the cursor to the field marked `COUNTY`. Type in `KENT` and press `F10`. The database screen will continue to show `Form 1`, but you will be asked

119

to select Next or Previous. Selecting Next takes you to the first form relating to a company in Kent. Next or Previous will move you through the forms that meet the search criteria. Press ESC to return to the Browse screen.

Ability doesn't recognise case when searching so you can search for KENT, kent, Kent or any other combination of upper or lower case letters you wish.

Wildcards

* replaces any number of characters, ? replaces just one character. Searching for:

    NEW*

will find, for example:

    NEWTOWN, NEWBURG, NEWBURY etc.

Searching for:

    N?WTOWN

Finds:

    NEWTOWN, NOWTOWN etc.

Avoid entering characters after the asterisk, as Ability finds only the last occurrence of the first character after the asterisk. Searching for:

    *WTOWN

will not find any forms for NEWTOWN or NOWTOWN. because it will start to attempt to match patterns starting from the last W in the names. In other words, it compares WTOWN with WN and of course they do not match.

Numeric Searches

Press F3-S again and move the cursor to the COUNTY field. Press:

    F2-C

to clear the field contents which remain from the last search. Now move to the INCOME field and type 20000. Press F10 and Ability will search for all forms with incomes of £20,000.

Relational Operators

You can search for forms where the value in a numeric field is not precisely known. To do this, use relational operators:

```
<          Less than
>          More than
=          Equal to
<=         Less than or equal to
>=         Greater than or equal to
<>         Not equal to
```

Table 8.1. Relational Operators

To return to our last example press:

```
ESC-F3-S
```

to return to the search screen press F4 to edit the INCOME field. Change the field contents to:

```
>10000
```

To search for those with incomes greater than £10,000, press F10 and you will see all the forms for people who meet that criteria. You may wish to mail different materials to people in different income brackets, to do this you need to connect the search criteria. There are three possible operators to connect search criteria.

```
OPERATOR   LOGIC     TRUE IF     EXAMPLE
&          AND       A AND B     A=B AND A=C
|          OR        A OR B      A=B OR A=C
~          NOT       A NOT B     A <> B
```

NOT is very useful as you can search, say, for all customers NOT in Kent. We'll use & as an example, so to search for all customers with incomes between £10,000 and £15,000, enter:

```
>10000 & <15000
```

121

Brackets

Brackets can be used to determine the order in which Ability evaluates search criteria when it tries to match forms. For example, you can use:

```
(>5000 & <10000) | >30000
```

to search for customers with incomes between £5000 and £10000 or over £30000.

Dates

You can also search for dates in the same way as any other number. This is because Ability stores the date as the number of days from the beginning of 1900. You can enter the date in the Date Search field in either American (month-day-year) or Long format (January 1, 1976).

Multiple Field Searches

You can, of course, use several search fields to refine the search so that you only find the forms that apply to the particular class of customers you require. For example, all Analytical Chemists living in Kent with incomes in excess of £30000 p.a. who have enquired about temperature gauges since May 1987.

Subsets

You don't have to send letters to all of your database; you can also restrict the mail to a limited class of subjects. The subjects are loaded into a new database called a Subset. Subsets contain a group of forms that are selected by one or more criteria that you choose in exactly the same way as you chose the search criteria.

To select a Subset press:

```
F2-M
```

Enter search criteria in the form.

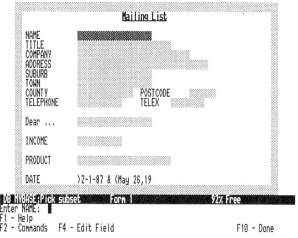

Figure 8.7. Make Subset Form

Once you have selected the Subset, press F10 and you will be presented with a new Browse screen. This is effectively a new database that only contains forms that match the criteria you specified for the Subset. You can do virtually anything with the subset that you can do with the original database. If you wish, you can save it as a new database using:

[A]   F2-W

[A+]   F2-FW

You can exit from the Subset by selecting Make-subset again and pressing:

    F2-C

to clear the form.

What can you do with a Subset?

How about selecting a Subset covering all those customers who enquired about your products two weeks ago? You can then use the mailmerge facility to send them another letter. Type:

    F2-RM

to select Report and Mailmerge to start a new letter called CHASE.

Start in the top left of the letter with a field referring to a field in the subset:

[A]   Press F2 and select FIELD

[A+]   Press F2, select INCLUDE then select FIELD.

Type: NAME=

to name the field.

Move the cursor down one line and start another field named TITLE. Repeat this operation for all the following fields:

```
COMPANY
ADDRESS
SUBURB
TOWN
COUNTY POSTCODE
```

Note that the last line has two fields, COUNTY and POSTCODE, separated by a space. On the next line move the cursor to column 50 and start a new field. This time, instead of naming the field, type:

```
+TODAY()
```

Then press: F4-FDL

to set the date format.

Now we can start the letter proper. I'll enclose fields in square brackets containing their name:

Dear [SALUTE=],

A short time ago we sent you some information on our [PRODUCT=]. We are writing to ensure that you have received the information and to enquire whether you would like any further information on this or any of our other products on the enclosed list.

Assuring you of our best attention at all times,

Yours sincerely

Donna Wannu
Sales Administrator

Pressing F10 will put you into the menu to print the letters.
Alternatively:

F2-V

will "print" the letters one at a time on the screen for inspection.

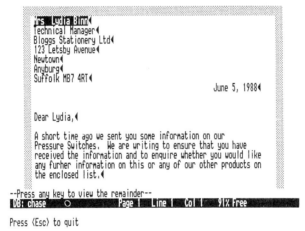

Press ⟨Esc⟩ to quit

Figure 8.8. Mailmerged Letter on Screen

There may come a time when you need to use the same field twice in
one letter. Ability won't let you! There is a mechanism that will allow
you to do this: linked fields. Chapter 11 will deal with linked fields in
detail; for now just precede the second fieldname with an exclamation
mark (!). The two fields will contain the same information but now
have different names.

Reports

Mailmerge is one example of a DATABASE Report, there are two
others. Press F2 and select Report, you will see a menu:

Forms	Print current database/ subset using forms layout
Mail-merge	The mailmerge option
Summary	Print a summary report

A summary report is a list of part of the data in a database or subset. We will produce a telephone directory from our database.

Sort the MYBASE database on the COMPANY field only. Choose Report from the F2 menu and select Summary. Call the report NUMBERS. You will then be presented with a blank form on which to select the fields you wish to include. Select Fields by typing a number into the appropriate field. The number determines the column of the summary in which the field will appear. In this case number the fields like this:

```
NAME            1
COMPANY         2
TELEPHONE       3
```

You can correct mistakes either by typing a new number or by using F4 and editing the fields using the Del, Del left or Ins keys.

Having done this, either press F10 to go to the Print menu or F2-V to see the report on the screen.

If you select a large number of fields the Sideways printing option might be useful.

Report Column Headings

It is often useful to have headings at the top of each column. Ability allows you to specify a heading in each field of the report. Return to the NUMBERS report by selecting a summary report and typing NUMBERS when asked for the name of the summary report. Move to field 3 (TELEPHONE) and type:

```
3,Telephone
```

Select F2-V to see the report on screen and notice that the telephone number column now is headed **Telephone**. It might be nice to change this heading to Telephone Number, but this would take the heading off the page. What we need to do is arrange things so that the heading is printed on two lines like this:

```
Telephone
Number
```

This is very easily accomplished. Press ESC to return to the Summary screen, then press F4 to edit the Telephone field. Change the field so that it now reads:

```
3,Telephone\Number
```

Type F2-V again and you will see that we have achieved the desired result. The backslash tells Ability to move down one line and centre what follows in the same column. You can add as many backslashes as the field will take and each one has the same effect.

We need to add headings to the other two columns but, as these are short headings in relation to the width of the column, we only need one line. To print on the second line we simply precede the heading with a backslash. Move the cursor to the NAME and COMPANY fields and change them to read as follows:

```
1,\Name
2b,\Company Name
```

Report Grouping

You may have noticed that we did something a little different with the COMPANY field. We added an extra b to the column number. This has the effect of putting a blank line in the report between each group. As we put the b in the COMPANY field, each company will be separated from the next by a blank line. You can put a b in any or all of the fields, so that you can separate by department or income or whatever. The only requirement is that the database has been sorted by that field. It obviously makes sense to specify grouping by sort priorities.

```
Database: MYBASE                                        Page 1
                                              Telephone
          Name              Company Name       Number

     Mr. Fred Bloggs    Bloggs Stationery Ltd   0012 345 667
     Mrs Lydia Binn     Bloggs Stationery Ltd   0012-345-667
     Mr M O'Carte       Bloggs Stationery Ltd   0012-345-667



     Mr. D. Atherton    Dabs Press Ltd.         061-773-2413
     Mr. B. Smith       Dabs Press Ltd.         061-773-2413



     Mr. J Smith        Honey Hams Ltd.         098-789-1245


--Press any key to view the remainder--
              Choose fields to print    90% Free
```
Press <Esc> to quit

Figure 8.9. Summary grouped by company

Calculating Totals

In addition to separating the summary into groups, you can also total numeric fields within the groups. To do this, add a t to the column number in the field. We only have one numeric field, INCOME, so we will return to the Summary screen and type 3t into the field. Now move to the Telephone field and delete the contents using F4 and Del.

Pressing F2-V now displays the screen shown in Figure 8.10. Pressing F10 allows you to print the form.

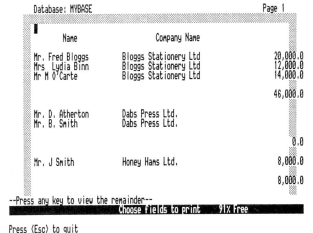

```
Database: MYBASE                                        Page 1

          Name              Company Name

     Mr. Fred Bloggs    Bloggs Stationery Ltd       20,000.0
     Mrs Lydia Binn     Bloggs Stationery Ltd       12,000.0
     Mr M O'Carte       Bloggs Stationery Ltd       14,000.0

                                                    46,000.0

     Mr. D. Atherton    Dabs Press Ltd.
     Mr. B. Smith       Dabs Press Ltd.


                                                         0.0

     Mr. J Smith        Honey Hams Ltd.              8,000.0

                                                     8,000.0

--Press any key to view the remainder--
              Choose fields to print    91% Free
```
Press <Esc> to quit

Figure 8.10. Summary Report with Totalling

[A+]

Ability Plus users can also employ some built in functions in their summary reports. To select a built in function simply type its name IMMEDIATELY AFTER the t flag. So to average the INCOME column type:

```
3tavg,\Income
```

Functions available are:

avg or average Calculate the arithmetic mean (Average) of the amounts in a column.

count Counts the number of items in the column. (works on numeric fields only)

max Give the maximum value in the column

min Give the minimum value in the column

total Calculate the total in the column

std Calculate the standard deviation of the figures in the column

sum Identical to total

var Calculate the variance of the items in the column.

In all cases, if result grouping is selected, a sub result is given on each group.

Summary of Database

The next three chapters go on to examine DATABASE in more detail, dealing largely with command keys and advanced facilities. We will use the rest of this chapter to review what we have learnt so far.

The most important thing to do before you start on a new database is to plan it. You should consider what the database is for and what information is needed. For example, MYBASE has a single field for names. In a large database this would make rapid checking impossible. J. Smith, John Smith, J.L.Smith and Mr. Smith would be widely separated in the database. In this case you could use three fields for names, TITLE, INITIALS and SURNAME. You could then sort the database by surname and search for a particular name. If, however, you are maintaining a small payroll, you could easily keep name as one field, perhaps searching on a department field.

You should avoid inserting fields that will be difficult to fill, for example, many of the records will not contain income information. If you need to categorise people by their likely buying habits, you can use other indicators, perhaps job or professional qualification.

Within the limits of these guidelines, include as much information as you think might be useful, but above all keep it simple!

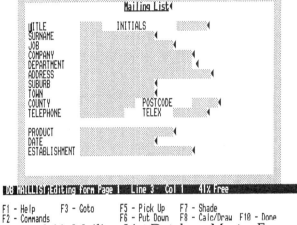

Figure 8.11. Mailing List Database Master Form

When adding forms to a database it is important to fill in as many of the fields as possible. Make sure that the fields you will want to search or sort on are filled. Also ensure that the fields are filled correctly. Putting county information in the TOWN field will cause real problems.

Finally, maintain your database accurately. Delete out of date entries, and watch for multiple entries of the same record, perhaps with different spellings.

Regular sorting of the database can help to maintain its accuracy, and you should, as a rule, use Search before entering a new record to minimise duplications.

Subsets are extremely useful for preparing mailshots and with a little imagination you can also use the printing facilities to write formatted files for other applications. Instead of printing to paper simply print to a file.

9 : The Master Form

DATABASE can be logically divided into two areas: the master form, which is used to define the data fields, and the rest of the database. The effect of the Ability Function keys F2 and F4 differ in their actions between the master form design and the rest of the database. There are also differences between the key usage in Ability and that in Ability Plus.

The vital thing to remember when designing a master form is that the user must be able to understand the forms you produce. Field identifier labels should be used and fieldnames chosen to reflect the contents of the field.

It is important to ensure that fields are sufficiently large to accommodate all the data you need without being too large.

Two function keys are vital in the design of the master form, F2 and F4, the Command and Edit keys. The menus produced by these keys are fairly self explanatory, but we will look at both in some detail later in the chapter. The F10 key is used to signify that you have completed the master form design.

If the master form is too long for you to complete its design in one session, you are probably trying to get too much data in one form, so think again! When dealing with database forms, small is beautiful.

The Done Key F10

Pressing F10 completes the master form. Only use this key when you have completely finished the design, as you will not easily be able to edit the fields afterwards.

If you do find that you have made a mistake, return to the Library screen by pressing F10 a second time, then use F2 to Rename the database file to any convenient name.

If you then select the renamed database file, you can use the change procedure described in the next chapter to rebuild the database under its original name. Don't forget to erase the extra unwanted file when you have finished.

[A] The Database Command Key F2

Pressing F2 when in the master form produces a menu of functions that can be used with fields.

Figure 9.1.Ability Database Command Screen

Field	Create a Field
Indent	Indent text
Center	Centre shaded Text
Typestyle	Bold, Italics or Underline
Other	Other functions

The Other option provides three more functions:

Page-Format	For setting master form
File	Load or save text file
Quit	Exit database without saving form

Text can be freely mixed with fields on the master form. The Indent and File functions can only be used with text, but all of the others are available for both text and fields. These functions are identical to those used in WRITE. When used in fields, typestyles act on the data in the field.

[A]

Fieldnames

Fields are identified by a name which must be unique on the master form. Move the cursor to the position where you want the field to be placed and select `Field`. You will then be asked to name the field. Names can be up to 13 characters long, but the first three characters must be underlines or alphabet characters. After naming the field you will be asked to set the field size. This is done using the cursor arrow keys.

[A+]

The Database Command Key F2

Pressing `F2` when in the master form produces a menu of functions that can be used with fields.

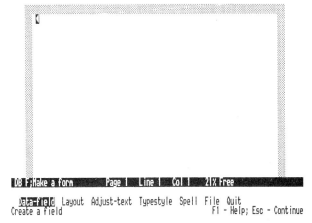

Figure 9.2. Ability Plus Database Command Screen

Data-Field	Create a Field
Layout	Page and Form
Adjust Text	Text formatting
Typestyle	Bold, Italics or Underline
Spell	Correct misspelt words
File	Load Save or Block Save text file
Quit	Exit database without saving form

Text can be freely mixed with fields on the master form. Some functions can only be used with text but others are available for both text and fields. All functions are identical to those used in WRITE.

In the Adjust-text menu, Center, Linespace and Break-page work on both text and fields, Indent and Justify work only on text. Spell of course works only on text, as do the File functions. The Layout menu affects only the form.

When used in fields, Typestyles act on the data in the field. You should use the F7 key to shade the field or fields in which you want the Typestyle to operate.

Fieldnames [A+]

Fields are identified by a name which must be unique on the master form. Move the cursor to the position where you want the field to be placed and select Data-Field. You will then be asked to name the field. Names can be up to 13 characters long, but the first three characters must be underlines or alphabetic characters. After naming the field, you will be asked to set the field size. A menu will appear giving the choice of three options. The easiest to use is the Set option, as you only have to type in the required width as a number. The other two options change the width by plus or minus one respectively.

The Edit Field Command [A]

On pressing the F4 key with the cursor on a field, you will see a menu of four options:

Edit	Change the contents of the field
Format	Change the Display format of the field
Width	Change the width of the field
Name	Change or remove the field name

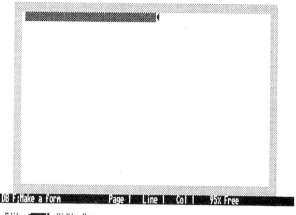

DB F:Make a form   Page 1   Line 1   Col 1   95% Free
      Edit Format Width Name
   Change the display format of the field(s)   F1 - Help; Esc - Continue

Figure 9.3. Database Edit Menu [A]

Edit	allows you to edit the field name when creating a master form, or field contents at other times.
Format	gives you further options:
Money	Select money format Standardeg, £1,234,567.89 Leading £ sign Negative numbers in Brackets

Leading-$-sign

Use a leading currency symbol (Yes or No option)
In the UK a £ is used in place of the $ sign which is
displayed in the option title

Negative-sign

Use accountancy standards for negative numbers,
ie, negative numbers in brackets. (Yes or No option)

Commas	Use commas to separate thousands (Yes or No option)
Fixed	Fix the number of Decimal places (0-12)

Variable   Variable number of decimal places

Scientific   Use Scientific notation with E indicating
                    the exponent. eg, 1,000,000 (or 10^6) is shown as 1E6

Percent   Show values as percentages

Date   Display the month, day and year
                    American 06/05/88
                    European 05-06-1988
                    Metric 88-06-05
                    Long June 5, 1988

Justify   Right or left justify field
                    Left Right

Width   Set the field width using the cursor key

Name   Change the name of the field

[A+]

On pressing the F4 key with the cursor on a field in the master form, you will see a menu of six options, in other areas of the database only five options are available:

Edit   Change the contents of the field
Format   Change the Display format of the field
Width   Change the width of the field
Name   Change or remove the field name
Global-Format   Make this format global
Type   Specify or change the contents of advanced field
                 types. A new menu results.

The Type option only appears on the master form.

[A+]

Edit Menu

The Ability Plus `Edit` menu is obtained by pressing `F4` whilst in the master form screen:

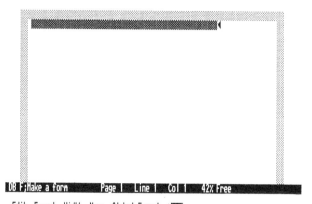

Figure 9.4 Ability Plus Edit Menu

Many of the `F4` options have subsidiary menus. We will look at these in turn:

`Edit`   Allows you to edit the field name when creating a master form, or field contents at other times.

`Format`   gives you six further options:

    `Money`   Select money format

        `Standard` eg, £1,234,567.89
                  Leading £ sign
                  Negative numbers in Brackets
        Currency-sign
                  Leading £

    `User`   Display with user-defined symbols, options 1-7 are described on the `Hints` line.

`Percent`
>   Show values as percentages

`Date`   Display the month, day and year in the style set up
        in the `Library` screen. For example:
        Long   June 5, 1990
        Short   05-06-90

`Reset`   Display without formatting symbols

`Number`   Punctuation and scaling menu, as follows.

`Decimal`	
`Fixed`	fixed number of decimal places
`Variable`	variable number of decimal places
`Scientific`	displays numbers as a mantissa (a number) followed by an Exponent preceded by an E. eg, $1E6=1 \times 10^6=$ 1,000,000
`Separator`	use a separator to display thousands, eg, 1,000s or No option)
`Negative`	Use accountancy standards for negative numbers ie, negative numbers in brackets. (Yes or No option)

`Justify`   Right or left justify field

>   `Left Right`

`Width`   Set the field width either by entering the number or
        selecting the width. A secondary menu is produced
        as follows:

`Set`   Type in Field width

`Increase-by-1`   Change width by 1 column
`Decrease-by-1`   Change width by 1 column

`Name`   Change the name of the field
`Global-Format`   Make this format global. This option produces the
        same secondary menu as `Format`.
`Type`   Specify contents of Advanced Fields.

Advanced Field Types [A+]

Ability Plus allows you to define the type of entry required for a field. These are called, by Ability Plus, Advanced Fields and can be defined from the `Type` option on the `F4` Edit menu. Four options are revealed after selecting `Type`:

`Default`   Return to default field type. This is the field type normally defined by Ability, in which the entries may be text, characters, or formulae.

`Mandatory`
              Make the field mandatory. Mandatory fields must contain data, otherwise it is not possible to save the form. Use this option for essential information only. Do not use it for all fields, as the available data length may vary. Address fields are a prime example of this. An address can take as few as three fields, or as many as nine.

`Set`   Define a set of possible entries. There will be some fields which will have a limited possible set of entries. For example, there are only two possible entries for a field that asks if the subject has a right eye. In this case, you would define a set of two options, Yes OR No. Up to 24 entry options can be specified, each being separated by a vertical bar (|) which signifies an OR condition. When you enter or edit the field you may only use one of the options. If you try to enter something which is not in the set, the available options are displayed at the bottom of the screen and the one applicable may be selected by typing a number.

`Picture`   Define characters acceptable in a field. This option complements the SET option in many ways. Instead of restricting the entries to a set, the user is allowed to enter any data he or she requires, provided that it matches the template that was set when designing the master form. The template is set by defining a pattern of special

141

characters in the field to represent the characters that are allowed. Non-special characters define themselves: in other words they will automatically be inserted in the field in the position defined. The special characters are:

Char	Accepts
?	Any character
9	0-9 and space
N	0-9, space, full stop and comma
A	All alphabetical characters
C	As A but lower case characters are converted to upper case
c	As A but upper case characters are converted to lower case
X	As ? but lower case characters are converted to upper case
x	As ? but upper case characters are converted to lower case

The `Help` screen for the `Picture` option suggests that an extra character is available, Z. This should insert a 0 if a space is found. It does not appear to work in the current release.

To define, say, a telephone number you could define the `Picture` template as (99+)-999-999-9999. If you enter the number 448981234567, Ability will enter:

(44+)-898-123-4567

in the field. If you are defining telephone numbers be careful, as there seems to be little logic in the length of telephone numbers in the UK. If in doubt, add a few extra 9s to the picture definition. If the picture definition does not fill the field, any additional characters you try to enter will be lost.

The completed field will always be regarded as a text field by Ability Plus. It cannot therefore be used for calculations.

The `Type` option is very useful if you need to search or sort a database on a particular field, as it enables you to ensure that the contents of certain fields are both present and of a predictable type.

10 : Other Screens

Entering the DATABASE (after completing the master form) is simply a matter of selecting the appropriate file from the `Database` menu and pressing `RETURN`. You will find yourself in the `Browse` screen.

Browse

In the `Browse` screen all the function keys are available except `F7`, `Shade`. You can edit forms by retyping or by using `F4 Edit`. Pressing `DEL` in any form will offer you a Yes/No choice on whether or not to delete the form. You can recover deleted forms.

F1 Help

Interactive help on the DATABASE system. Simply press `F1` from any function.

F2 Commands

The `F2 Command` key produces a menu of functions. Ability and Ability Plus have different menus so we will examine them separately.

[A]

Ability Command Menu

`Add`   Enter the `Add Forms` screen.

`Sort`   Enter the `Sort` screen.

`Make-subset`
                  Enter the `Make-subset` screen.

`Write Subset`
                  Write the current subset into a new database. You will be asked for the name of the file to contain the new database. The forms written are copied from the original database, which is not altered.

`Report`   Report produces a new menu with three options:
                  `Forms`   Print the subset in forms.

Summary   Enter the Summary screen.

Mail-merge Print letters using the subset data.

Change   Enter the Change screen.

Print   Print allows you to print an individual form. The sub commands are exactly the same as those for WRITE.

Recover   Ability keeps a copy of the forms you delete. This allows you to recover them at will. On selecting Recover, you will enter a new subset containing only those forms which have been deleted. You can use SEARCH or PgUp and PgDn to find forms you wish to return to the database. Once you have found them, press Ins to Recover the form.

Selecting Recover a second time returns you to the Browse screen and F10 returns you to the Library screen.

Backup   Deleted forms take up disc space so it is wise to remove them entirely from time to time. Backup makes a complete copy of the database, leaving out deleted forms. After making a copy of the database, Ability adds the extension BAK to the original database file. The file can be found in the Files column of the Library screen.

Validate   Validate updates all the fields that contain formulae throughout the whole database. This is exceptionally useful, even vital, if you use spreadsheet fields in a database. If you have a large database, the Validate function takes some time to complete.

Ability Plus Commands

Database   The Database option produces a menu of two further options: Add   Enter the Add Forms screen.

Change   Re-edit master form (see [A] description).

Sort   Enter the Sort screen [A+]

Make-subset

Enter the Make-subset screen

Report   Report produces a new menu with three options:
Forms   Print the subset in forms
Summary   Enter the Summary screen
Mail-merge Print letters using the subset data

Print   Print allows you to print an individual form. The sub commands are exactly the same as those for WRITE.

File   File produces a sub menu of four options

Write   Write the current subset into a new database. You will be asked for the name of the file to contain the new database. The forms written are copied from the original database, which is not altered.

Recover   Ability keeps a copy of the forms you delete allowing you to recover them at will. On selecting Recover, you will enter a new subset containing only those forms which have been deleted. You can use SEARCH or PgUp and PgDn to find forms you wish to return to the database. Once you have found them press Ins to Recover the form. Selecting Recover a second time returns you to the Browse screen and F10 returns you to the Library screen.

Backup   Backs up database. Details as Ability.

Validate   Validates database. Details as Ability.

Quit   Exit DATABASE without saving.

F3 Goto

Goto allows you either to find a form by number or to search for a record or records that meet criteria that you select. Pressing F3 gives you two options:

Form   Enter the number of the form you want
Search Enter the Search screen

F4 Edit Field

The contents of the field are copied to the edit line under the Status Line. You can use the horizontal cursor movement keys and the DEL left, DEL and Ins keys to edit the line. Pressing RETURN puts the edit line back into the field.

F5 Pick-up

F5 pick-up and put-down F6 are used to transfer data from database to spreadsheet and *vice-versa*. Pressing F5 picks up all of the information in a database. If you only want to Pick-up part of it, you must make a subset and Pick-up from that.

You can also transfer data from spreadsheet to database. To do this, set up a database master form to contain the fields you want to copy. Use F7 to Shade the appropriate fields before pressing F5 to pick up the data. You must ensure that the database fields appear in exactly the same order they do in the spreadsheet and the database fields must also be wide enough to accommodate all the information.

F6 Put Down

F6 Put-down is the reverse of the F5 option. To Put-down a database in a spreadsheet, open a spreadsheet file and move the cursor to where you want the first field to begin. Press F6 and the whole of the picked up information is listed, like a summary report, in the spreadsheet. Column widths are set to match the database fields.

To Put-down a spreadsheet in a database, select the database containing the fields you wish to transfer and press F6. Information from each row of the spreadsheet is read into individual forms. Note that it is also possible to Pick-up and Put-down information in a database to replicate all the forms in the database.

F8 Calc/Draw

`F8 Calc/Draw` Used to update calculations in a single form. Compare this to the `F2 Validate` option which updates the calculations in the whole database.

F9 Flip

`F9 Flip`   as in WRITE, to transfer between applications or databases.

F10 Done

This key exits from database back to the `Library` screen.

The Add Forms Screen

`Add forms` provides you with a blank form into which you can enter data. Pressing `F10` moves to the next blank form. Pressing `ESC` or `F10` whilst a blank form is on the screen will return you to the `Browse` screen.

`Add forms` allows the use of only four function keys. These act in the same way as they do in the `Browse` screen:

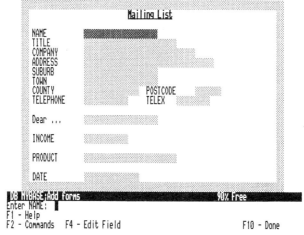

Figure 10.1. The Add Forms screen

F1 Help

Provides on line help for Ability Plus.

F2 Commands

Both Ability and Ability Plus allow only one option when adding forms. This is `Clear form`, which, as its name suggests, is used to clear data from a particular form.

F4 Edit Field

Allows the contents of the field under the cursor to be amended.

F10 Done

Press F10 once to move to new blank form. Pressing `F10` (or `ESC`) takes you to the `Browse` screen if you have a blank form on the screen.

The Sort Screen

The `Sort` screen is a blank master form. You number the fields in the order in which you wish them to be sorted. For example, if you want to `Sort` by county, then by town, then by company, and finally by surname, you would number the fields 1,2,3 and 4 respectively. Ability would sort all the surnames in each company, in every town, and in each county into alphabetical order. All the towns in Essex would be listed in alphabetical order within the Essex group. Within each town, all the companies would be listed in alphabetical order, and within each company each employee's surname would be listed in alphabetical order.

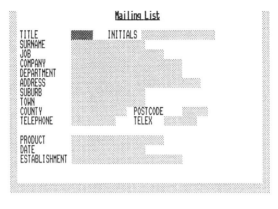

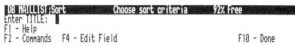

Figure 10.2. The Sort Screen

For example:

Essex	Chelmsford	Bloggs and Son	Adams
	Barker		
		Cray-pens	Arnold
			Crisp
	Dagenham	Ford Motor Co.	Akehurst
			Aston
			Atkins

and so on ...

This is called a sort in ascending order. You can also Sort in descending order by putting a d after the sort number.

Sort allows the use of only four function keys. These act in the same way as they do in the Browse screen:

F1 Help

Provides on-line help.

F2 Commands

Both Ability and Ability Plus allow only one option when in the Sort screen forms. This is Clear form which, as its name suggests, is used to clear the Sort form.

F4 Edit Field

Edit the current field.

F10 Done

Press once to `Sort` the database. You will be asked for the name of a file into which the `Sort` information should go. Be warned that this file only contains a series of pointers to the data in the database. If you delete the database you will lose all the information in the database.

If you want to re-enter the `Sorted` database from the `Library` screen, point the cursor at the sorted file name.

Within the sorted database only 3 `F2` options are available:

```
Make-subset
Write
Report
```

These work in the same way as they do on the Browse screen. The `Write` option allows you to create a new `Sorted` database. If you use this option, you can safely delete the original database and the `Sort` file with no problem.

The Search Screen

`Search` produces a blank form identical to the `Sort` form. Use this to define the criteria for the search. Search in DATABASE is very similar to the `Search` facility in WRITE. You can Search for forms in which one or more patterns are matched in designated fields. There are two basic types of pattern: `Text` and `Numeric`. These are covered in detail in Chapter Eight so we will not spend a lot of time on them here.

Text Searches

`Text` patterns can be either wholly defined or wildcards may be used. Type in your search criteria and press `F10`. The `Database` screen will continue to show form 1, but you will be asked to select `Next` or `Previous`. `Next` will take you to the first form matching your search criteria. `Next` and `Previous` move you through the forms. `ESC` returns to the `Browse` screen. Ability does not recognise case when searching.

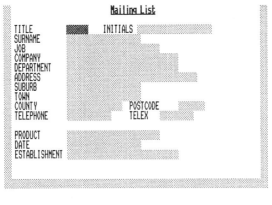

Figure 10.3. The Search screen

Wildcards

* replaces any number of characters, and ? replaces a single character. You should avoid entering characters after the asterisk, as Ability finds only the last occurrence of the first character after the asterisk.

Numeric Searches

Numeric searches are searches for a number. You can search using the default, when the number in the field is equal to the number in the search form field. Alternatively, you can use relational operators to modify the search.

Relational Operators

You can search for forms where the value in a numeric field is not exactly known. To do this, you use the relational operators.

<	Less than
>	More than
=	Equal to
<=	Less than or equal to
>=	Greater than or equal to
<>	Not equal to

You can connect the search criteria to search for a number meeting two or more criteria. There are three possible operators to do this:

```
OPERATOR        LOGIC          TRUE IF        EXAMPLE

&               AND            A AND B        A=B AND A=C
|               OR             A OR B         A=B OR A=C
~               NOT            A NOT B        A <> B
```

NOT is very useful as you can search for all records NOT meeting specified search criteria.

Brackets

Brackets can determine the order that Ability evaluates search criteria when trying to match forms. Items in brackets are evaluated first.

Dates

You can search for dates in the same way as any other number, because Ability stores the date as the number of days from the beginning of 1900. You can enter the date in the Date Search field in either American (month-day-year) or long format (January 1, 1976).

Multiple Field Searches

You can use several search fields in combination to more accurately define the search requirements.

Make-subset Screen

You can select a limited class of subject from your database. The subjects are loaded into a new database called a subset. Subsets contain a group of forms that are selected by one or more criteria that you choose, in exactly the same way as you chose the search criteria.

When you have selected the subset, press F10 and you will be presented with a new Browse screen. This is effectively a new database containing only forms matching the subset criteria. You can do virtually anything with a subset that is possible in the original database. If you wish, you can save a subset as a new database using WRITE.

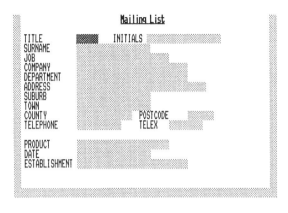

Figure 10.4. Make Subset Form

Functions available are:

F1 Help

F2 Commands

(Only one option is permitted, Clear Form)

F4 Edit Field

F10 Done

The Summary Screen

The Summary screen is dealt with in detail in Reports, Chapter Eight. For completeness, we will include a brief resumé here.

A summary report is a list of part of the data in a database or subset. On selecting Make-subset you will be presented with a blank form on which to choose the fields you wish to include. Select Fields by typing a number into the appropriate field. The number determines in which column of the summary the field will appear. You can correct mistakes, either by typing a new number or by using F4, and edit the fields using the DEL or DEL left and Ins keys. Pressing F10 will take you to the Print menu. If you select a large number of fields, the Sideways printing option might be useful.

Report Column Headings

Ability allows you to specify a heading in each field of a report. Type a comma (,) after the column number and type in the title. If you wish to include a new line, insert a backslash (\) in the title.

Report Grouping

Adding a b to the column number has the effect of putting a blank line in the report between each group. If you put the b in a field on which the database has been sorted, each group of matching fields will be separated from its neighbour by a blank line. You can put a b in any or all of the fields, provided the database has been sorted by that field.

Calculating Totals

As well as separating the summary into groups, you can total numeric fields within groups, by adding a t to the column number in the field.

The usual four command keys are available:

F1 Help	Provides the usual on-line help.
F2 Commands	Clear Form
	View View Summary report on screen
F4 Edit Field	Edit the current Field.
F10 Done	Press F10 to exit the screen.

[A+]

Ability Plus users can also employ some built-in functions in their Summary reports. To select a built-in function, simply type its name *immediately after* the t or b flag. So to average a column type:

```
tavg
```

11 : Advanced Database

Ability allows you to consolidate data on a database, to join databases, to change a master form and to perform calculations on fields. Ability Plus allows you to export or import files and to conditionally join databases.

We have already dealt with the change master form and calculations functions earlier; we can now take a look at some of the other features.

Joining Databases

Ability allows you to join two databases. This technique allows you to store information in different databases and to join them in order to produce the forms you require. For example, you could store account information in one database and invoices in another.

Joining the two databases would then add some of the information on the account file to the invoice file so that you could produce printable invoices. Adding payments as negative invoice values and producing a totalled Summary Report would then give you a debtors' statement.

Using the same technique on your purchase ledger would give you a creditors' report.

To look at the way we can join two databases we will start by writing two new ones.

The Accounts Database

This database contains information on all your customers. It is in fact a modification of the MYBASE database we wrote earlier, and was written by using the CHANGE option and naming the new form ACCOUNTS. This is a very useful way to produce new databases that contain information from others.

There are only five new fields on this database, five new field identifiers, and a new heading.

The heading is the name and address of the company. This is not necessary if this is a stand alone database, but essential if we are going to send our forms to somebody else.

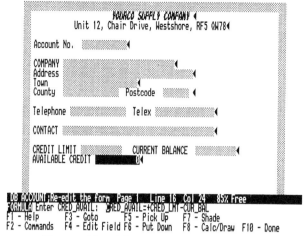

Figure 11.1. The Accounts database

The Fields are:

`Account number`

This is the number which defines the customer. Names can be misspelt, as we saw earlier. In an accounts database this can lead to the form being incorrectly filed and invoices or payments being credited to the wrong account. Mistakes on numbers are a little easier to detect.

> Field name   ACCT_NO
> Contents   Text

`Contact`

A little idiosyncrasy of mine. It is always useful to record the name of the contact who deals with your account at the customer's premises. Establishing a good relationship can pay dividends in cash flow terms.

> Field name   CONTACT
> Contents   Text

`Credit Limit`

How much they can afford to pay you back, and how much you can afford to lend them! Keep this just above the customer's average spending level.

A sudden high level of purchasing or low payment could spell trouble. The customer is either suddenly doing well or they need to use your money to stay in business. You don't want to go to a creditors' meeting do you? Keeping a close eye on credit limits can save a lot of money.

A useful tip is to recheck credit ratings before raising credit limits.

Field name	CRED_LMT
Contents	Number
Format	Money, Standard

Current Balance
How much they owe you.

Field name	CUR_BAL
Contents	Number
Format	Money, Standard

Available Credit
How much more they can owe you.

Field name	CRED_AVAIL
Contents	Formula+CRED_LMT-CUR_BAL
Format	Money, Standard

Figure 11.2. Completed Accounts form

This database should contain the details for three of the companies in the MYBASE database.

COMPANY	ACCOUNT NO.
Bloggs Stationery	B01234
Sow Bacon	S01246
Honey Hams	H01234

You can make up your own entries for the other three fields, the fourth is calculated for you.

Invoice Database

The invoice database is a new one. It contains all the information you will need to invoice for goods and services. We will take a look at the form in detail.

The first thing we have to do is decide the page dimensions. The demonstration form is 19 lines deep and 64 columns across. You could make the form much deeper, or wider to suit your needs and your printer. A page length of 64 would allow you to have 47 invoice lines and leave room for a footer containing the page number, VAT number and Company Registration number.

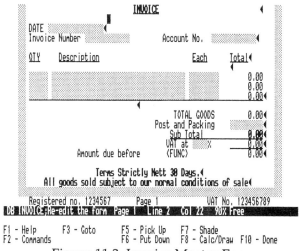

Figure 11.3. Invoice Master Form

Line 1 of the form contains the word INVOICE which is underlined
and in Bold print. Line 6 contains the words QTY, Description, Each,
and Total starting in columns 1,9,45 and 55, the invoice line fields fall
under these columns. The rest of the fields are:

Identifier	Fieldname	Format	Contents	Line
DATE	DTE	Long Left	date	3
Invoice Number	INVOICE			4
Account No	ACCT_NO			4
	QTY1			8
	Desc1			8
	PRC1	Money		8
	TOT1	Money	+PRC1*QTY1	8
	QTY2			9
	Desc2			9
	PRC2	Money		9
	TOT2	Money	+PRC2*QTY2	9
	QTY3			10
	Desc3			10
	PRC3	Money		10
	TOT3	Money	+PRC3*QTY3	10
TOTAL GOODS	TOT_GOODS	Money	+TOT1+TOT2 +TOT3	12

Post and Packing P_P	Money			13
Sub Total	SUB_TOTAL	Money	+P_P +TOT_GOODS	14
VAT at	VAT			15
	VAT_AMT		+SUB_TOTAL *VAT%	16
Amount due before	DUE_DATE	Left Long date	+DTE+30	17
	INV_TOT	Money	+SUB_TOTAL+ VAT_AMT	17

The last two lines of the form contain business terms and a statement of conditions of sale. Underlines are set below the last invoice line and sub totals and VAT. Notice the formula in the DUE_DATE field. This is a very convenient reminder for your customers of when they are supposed to pay you, and illustrates the use of calculations on dates. You could use +today()+30 but as this date will change every time the form is updated, it is probably better to let the user enter the date manually.

Notice also that TOT_GOODS is calculated by adding together all of the individual totals. The issue of Ability used in the writing of this book did not allow the use of SUM or TOTAL with a range of database fields. Both SUM and TOTAL could be used with a defined list.

ie,	+TOTAL(tot1..tot3)	does not work
	+TOTAL(tot1,tot2,tot3)	does work
	+tot1+tot2+tot3	does work

After completing the Master Form, enter a few invoices using fictitious items, quantities and prices. Note the automatic calculation of Due_Date and other calculated fields. Make sure that you only use the account numbers below:

COMPANY	ACCOUNT NO.
Bloggs Stationery	B01234
Sow Bacon	S01246
Honey Hams	H01234

Figure 11.4 Completed Invoice Form

Joining Field

The essential, in joining two databases, is that there are two identical fields. In our case we have used the Account Number (ACCT_NO) field to ensure that we do have identical fields. When we join the databases, data from each will be added together to produce a new database of forms.

The new forms will contain data from each database that relates to a particular Account number. The Account number field is therefore called the JOINING FIELD. As previously explained, it is vital that this field is selected with some care.

Making the Join

Joining databases will make a new Master form containing all the fields from each database. You can edit this in the normal way, but in the current issue of Ability, moving fields caused problems as the computer tended to run out of memory. It makes sense, therefore, to start with the database that contains the information you require at the top of the new master form.

[A]

This appears to be a 'bug' (a program error) in the Ability software. Ability Plus seems to be free of this problem. If you press F10 to save the new database master form then use the F2 Change facility to edit it, the above problem does not occur. This is dealt with later in this chapter.

To make the join, go to the Library screen and select the ACCOUNTS database. When the word Browse appears in the status line press:

[A]   F2,C

[A+]   F2,D,C

(do not type the commas) to CHANGE the database. When asked for the name of the new database type:

    MAIL RETURN

You will now see a Master form on the screen. Press:

    F2 J

to select join. Ability and Ability Plus differ slightly in their way of obtaining user information for Join.

[A]

When asked which file you wish to join with type:

    INVOICE RETURN

You will now be asked for a common field to base the join on. Move the cursor to point at ACCT_NO (the account number field) and press RETURN. Repeat the operation when asked for the join field on the second database. You may now have an error message:

    'Some of the fields in the join database had to
    have their names changed Please check all fields
    that contain formulae'

[A+]

When asked for a common field to make the join on, move the cursor to point at ACCT_NO (the account number field) and press RETURN.

You will now be asked which file you wish to join with, type:

```
INVOICE RETURN
```

You will then be asked to select the join field on the second database. Move the cursor to ACCT_NO and press RETURN. You may now have an error message:

```
'Duplicated field names will be renamed in the
join database. Please check all fields that
contain formulae'
```

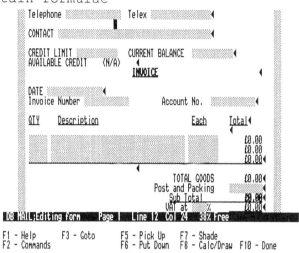

Figure 11.5. Joined Master Form

[A][A+]

Ability will not allow two fields with the same name on one master form. When joining databases, Ability will rename any fieldname duplicates. You should not try to rename any fields on the new database, as the data for those fields will be lost.

You will, of course, have two joining fields. You can delete either without effect.

If you have an error message on the screen press Esc to clear the message and you should see the combined master form.

This master form can be edited in the usual way. In this case we remove the Account number field and field identifier, from line 4, and the field identifiers from the Company name and address fields. Now delete lines 9 to 14 which contain Telephone, Telex, Contact and Financial fields.

[A+]

If you have Ability Plus move the Date field and its identifier by shading it and pressing `Del` then move the cursor to column 40 and line 4 and press `F6` to put the date alongside the COMPANY field.

Figure 11.6. Edited Master Form

[A]

On the issue of Ability used for this book, moving a field resulted in a memory error. This appears to be a bug in Ability. It has not been possible to ascertain the exact conditions that cause the problem, but if this happens to you do not attempt to move fields but save the form using `F10`. Now use `F2 C` to re-enter the change screen under a different filename. This file can then be edited without problems, so move the Date field and its identifier by shading it and pressing `Del`, then move the cursor to column 40 and line 4 and press `F6` to put the date alongside the COMPANY field.

Finally, use `F4` to format all of the money fields to the money format.

Press `F10` to complete the join and enter the Browse screen. As you can see, all of our invoices now have names and addresses.

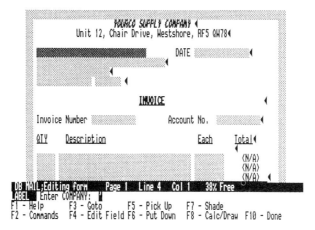

Figure 11.7. Completed invoice

Debtors' Report

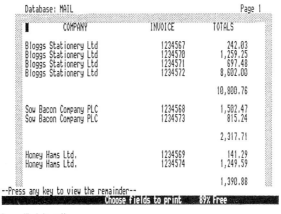

Figure 11.8. Debtors' Report

Having joined the databases, we can prepare a debtors' report for the month. Make a Subset for dates greater than 31-May-1988 and less than 1-July-1988. Sort the subset by Account number and Invoice number then select a summary report. Name the report DEBTORS. Fill in the following fields:

```
COMPANY      1b,COMPANY
INVOICE      2,INVOICE
3t,TOTAL     3,TOTAL
```

165

When you print this you will get a list of your debtors.

In order to show a report screen I have limited the report to the above fields. You will doubtless wish to include VAT and other fields in this report for completeness.

[A+]

Conditional Joining

Ability Plus allows you to conditionally join databases. If you conditionally join two databases, you do not create a third database, you simply relate and link fields from your current database with another. This produces a virtually joined database.

The key to a virtual join is the relational expression which tells Ability Plus what database to use and which field to use as the form identifier. The relational expression is entered as the field name. It has the form:

```
#<Filename>\<Fieldname>
```

The Hash character (#) tells Ability Plus that the expression is relational. `<Filename>` is the name of the database you want to relate to and `<Fieldname>` is the name of the field that you want Ability Plus to search through.

When you enter something in a related field, Ability Plus searches through the field in the related database.

When it encounters a field of the same value, it transfers the values of the fields in the original database into the linked fields in your current database.

A linked field expression has the form:

```
+<Filename>\<Fieldname>
```

You can only link to a file that you have set up a relation to. The Plus sign (+) defines the expression as a link, `<Filename>` is the name of the database you want to link to and `<Fieldname>` is the name of the field whose contents you want copied into the current field.

That is the theory; now we can try some practice. We will make a report showing the current balance and available credit.

First select new, in Database, and enter the filename DEBTORS. In the master form enter on line 1 the field Identifier ACCOUNT NUMBER, then start a field of width 7 called:

```
#ACCOUNTS\ACCT_NO
```

On the next line, type COMPANY and start a field of width 25 called COMPANY containing +ACCOUNTS\COMPANY.

Three more fields, each 12 characters wide are required. CURRENT BALANCE (CUR_BAL), AVAILABLE CREDIT (CRED_AVAIL) and CREDIT LIMIT (CREDIT_LMT). These should be entered as:

```
+ACCOUNTS\CUR_BAL        and
+ACCOUNTS\CRED_AVAIL
+CRED_AVAIL +CUR_BAL
```

On each of these fields, type:

```
F4,F,M,S,Esc,Esc
```

(without the commas) to set the Money format.

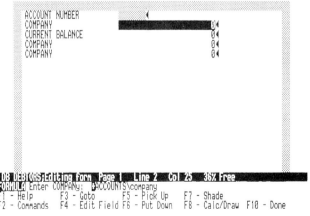

Figure 11.9. Conditional Master Form

Pressing F10 takes you into the Add Forms menu. Type H01234 into the ACCOUNT NUMBER field and the rest of the form will be completed for you. Any other account number, or partial account number, will fill the form with different details.

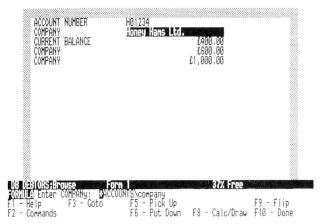

Figure 11.10. Conditional Form

You can obviously use any of the fields for the relational expression. In fact you can relate to more than one database at a time. You can link fields to produce another relation if you wish!

The CREDIT_LMT field could have been written as:

```
+ACCOUNTS\CRED_AVAIL +ACCOUNTS\CUR_BAL
```

as you can operate on two linked fields if you so desire.

One thing you must remember is that the order in which you create fields is the order in which Ability Plus steps through them. Be careful not to invoke data that has not yet been calculated.

[A][A+]

Consolidating Databases

You can consolidate a database to produce a summary of information about groups of forms that contain the same information in the consolidate field. If you consolidate databases, Ability produces a new database that contains one form for each group of forms in the original databases which contain identical information in the consolidate field. Each of these forms contains a group total for all the fields on the database which contain a numeric value.

You will usually use a consolidated database to produce sub-totals which you can then transfer to a text file in WRITE or a field in

SPREADSHEET. Ability does not attempt to consolidate text fields: the consolidated database will just contain text from the last form on the database.

We will use the MYBASE database to demonstrate this.

First get the MYBASE database on screen, then select the Sort menu by entering:

```
F2,S
```

(without the comma). Move the cursor to the COUNTY field and type:

```
1c
```

This defines the consolidate field. The consolidate field can, of course, have any sort priority.

Now select any other fields you wish to sort.

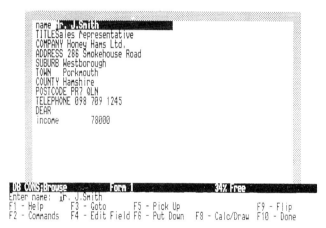

Figure 11.11 Consolidated Sort Criteria

Press F10 and select a file name. (CONS perhaps?) Press RETURN and you will see the consolidated report. The only significant field in this case is the income field.

[A+]

Exporting Files

Ability allows you to export files to other software. Exported files are placed in the files column of the Library screen. To export files, you must set up the translation parameter in the Library menu. You have a choice of dBASEII, dBASEIII or Comma Separated file formats.

Exporting files is simply a matter of positioning the cursor over the appropriate database file and pressing:

F5

The name of the file will appear in the command area. Now move the cursor to the files column and press:

F6

You may put the file down on any drive, the current directory, or the root directory.

Putting down the file automatically translates it.

[A+]

Importing Files

Import file translation is automatic. All you do is to position the cursor over the filename in the Library Files column. Press:

F5

then move to the appropriate application and press:

F6

to import and translate the file.

If you attempt to import a file into an unsuitable location, Ability will produce an error message.

12 : Built-in Functions

This Chapter deals with Ability's built-in functions. It is not necessary to read and understand it before using the software. In fact, you could well skip this chapter altogether and return to it when you need to refer to any of the functions.

Ability has a very wide range of built in functions to perform complicated calculations. These functions are formulae and must be preceded by either a plus sign (+), or an at sign (@). You can use the built-in functions to perform date, financial, logical, mathematical, trigonometric and other calculations.

We will use computer symbols for mathematical operators:

> a * b   Multiply a by b
>
> a / b   Divide a by b
>
> a + b   Add a to b
>
> a - b   Subtract b from a

Rules for Built-in Functions

You may use the built-in functions in formulae to determine the contents of a field. You must follow specific rules in order to include the built-in function:

First create a field then enter the function. You must precede the function name with + or @ to indicate that it is a formula.

Type the function name exactly. Ability will not accept abbreviations. The one exception is that you can use AVG for AVERAGE.

The function name must be followed by brackets enclosing any arguments necessary. The arguments are the information Ability needs to perform the calculation, eg, the TOTAL function requires a list of the values to add. The list can comprise numbers, field addresses, ranges and field names. To find the sum of the values between D1 and D20 of a spreadsheet, for example:

```
+TOTAL (D1..D20) or @SUM (D1..D20)
```

Some functions do not require arguments, but for these you must still include the brackets.

eg,   +TODAY()

You can use more than one function in a formula by using brackets to group the various functions and to control the order of calculation. If you wish to calculate the average of a row of eight numbers and display the absolute value of the result, for example:

+ABS (AVG(A1..A8))

If Ability cannot perform the calculation you request, an error message is displayed in the field instead of the result of the formula. A list of error messages can be found later in this Chapter.

Date Functions

Ability's built-in date functions generate a date code which is a number representing the number of days since December 31, 1899.

To translate date codes into recognisable dates, use any of the date formats available in the Format menu:

DATE(Year,Month,Day)
>   The DATE function calculates a date code for the given day, month, and year: +DATE(88,1,23)

DAY(datecode)
>   DAY calculates the day of the month of the date code entered.

MONTH(datecode)
>   MONTH calculates the month for the date code you enter.

TODAY()
>   The TODAY function calculates a date code for the current day. The current day is the system date. This is either the date from the system clock, if you have a real time clock in hardware (eg, Amstrad machines), or the date you type when you first start the computer (eg, IBM PC machines). If the system date is not correct, Ability naturally calculates an incorrect current day.

WEEKDAY(datecode)
> The WEEKDAY function calculates the day of the week of the date code you enter. Days of the week are numbered sequentially from Sunday (1) to Saturday (7).

YEAR(datecode)
> YEAR calculates the year of the date code you enter.

Financial Functions

The built-in financial functions calculate compound amounts and net present values of investments. They can be used in forecasting and analytical calculations.

COMPOUND(principal,interest,periods)

The COMPOUND function calculates the resultant compound value if you invest or borrow principal at a specified interest rate for a specified number of periods.

The formula is:

    COMPOUND=Principal x (1+interest)^{periods}

To find the compound amount on £500 at 15% interest per annum over five years enter:

    +COMPOUND(500,15,5)

FV(payment,rate,periods)

The FV function calculates the future value of an annuity or savings scheme, based on the payments per period and the number of periods for which you want the value calculated. The formula is:

    FV = payment x ((1 + rate)^{periods}-1)/rate

For example, to calculate the future value of an annuity with £500 payments at an interest rate of 15% per annum compounded monthly over five years enter:

    +FV(500,15%/12,60)

IRR(guess,list)

The IRR function calculates the internal rate of return of a series of cash flows represented in a list. The calculation uses as a starting point a guess at the correct answer. The internal rate of return is the effective interest rate such that the net present value of the cash flow is zero. This function is the inverse of the net present value function, which follows.

The initial cash flow should be included in the list of payments as a negative number to indicate that it is money received, rather than money paid out.

NPV(rate,list)

The NPV function calculates the net present value of a set of future cash flows. Ability assumes the first cash flow occurs at the end of the first period, which means the initial payment is not usually included. (Compare with the IRR function.) In this function:

rate	is the effective interest rate per period
list	is the value of the payments in the order they appear, one payment for each period.

If you enter list as a range including several rows and columns, Ability reads the range from left to right and top to bottom. If there are blank fields in the range, Ability ignores them when calculating the net present value.

For example, to find the net present value of cash flows of £900, £200, £300, and £500 in each period at a rate of 16.55%, type the following formula:

```
+NPV(16.55%,900,200,300,500)
```

PMT(principal,rate,periods)

The PMT function calculates the amount of each payment needed to pay off a loan at the given principal, interest rate per period, and number of periods. Ability uses the following formula to calculate the payments:

```
.PMT=principal x rate / (1 - (1 + rate)-periods)
```

If the payment amounts are fractional numbers, use the ROUND function in order to make the payments even amounts.

To find the payment required to pay off a £29,000 mortgage at 9.25% interest per annum compounded monthly, over a period of 240 months, use the following formula:

```
+PMT(29000,9.25%/12,240)
```

PV(payment,rate,periods)

The PV function calculates the present value of an annuity. The value is calculated from the amount of the payment, the interest rate per period and the number of periods. Ability computes present value using the following formula:

```
PV=payment x(1 - (1 + rate)-periods/rate
```

For example, to find the present value of an annuity with payments of £400, at 12.5% interest per period, after four periods, type:

```
+PV (400,12,5%,4)
```

Logical Functions

The two built-in logical functions may be used to check for specific conditions in a calculation and to test for errors.

IF(x,true,false)

The IF function calculates x and evaluates it; if x is true (not zero), the true value is displayed; if x is false (zero), the false value is displayed.

If you enter the formula:

```
IF (x >y, x, y)
```

Ability displays either x or y, whichever is the larger.

Logical and relational operators may be used in an IF function.

For example, you can type:

```
+IF (C5 > 10 & C5 < 20,0,1)
```

If the value in the field is greater than 10 and less than 20, Ability displays the true value (0), otherwise Ability displays the false value (1).

You can also write a formula such that the true and false values will return labels which reference other data, such as error messages.

To do this, you should enter field addresses instead of values for true and false. For example, type the word PROFIT in Field F20 and the word LOSS in Field F21. Then type the IF function:

```
+IF (A2 > 0,F20,F21)
```

When Ability evaluates the formula, you will see the label PROFIT displayed if the value is positive. If the value is negative you will see the label LOSS.

ISERR(list)

The ISERR function checks the list and counts the number of fields that contain:

N/A, CIRC FUNC, DIV O, OVER UNDER or ERR

error messages.

The list can be field addresses, ranges, or field names. To check an entire spreadsheet for errors, enter list as a range of fields covering the whole spreadsheet.

You can combine the IF function and the ISERR function to check for errors and return an error message if something is incorrect. For example, in a spreadsheet that runs from A1 to X50, you can use a formula like this:

```
+IF (ISERR (A1..X50), Errors, No Errors)
```

Put the text of the error messages in the fields you have named ERRORS and NOERRORS. For example, you might type the following in Z51:

```
ERRORS= You have a problem!
```

and this in Z52:

```
NOERRORS=No problems
```

On evaluating the formula, Ability either displays the ERRORS message if the spreadsheet contains errors, or the NOERRORS message if there are none.

Mathematical Functions

The built-in mathematical functions are provided to enable you to perform arithmetic and other calculations. These functions automatically find the average, the minimum and maximum, the number of permutations, and other complex computations. You may not need any of these functions in your work, so don't spend a lot of time on them unless you do need to use them.

ABS(x)

The ABS function calculates the absolute value of a number or the value of a field. This can be a very useful function. The Absolute value is a value with a positive sign, regardless of whether the original value was positive or negative.

For example:

```
+ABS(31) = +ABS(-31)  (=31)
```

AVERAGE (list) or AVG (list)

The AVERAGE function calculates the unweighted arithmetic mean (average value) of one or more values in a list. The list may contain numbers, ranges, fieldnames or field addresses and any mix of these.

The function can be abbreviated to AVG.

The average is calculated by adding together all the values and dividing by the number of values.

For example:

```
+AVERAGE(10,20,30) or +AVG(B6..D6,SALES,C8)
```

COMB(n,m)

The COMB function calculates the number of combinations of n items, taken m at a time. It uses the following formula:

```
COMB= n!/(m! x(n - m)!)
```

The ! sign is the standard mathematical symbol for a factorial. N! means N factorial or N*(N-1)*(N-2)*(N-3)....*1.

```
eg, 5!= 5*4*3*2*1 = 120
```

COUNT(list)

The COUNT function counts the number of items in a list. The list may contain numbers, field addresses, ranges and field names. Ability counts only the fields that contain information; it does not count blank fields.

For example:

```
+COUNT (B3..D9) or +COUNT(24.50,36,A1..A6)
```

EXP(x)

The EXP function calculates the value of e^x, where e is the exponential function or to the base of natural logarithms, 2.71828. Natural logarithms are used extensively in scientific applications.

FACT(n)

The FACT function calculates the factorial of number n. n can be any positive integer, and is defined as 1 for FACT(0).

A negative number causes an error <FUNC> in the field.

Factorial calculations can lead to very large numbers, some of which may be too big for Ability to handle. In this case, Ability displays OVER in the field.

```
FACT(x)  =  !x  =  x*(x-1)*(x-2).....1
FACT(5)  =  !5  =  5*4*3*2*1 = 120
```

INT(x)

The INT function produces only the integer part of the value you enter as x.

For example, entering:

    +INT(3.12543)

    produces the result 3

LN(x)

The LN function calculates the natural logarithm of the number x. Do not confuse natural logarithms which use the base e, with logarithms that use the base 10. Natural logarithms are used frequently in science.

    LN=LOG$_e$
    LN(10) = 2.303
    LN(x)   = 2.303*Log$_{10}$(x)

LOG(x)

The LOG function calculates the logarithm (base 10) of the number x.

    LOG(10) = 1

MAX(list)

The MAX function calculates the maximum value in a list. The list can include numbers, field addresses, ranges and field names. The largest value is defined as the most positive or least negative number:

For example,

    +MAX (1,2, -16,8)

Ability displays the largest value, eight.

MIN(list)

The MIN function calculates the minimum value in a list. The list can include numbers, field addresses, ranges, and field names. The smallest value is defined as the least positive or most negative number:

For example,

```
+MIN (1,2, -16,8)
```

Ability displays the minimum value, -16.

MOD(x,y)

The MOD function calculates the remainder when x is divided by y. The calculation is made to this formula:

```
MOD(x,y) =x -(y*INT(x/y))
```

You can calculate the fractional part of a number x by typing +MOD(x,1.).

PERM(m,n)

The PERM function calculates the number of permutations of n items, taken m at a time. It uses the following formula:

```
PERM = n!/(n - m)!
```

The ! signifies a factorial. N! means N factorial or N*(N-1)*(N-2)*(N-3) … *1.

```
eg, 5!= 5*4*3*2*1 = 120
```

PI()

The PI function always returns the constant PI or 3.14159265359. This function is used to convert angles between radians and degrees when you use the SIN, COS, TAN and other trigonometric functions. It is frequently used in science and mathematics. PI is defined as the circumference of a circle divided by its diameter.

RAND(x)

The RAND function calculates a random number between 0 and x (including 0 but excluding x). Each time you recalculate, Ability will find a different random number. Random numbers are used in statistics and sampling, and by some professions to calculate charges!

ROUND(x,y)

The ROUND function calculates the value of x rounded to the nearest y. If you want to round to an integer, y should be 1. The ROUND function is very useful in calculated prices, for example, to ensure that fractions are always to the nearest penny.

For example:

```
+ROUND(2.56,.5)
```

will return 2.50. It is also useful to correct errors when you use fixed precision calculations.

SQRT(x)

The SQRT function calculates the square root of x. x must of course be equal to or greater than zero. If it is not, Ability displays FUNC in the field to indicate an error. The square root of a negative number is, of course, imaginary and can only be defined as the square root of a positive number multiplied by the square root of -1 (which cannot be calculated but is defined as i or j).

STD(list)

The STD function calculates the standard deviation of the sample represented by the list. which may consist of numbers, ranges, fieldnames or field addresses or any mix of these. Ability defines standard deviation as the square root of the variance (see the VAR function).

SUM(list)

The SUM function calculates the total of the values in the list. The list may contain numbers, ranges, fieldnames or field addresses or any mix of these. The SUM function is identical to the TOTAL function.

For example:

```
+SUM (122,25,190)
+SUM (B1..C19)
+SUM (Sales,D5<Expenses,Equip)
```

181

TOTAL(list)

The TOTAL function calculates the total or sum of the list. The list may contain numbers, ranges, fieldnames or field addresses or any mix of these. This function is the same as the SUM function.

VAR(list)

The VAR function calculates the variance of the list. The list may contain numbers, ranges, fieldnames or field addresses or any mix of these. Ability calculates variance according to the formula.

$$VAR= n* \frac{(sum\ of\ x^2) - (sum\ of\ x)^2}{n^2}$$

where each x is an item in the list and n is the total number of items in a list. Variance is a measurement of the spread of values.

Trigonometric Functions

Trigonometric functions are used to solve standard trigonometry problems, such as computing the sine or tangent of an angle. You may never need to use any of these but it is good to know they are available. Many of the functions use or give radians in the result. There are 2*PI radians in 360 degrees. One radian is 57.3 degrees.

ACOS(x)

The ACOS function calculates the inverse cosine of the number x. The result is given in radians. To convert to degrees multiply the result by 57.3.

ASIN(x)

The ASIN function calculates the inverse sine of the number x. The result is in radians. To convert to degrees multiply the result by 57.3.

ATAN(x)

The ATAN function calculates the two-quadrant inverse tangent of the number x. The result is given in radians. To convert to degrees multiply the result by 57.3.

ATAN2(x,y)

The ATAN2 function calculates the four-quadrant determination of the angle formed by the point (x,y) and the x-axis. The result is given in radians. To convert to degrees multiply the result by 57.3.

COS(x)

The COS function calculates the cosine of the number x, where x is an angle given in radians. If x is in degrees divide it by 57.3.

SIN(x)

The SIN function calculates the sine of x, where x is an angle given in radians. If x is in degrees divide it by 57.3.

TAN(x)

The TAN function calculates the tangent of x, where x is an angle given in radians. If x is in degrees divide it by 57.3.

Lookup Functions

The next set of built-in functions are FIND, INDEX, and LOOKUP. These are used to search for the location of specific information. These functions are most useful if you're working with tax tables or other kinds of spreadsheet tables that you want to use for cross referencing with other information.

FIND(value, list)

The FIND function searches the list for a number that is less than or equal to the test value. A list can contain numbers, field addresses, ranges and field names. The list must be sorted into ascending order, or the results may be incorrect.

Each item in the list must occupy a specific position. In other words, the first item is in position 1, the second in position 2, the third in position 3 and so on. Ability uses the position number to tell you where the test value is located in the list. When Ability searches, it finds the last value that is less than or equal to the test value and displays its position.

For example, if you have a list containing the numbers 1, 15, 20, 30, 35, 40, and you want to find where the test value 19 occurs, use the following FIND function:

```
+FIND (19, 1, 15, 20, 30, 35, 40)
```

In this example, Ability displays 2. The 2 refers to the second position in the list, or the number 15. The 15 is the last value in the list that is less than or equal to the test value. If the list you want to search is a range that contains several rows and several columns, Ability searches the range from left to right and top to bottom.

The FIND function is similar to LOOKUP, except that LOOKUP returns an actual value, whereas FIND returns the position of the value. The INDEX function is the inverse of the FIND function, in that with INDEX, you enter the position in a list, rather than a value.

INDEX(x,list)

The INDEX function finds the value in a list that is in the xth position. The list can be numbers, field addresses, ranges and field names. Ability searches the list and displays the value that occurs in the specified position. For example, if you type:

```
+INDEX (2,1,15,30,35,40)
```

Ability displays 15, which is in the second position in the list.

LOOKUP(x,inrange,outrange)

The LOOKUP function is similar to the FIND function. LOOKUP searches the specified range, called the inrange, to find the last value that is less than or equal to the specified value, x. Ability next looks up the corresponding position in another location, called the outrange and displays the value in the field. The inrange must be sorted into ascending order. If it isn't, Ability displays the <FUNC> error in the field.

LOOKUP equates to combining INDEX and FIND functions in this format:

```
+INDEX(FIND(x,inrange),outrange)
```

Operators

Ability allows a full range of mathematical and logical operators. These are listed in the following charts together with relational operators and wildcard characters. Operators can be used in formulae and can help you write complex mathematical or logical expressions. You will need to use some or all of these operators from time to time.

Mathematical Operators

The following mathematical operators are used in formulae which are built into fields. The operators are listed in their order of priority from the highest (calculated first) to lowest (calculated last). You can use brackets to control the order of calculation and to group information.

Operator	Meaning
-	Negation/Change Sign. Changes the sign of a number, for example -∧9 or -INCOME.
%	Percent. The percent sign divides the value to its left by 100. For example, 5% is the same as 0.05.
∧	Exponentiation. The exponentiation sign (called a caret) raises the number to its left to the power on its right. For example: 3^2 is 3^2 or 9
*	Multiplication
/	Division N.B. * and / have equal priority.
+	Addition
-	Subtraction N.B. + and - have equal priority

(Note: Where operators have equal priority, use brackets as necessary to control the order of calculation.)

Logical Operators

Logical operators can be used in searches for information in Ability files, or in the IF function. The logical operators are listed in their natural order of evaluation. If you combine either AND or OR with relational operators in an expression, Ability evaluates the relational operators before evaluation of the AND or OR.

OPERATOR	LOGIC	TRUE IF	EXAMPLE

&	AND	A AND B	A=B AND A=C
		OR	A OR B	A=B OR A=C
~	NOT	A NOT B	A <> B

NOT is useful for searching, say, for all customers NOT named Smith.

Relational Operators

Use the relational operators when you search for information in an Ability file, or in the IF function. If you combine relational operators with mathematical operators in an expression, Ability performs the mathematical operations before evaluating the relational operators.

Operator	Meaning
<	Less than
>	Greater than
=	Equal to
<=	Less than or equal to (or, not greater than)
>=	Greater than or equal to (or, not less than)
<>	Not equal to
~=	Not equal to

Wildcard Characters

Wildcard characters can be used when you need to search for information in an Ability file and you don't know one or more characters. The wildcards replace the characters you don't know.

Wildcard	Meaning
*	Replaces zero or more characters and finds any whole word (in a document) or field (in a spreadsheet or database). For example, 'the*' would find the words the, these, thesis, and thermonuclear (in a document) or any field that begins with 'the' (in a spreadsheet or database).
?	Replaces a single character. For example, 'the?' would find the words 'then' and 'them' (in a document) or any

field that begins with 'the' followed by a single character (in a spreadsheet or database).

Error Indicators

Ability has a range of error messages which it displays in the field containing the error, if Ability cannot perform the calculation or evaluate the formula you have requested. There are seven error messages.

Error	Explanation
<N/A>	Either the formula refers to a field that doesn't exist, or it attempts to use a label field in a calculation.
<CIRC>	The formula contains a circular reference - that is, it refers to its own value. Circular references usually occur when a formula refers to a field that in turn refers to the field in which you enter the formula. Only one of these two fields shows <CIRC>. Normally, circular references are created accidentally, but you can use them to solve certain types of problems that involve iterative calculations.
<FUNC>	The formula contains an error in the built-in function. For example, the built in function may have. - Too many or too few arguments, eg, DATE(May, 1985) - Incorrect arguments, eg, DATE(1984,OCT10) - Invalid arguments, eg, SQRT(-1) - Improper use of exponentiation, eg, 1^.5 - Illegal date codes which you try to format, eg, -1
<DIV 0>	The formula attempts to divide by zero.
<ERROR>	The formula refers to a field that previously contained a value or formula, but the field has changed to a range, or a list, making the formula invalid.
OVER	The formula calculates a number that is too large or too small for Ability. This results in an overflow or underflow. The largest number possible is approximately 1×10^{308}.
UNDER	The formula calculates a number that is too large or too small for Ability to handle, resulting in an overflow or

underflow. The smallest possible number is approximately 1×10^{-308}

13 : Spreadsheet

A spreadsheet is simply a collection of fields, more usually called cells, arranged in rows and columns. Ability allows over seven million cells arranged as 9999 rows by 702 columns. Rows are numbered 1 to 9999 and columns A to ZZ. Cells are addressed by their column and row numbers. The cell in the top-left corner being A1 and the bottom right cell ZZ9999.

With such a large number of cells it is unlikely that you will fill a complete spreadsheet with data. Unless, that is, you have a large amount of memory and a masochistic streak. It is possible to run out of memory but on most machines you will find that recalculations take so long with large spreadsheets you will want to simplify the spreadsheet long before you have memory problems.

Cells

Spreadsheet cells are very similar to database fields in that they can contain text, data, formulae or references to other spreadsheets or cells. Cells can be referred to by their address or by names that you allocate. To enter data in a cell all you have to do is move the cursor to that cell and enter the data.

Formulae

A formula is simply a calculation in which cell names or addresses can take the place of numbers. Instead of writing:

```
1+2+6
```

you can write:

```
A2+C4+E7
```

Formulae can contain built-in-functions, cell addresses, numbers or arithmetic operators.

Formulae must start with +, -, @, $ (or a number)

Building a Formula

If you enter any of the characters, +, -, @, $ or a built in function then move the cursor to a cell, the cell address will appear in the edit line. Pressing non cursor movement keys enters characters into the formula until you use the cursor moving the keys again. This facility, called pointing, allows you to rapidly build formulae without having to remember cell addresses; you simply point the cursor at the relevant field and enter a character.

If you enter any other character than the above and move the cursor, the character will be entered as text, or data if the character is a number.

The following arithmetic operators can be used in spreadsheet formulae:

+	Addition
-	Subtraction
*	Multiplication
/	Division
%	Percent, divides the preceding number by 100
()	Brackets are used to enclose parts of a formula and to define the order in which calculations are made.

For example, C3*(A1+A2) would ensure that A1+A2 was calculated before the multiplication.

^ Raise the preceding number to the power of the following number, eg, $2 \wedge 4 = 2^4 = 16$

Ranges

A block of cells is called a range. You can operate on a range in the same way as a single cell for various functions. To define a range for MOVE, COPY, BLANK or FORMAT, use F7 to shade it.

To specify a range in a formula, define it as the top-left cell followed by two full stops then the bottom-right cell, eg,

```
+TOTAL(A10..C25)
```

You can use the point technique with full stops to build the range formula.

Lists

If the cells are not in a continuous block, you can define them as a list. Items in a list are separated by commas. A list of cells may also contain ranges, eg,

```
+TOTAL(D4..D7,D9,D11,D15..D17)
```

Commas

As you can see above, commas have a special meaning in Ability. If you use a comma in a number, Ability will treat the number as a list and you will see an error:

```
[.........]
```

All you can do is retype the number without the comma.

Moving Around the Spreadsheet

With over seven million cells, rapid and efficient ways of moving around the spreadsheet are essential.

Ability uses the following keys:

↑←↓→	One field in the direction of the arrow.
PgUp	Up a page (20 rows).
PgDn	Down a page of rows.
Home	To the first cell in the current row.
End	To the last non-empty cell in the current row.
Tab	To the right one cell
Shift-Tab	To the left one cell
Ctrl-Home	To cell A1
Ctrl-End	To the last non-empty column in the last row
Ctrl-PgUp	To the first field in the current column.
Ctrl-PgDn	To the last field in the current column.
Ctrl-→	To the right one screen of columns.
Ctrl-←	To the left one screen of columns.

Searching

You can move rapidly to any cell by pressing the goto key:

    F3

This gives you a choice of two options:

Goto   Enter a cell address or field name and press RETURN. Ability will move to the named field or address.

Search   Search for a cell containing a label or value. You cannot search for formulae. After entering the search criteria you will be presented with a new menu:

Row   Search just this row

Column   Search just this column

Both   Search rows and columns

Next   Search forward

Previous   Search backwards

Ability will find all occurrences of the search pattern. Case is ignored when searching for text; fred is equivalent to Fred and FRED etc.

Wildcards

Like database, Spreadsheet allows the use of two wildcard characters:

    *   replaces any number of characters,
    ?   replaces just one character.

You should avoid entering characters after the asterisk as Ability finds the last occurrence of the first character after the asterisk. In a spreadsheet containing a label, PRESSURE, a search for:

    *ressure

would be unsuccessful.

Relational Operators

You can search for cells where the numerical value is not known precisely. To do this you use relational operators.

<	Less than
>	More than
=	Equal to
<=	Less than or equal to
>=	Greater than or equal to
<>	Not equal to

For example, searching for:

    >1

would cause Ability to find all those cells where the value was greater than 1.

Logical Operators

You can connect the search criteria to allow a search for a number meeting two or more criteria. To do this you can use one of the three logical operators provided by Spreadsheet:

Op	Func	Example	Meaning
&	AND	>12 and <15	Greater than 12 and less than 15
|	OR	>12 or <3	Greater than 12 or less than 3
~	NOT	~Temperature	Not Temperature

A Basic Spreadsheet

Having dealt with the basics of moving around and searching through a spreadsheet, we can now get to work on a simple example. Spreadsheets are often described as tools for financial modelling. However, this minimises their capabilities. To prove that there are other uses, we will write a small spreadsheet that contains no financial information whatever, but models the variations in volume, pressure and temperature of an ideal gas. This is not a practical application

193

unless you are a balloonist, tyre or aircraft designer, but it is a fairly simple way of illustrating the principle of spreadsheets.

The first job when writing a spreadsheet is to plan it carefully. Once again you should put pen to paper before fingers to keyboard. Necessarily, I have used scientific formula, so the maths may look a little strange, but don't worry about that.

The basic gas equation is:

```
PV=nRT
```

There are only four variables in this spreadsheet, P,V,T and n. P is the pressure, V volume, T is the absolute temperature, R=0.082 and n is the amount of gas in moles (One mole of anything contains the same number of molecules as one mole of anything else). The other units of measurement we'll come to shortly.

A little algebra reveals that:

```
P=nRT/V
V=nRT/P
T=PV/nR
n=PV/RT
```

These are the four calculations we will need in the spreadsheet. We will need a column to enter the data, a column to read the results and two columns of text for labels.

Now we can start the spreadsheet:

Getting Started

Position the cursor over NEW under the Spreadsheet column on the Library screen. Press RETURN and enter the new filename GAS.

Labels

Use the cursor keys to move to field B1 (you will see Enter B1: immediately below the Status line. Type the title:

```
Ideal Gas Equation
```

Notice that the label overlaps the end of the field. Labels always do this if the following field is empty.

Any text you enter will be regarded by Ability as a label, unless you prefix it with a + or a -.

A number will usually be accepted as data, unless you precede it with a character to mark it as a label.

In this case, the characters used indicate the position in the field that you wish the label to occupy and are known as formatting characters.

These formatting characters must be the first character in the field, and are not reproduced as part of the field. They can be used on text labels in addition to numbers. The available characters are:

Character	Effect	Example
'(single quote)	Left Justify	'Volume
"(double quote)	Right Justify	"Volume
^(caret)	Centre	^Volume

Unless you tell it otherwise, Ability assumes left justified labels. Label fields may not be referenced in formulae.

If you need to justify numbers you can use the Format option from F4.

A fourth formatting character is available, *. If this is the first character in the field, it reproduces the character immediately following itself across the field. It is most often used thus:

*_	Draw a line across the field
*=	Draw a double line across the field

However, any character may be used in this way, including * itself.

Now we can put the labels in the following cells:

A3	Pressure
A8	Volume
A11	Temperature
A15	Moles
A17	R
B4	mm Hg

195

B5	Psi
B6	Psig
B7	bar
B9	litres
B10	Cu ft.
B12	deg. C
B13	deg. K
B14	deg. F

Under the pressure heading, Psig is the pressure in pounds per square inch above atmospheric, Psi is the absolute pressure. Bar is the pressure in atmospheres and mm Hg is the pressure in millimetres of Mercury. Under Temperature, deg K is the temperature in Kelvin (Celsius degrees above Absolute Zero).

In this scale one degree Kelvin (or one degree Absolute) is the same change in temperature as one degree centigrade (or Celsius) but zero degrees Kelvin is -273 degrees centigrade. Absolute zero is a very important temperature in physics and chemistry.

Entering Formulae

We can now start entering some formulae:

C5	+C4/760*14.7
C6	+C5-14.7
C7	+C4/760
C10	+C9/28.32
C13	273+C12
C14	9*C12/5+32

The spreadsheet requires entry in millimetres of Mercury, litres, degrees centigrade and moles. The above formulae convert to other units. In particular, the calculation needs temperatures in degrees Kelvin (degrees absolute), pressure in bar and volumes in litres.

Naming Cells

If we name some cells, it will make life a little easier when we come to write the major part of the formulae.

Fieldnames can be up to 13 characters long but the first three characters must be letters or underlines. Press:

    F4,N

and name the following cells:

    C7   P
    C9   V
    C13   T
    C16   n
    B17   R

We now need to define constants, in our case just one. Enter 0.082 in cell B17:

If you make a mistake and want to delete a field name type:

    F4,N,DEL

Naming a Range of Cells

You can also assign a name to a range or list of cells and can then refer to all the cells by the range name.

To do this, move the cursor to a cell outside the normal spreadsheet area and enter the name you wish to call the range, followed by an equals sign and the range addresses in brackets, eg,

    CALCULATION=(D4..D16)

You can use this name in functions and in formulae.

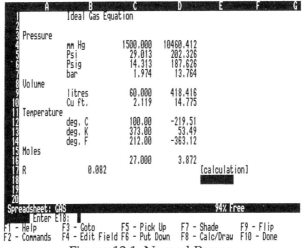

Figure 13.1. Named Range

Range Intersections

If you have two named ranges, you can indicate the intersection using a semicolon (;). For example, if you name two ranges:

```
FRED        A1..B10
JIM         B1..C15
```

Entering FRED;JIM identifies the intersection of the two ranges, in this case B10. You can use this intersection in a formula in the same way that you use a range.

Copying Cells

We can copy a single cell to a single cell or a range of cells, or can copy a range of cells to a range of cells.

The Copy option is found on the F2 Commands menu. If you want to copy a range, use F7 to Shade the range before pressing F2.

If you want to copy to a range of cells, Copy gives you the opportunity to mark the limits of the range using the cursor movement keys and F7. If you are copying a range of cells, you can simply move the cursor to the first cell of the range.

[A]

Ability allows you to use just the cursor movement keys and F7 to define the range to copy to.

[A+]

Ability Plus allows you to use F3, the cursor movement keys and F7 to define the range to copy to.

Move the cursor to C5 and press F7. Move the cursor to C17 by pressing Ctrl-End. Move the cursor back to C14. You should now have column C shaded between C5 and C14. Next press:

```
F2,C
```

to copy. Move the cursor to D5 and press RETURN.

[A+]

If you have Ability Plus you can use:

```
F3-GC14
```

to move to cell C14.

[A][A+]

You should now have a copy of column C in column D. We do not need all of these cells but it is a simple matter to overwrite the ones we don't need. This technique is a very useful time saver.

If you look through the cells you will notice that all the formulae have changed to refer to the new column.

Absolute Addresses

There may be some cells that you do not wish to change when copied. You can specify these by including the $ character in the cell address when you refer to it. The $ character makes the address absolute. You can define a cell address in four ways. We'll use cell C1 to illustrate:

C1	Non-absolute address
$C1	Absolute column address
C$1	Absolute row address
C1	Fully absolute address

Cells which are named are also treated as absolute.

Moving Cells

Moving cells is identical to copying cells, except that the original cells are blanked.

Editing Field

Now we enter the calculation formulae. Remember our original equations:

$$P=nRT/V$$
$$V=nRT/P$$
$$T=PV/nR$$
$$n=PV/RT$$

Move the cursor to D7 to enter the pressure calculation:

```
+n*R*T/V
```

Move the cursor to D4 and press:

```
F4,E
```

to edit the field. Enter 760*D7.

Move to cell D9 to enter the volume calculation:

```
+n*R*T/P
```

Move to cell D13 to enter the temperature calculation:

```
+P*V/(n*R)
```

Finally move to D16 and enter:

```
(P*V)/+R*T
```

One point to note is that the formula in cell D4 refers to the contents of cell D7. In general, spreadsheets are calculated in sequence from A1. A2,B1 is always calculated after A1. If the spreadsheet is calculated by rows, B1 is calculated before A2, and if calculated by columns, A2 before B1. In our case, D7 must be calculated after D4. There is a danger that D4, which uses the value in D7, may produce an incorrect value because the contents of D7 have not been recalculated when D4 reads them.

This is called forward referencing and can be extremely embarrassing with some spreadsheets, if you are not aware of it. You may print a spreadsheet that contains incorrect information because of forward references. The solution is to force recalculation twice.

Ability appears to resolve forward references without problems but if you ever use another spreadsheet, be aware of this potential problem.

Recalculation

Ability automatically recalculates the entire spreadsheet every time you enter or change information in a spreadsheet. With large spreadsheets, this can take some time, so it is often worth disabling the automatic recalculation. To do this press:

[A]   F2,O,R

[A+]   F2,S,R

This presents you with a new menu:

Yes   Automatic Recalculation
No   Manual Recalculation
Many   Recalculate a fixed number of times
Until-zero Recalculate until the result in a specified cell is zero.

The last two options enable you to make iterative calculations. That is, calculations where several recalculations have to be made. We will deal with iteration later in this chapter.

If you wish to force a recalculation press:

    F8

Locking Cells

All that remains is to lock all the cells. Press:

    F3,G

enter the cell address B3. Now press F7 followed by Ctrl-End. Finally press:

[A]   F2,O,L,F,L

[A+]   F2,R,L,F,L

to lock the formulae.

Move the cursor to B17 and press:

[A]   F2,O,L,N,L

[A+]   F2,R,L,F,L

to lock the data.

Locking a cell means that you cannot change an entry. You should routinely do this for cells containing formulae or constants that you should not change.

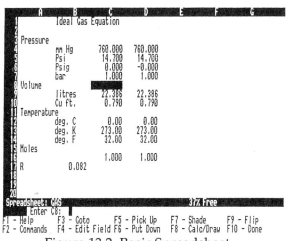

Figure 13.2. Basic Spreadsheet

[A]

The Lock menu is found on the OTHER sub menu from the F2 Commands menu.

[A+]

The Lock menu is found on the RANGE sub menu from the F2 Commands menu.

After selecting `Lock` you will be given a choice of the type of cell to lock:

All	Lock all cells
Non-Formula	Lock all cells containing text or data
Formula	Lock all cells containing formulae

You will now see another menu with just two choices:

Lock	Lock cells
Unlock	Unlock cells

If you move the cursor to a Locked cell you will see the word LOCK on the left of the `Status` line. Unlocking is, of course, the reverse of locking.

Testing the Spreadsheet

The spreadsheet is designed to enable you to enter any three parameters in column C. The fourth is then read from column D. To test the spreadsheet, all we need do is to set up a problem for which we already know the answer. Enter the following data:

C4	760
C9	22.386
C12	0
C16	1

If you look at column D you should see the same data presented.

Computer Modelling

If we increase the amount of gas by typing `2.75` into C16 we will see that, if we keep the pressure and temperature constant, we need a larger volume and, to keep volume and temperature constant, we need to increase pressure to about the tyre pressure of a modern car. If we assume that the gas is air in a car tyre and increase the temperature from water's freezing point to 25 degrees C, the temperature of a warm summer day, we see that the pressure has increased by more than 10%. By varying temperatures and pressures we can predict the behaviour of our tyre. We could obviously expand our model to include road-holding, and longevity. The spreadsheet could then be regarded as a simple computer model of a car tyre. We could get the same information by building a model and varying the gas parameters, but our computer model is quicker and cheaper.

Formula Display

You may wish to examine the spreadsheet formulae in some detail. Ability allows you to choose whether to display values or formulae on the screen. Press:

[A]   F2,O,V

[A+]   F2,S,V

You can then choose values or formulae for display.

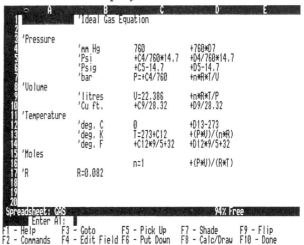

Figure 13.3. Formula Display

Iterative Calculations

Iterative calculations are ones which contain circular references. These normally require several calculations in order to reach the correct result. To illustrate this, we will write a small spreadsheet to calculate the amount of VAT in a purchase. Note that this is not the easiest way of performing this calculation!

Press F10 to exit from the GAS spreadsheet. Start a new spreadsheet called NEW. Enter the following data:

A2	TOTAL
A3	GOODS
A4	VAT

```
B1              Iterative
B3              +B2-B4
B4              +B3*E2%
```

As we are using circular calculations we will expect to get an error message in B3. The value will be calculated however, so we will just read it into another cell. In fact, we will copy all the results into column C:

```
C2              +B2
C3              +B3
C4              +B4
```

Just to show the fastest way of calculating VAT, we will add another column to calculate the figure in one pass.

```
D1              CALCULATED
D2              +B2
D3              +D2/(1+E2%)
D4              +D2-D3
E1              "VAT %
```

Set columns B to E to Money format using:

```
F4-FMS
```

Now enter the VAT percentage in E2 and the total cost of the goods in B2.

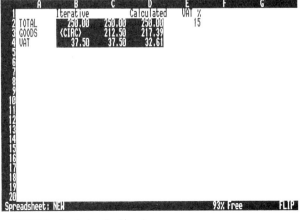

Figure 13.4.Iterative Spreadsheet

You will see the error message:

    CIRC

in B3 and figures in column c. Press:

    F8

The figures will change. Keep pressing F8 until the figures in column C stop changing. The figures using the iterative method should be identical to those calculated using the direct method in column D. The fact that we have chosen an example which is easy to calculate directly should not obscure the usefulness of the technique; some problems can be approached in no other way.

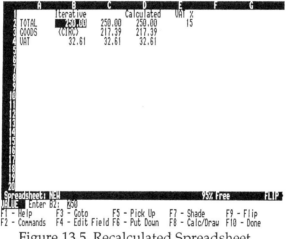

Figure 13.5. Recalculated Spreadsheet

Finally, you can speed up the process by pre-selecting a reasonable number of times to recalculate, say six, and use:

[A]   F2,O,R,M,6

[A+]   F2,S,R,M,6

In all these key sequence examples, don't type the commas!

14 : Spreadsheet Commands

SPREADSHEET allows the use of all ten function keys:

F1	Help
F2	Commands
F3	Goto/Search
F4	Edit
F5	Pick-up
F6	Put-down
F7	Shade
F8	Calculate/Draw
F9	Flip
F10	Done (Save and Exit)

F1

F1 allows the usual context sensitive help. We have dealt with F3, F7 and F8 in the last chapter. Keys F9 and F10 have the usual uses.

F5 Pick-up

Pick-up F5 and Put-down F6 are used to transfer data from SPREADSHEET to DATABASE or WRITE. Pressing F5 picks up all of the information in a shaded area of a spreadsheet. This can be transferred as a text copy to a WRITE document simply by opening the document and pressing F6.

To transfer data from SPREADSHEET to DATABASE, set up a database master form containing the fields you want to copy. Next, use F7 to shade the appropriate fields before pressing F5 to Pick-up the data. You must ensure that the database fields appear in exactly the same order as they do in the spreadsheet and that the database fields are wide enough to accommodate all the information.

F6 Put-down

To put down a spreadsheet in a database, select the database containing the fields you wish to transfer to and press F6. Information on each row of the spreadsheet is read into individual forms. F6 will also transfer data as text to a document.

F2 Commands

[A] Pressing the `F2 Commands` key displays a menu of eight options.

`Copy`	Copy range
`Move`	Move range
`Blank`	Range
`Titles`	Fix titles
`Insert`	Columns or rows
`Remove`	Columns or rows
`Print`	Print a spreadsheet
`Other`	

We have looked at `Copy` and `Move` in the previous chapter, so we'll now examine the others.

Blank

Blanks, or removes, the contents of a cell or a shaded range of cells.

Titles

Fixes on screen all `Row` and `Column` information to the left and above the cursor. This is most useful in larger spreadsheets as it keeps the row and column titles on the screen when you scroll through the spreadsheet.

If you want to fix vertical titles only, move the cursor to the next row one column to the right of the ones you want to fix. To fix the titles in column A, move the cursor to cell B1 and select `Titles`. To fix horizontal titles only, move the cursor to column A and the row immediately below the row you wish to fix. To fix horizontal titles in rows one and two, move the cursor to cell A3 and select `Titles`. To fix horizontal titles in rows one and two and vertical titles in column A, move the cursor to cell B3 and select `Titles`.

Unfreeze Titles

To unfreeze titles, move the cursor to cell A1 using `CTRL-Home` and select `Titles`.

Insert

The `Insert` command is used to insert one or more rows or columns at the position of the cursor.

To insert a row, move the cursor to the row where you wish the new rows to begin. Select `Insert Row`. Ability will ask for the number of rows to insert. Ability will automatically amend references to cells that have been moved.

To insert a column, move the cursor to the column where you wish the new columns to begin. Select `Insert Column`. Ability will ask for the number of columns to insert. Ability will automatically amend references to cells that have been moved.

Remove

Use `Remove` to totally remove one or more shaded rows or columns.

To remove one or more rows from the spreadsheet, place the cursor in a column and press `F7`. Move the cursor vertically to shade the rows you wish to delete. Select `Remove Rows`. Ability will automatically amend references to cells that have been moved.

To remove one or more columns from the spreadsheet, place the cursor in a row and press `F7`. Move the cursor horizontally to shade the columns you wish to delete. Select `Remove Columns`. Ability will automatically amend references to cells that have been moved.

Print

This is the option that allows you to print a spreadsheet. Ability removes `Row` and `Column` numbers from the printout. Selecting `Print` displays the standard print menu:

`Go`   Start Printing now

`To-File`   Print-to Menu

`Printer`   Print file on Printer.

File   This will produce an ASCII file that can be modified by a wordprocessor. You can send this file to people who don't have Ability.

Cpi   Select character size menu.

                Pica   10 characters per inch
                Elite   12 characters per inch
                Condensed   condensed print size

Range   Pages or whole file menu

Shaded   Print shaded range

All   Print whole file

Paper   Select paper type
                Continuous Continuous paper
                Single   Single sheet paper

Sideways   Print file upright or sideways
                Sideways   Print file sideways
                Upright   Print file upright

                The Sideways option relies on the graphics mode of the printer and so is not usable with a daisywheel printer, or impact printer incapable of graphics.

Printing Large Spreadsheets

Ability will print as many columns as possible across the paper. After printing the last row, Ability will feed paper to the top of the next sheet and start printing the next set of columns.

The F2 Other Menu

The Other option offers nine more options on a menu:

Data-fill   Fill cells with data
Sort   Sort a spreadsheet range

Transpose	Transpose data on a spreadsheet
Lock	Locking cells
Recalc	Recalculate a spreadsheet
Values	Displays Formulae or Values in cells
Consolidate	Consolidate spreadsheets
File	Load or Save spreadsheet
Quit	Exit without saving

Filling Cells with Data

Fill shaded cells with numbers. Shade an area then select Data-fill. You will be asked to nominate the start value and the increment. The cells will then be filled from left to right and top to bottom. This could be used to put month numbers or dates in a spreadsheet.

Sort

This option allows you to sort a spreadsheet by either row or column.

First Shade the area to be sorted, then select Sort from the menu. You will be asked which row or column you wish to sort. You will be asked if you wish an Ascending or a Descending sort. If you Sort a row, the contents of the shaded columns will be ordered; if you Sort a column, the row contents will be ordered.

Transpose

Transpose shaded formulae. This is similar to the move option except that column information is moved to a row, and row information to a column. Effectively the shaded range is rotated. Select the range to transpose using F7 and the cursor keys, then select Transpose. Move the cursor to the cell where you want the upper left corner of the transposed range to appear and press RETURN.

Lock

Lock allows you to lock or unlock cells. Locking cells makes it impossible for you to alter the contents. This should be done to prevent spreadsheets being damaged by erroneous overwriting of formulae. Define the cells you wish to lock by shading.

You can choose to lock:

All cells
Formula cells
Non Formula cells

Recalculating a Spreadsheet

`Recalc` allows you to set the recalculation mode of the spreadsheet. Normally Ability recalculates the whole spreadsheet each time you make an entry. If the spreadsheet is a large one, the delay caused by recalculation can be a little frustrating. For this reason you may choose to select when to calculate the spreadsheet. `Recalc` allows four options:

Yes   Turn on auto-recalculation

No   Turn off auto-recalculation

Many   Recalculate a set number of times. After entering a
             number Ability recalculates the spreadsheet that number
             of times. Once completed, the number of recalculations
             returns to one.

Until-zero   Recalculate until the contents of a chosen cell is zero.
             After selecting `Until-zero` you will be invited to select
             a cell. Use the cursor keys or type in the number.
             Recalculation will only stop when the chosen cell has a
             zero value. You can use an IF statement in the cell if
             necessary, eg,

             ```
             IF(cell=23,0,1)
             ```

             In this example, recalculation stops when cell=23.

The last two options are very useful for iterative calculations. You can also use `F8` to force recalculations at any time.

Values

The `Values` option allows you to choose whether to display `Values` or `Formulae` in cells. Displaying formulae is a very useful option when setting up or correcting (debugging) a spreadsheet. If you choose to print the spreadsheet, Ability will print whichever option is on the screen. You may have to increase the column width if you want to display formulae.

Consolidate

The Consolidate option allows you to add, subtract, multiply or divide two spreadsheets. The cells of spreadsheet 1 are compared with the cell at the same field address in spreadsheet 2. You will be asked to select Add, Subtract, Multiply or Divide followed by the names of the two spreadsheets.

File

File gives you two options:

Load   Load the contents of another spreadsheet into your spreadsheet. You can also translate .DIF files from Lotus 1-2-3 or Symphony. If you load an Ability spreadsheet, just type the filename when asked. For Lotus files you have to type the extension .DIF after the filename. Ability changes column widths to match the loaded spreadsheet.

Save   This saves a whole spreadsheet, if you want to export the file to Lotus 1-2-3 or symphony add the extension .DIF after the filename.

Quit

Use Quit to exit from the spreadsheet without saving it.

Commands

[A+]

Many of the Ability Plus commands are similar to the Ability commands. This section will therefore contain just a brief explanation of the command, further details being available in the Ability commands section of this chapter.

Pressing F2 presents a menu of eight options:

```
Spreadsheet
Range
Copy
Move
Data
Print
File
Quit
```

The Spreadsheet Option

[A+]

This allows further options.

Insert   Insert one or more rows or columns at the position of the cursor. Ability will ask for the number of rows or columns to insert.

Delete   Delete one or more shaded rows or columns.

Titles   Fixes on screen all Row and Column information to the left and above the cursor. This is most useful in larger spreadsheets.

Using Two Windows

Selecting Window allows you to split the screen vertically or horizontally into two windows. If another file is open in the other flip state it will appear in the other window. If you wish you can synchronise windows.

When you have selected either a Vertical or a Horizontal split, you will see a light coloured bar on the screen. Move this bar using the cursor movement keys and press RETURN when in the correct place.

To return to one window select Clear from the Windows menu.

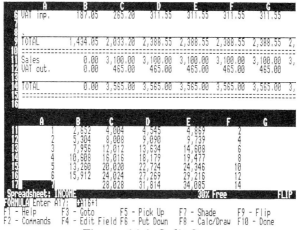

Figure 14.1. Split Screen

Other Commands

Range [A+]

Lock   Lock or Unlock cells

Blank   Deletes a cell or a shaded range of cells.

Copy and Move

        Copy and Move both act on shaded ranges. Both were
        discussed in the last Chapter:

        Copy   Copy range

        Move   Move range

Data [A+]

Data allows data manipulations. There are three options:

Fill

        Fill shaded cells with numbers. Shade an area then select Fill.
        You will be asked to nominate the start value and the increment.
        The cells are filled left to right and top to bottom.

Sort

        Sort spreadsheet by either row or column. First Shade the area
        you want to Sort then select Sort from the menu. You will be
        asked which row or column you wish to sort. You will be asked
        if you wish an Ascending or a Descending sort. If you sort a

row, the contents of the shaded columns will be re-ordered; if you sort on a column, the row contents will be ordered. There is no effect outside the shaded area.

Transpose

Transpose shaded formulae. This is similar to the move option except that column information is moved to a row, and row information to a column.

Print [A+]

Print produces the usual nine option menu:

Go   Start Printing now

To-File
Print to Disc or Printer

Printer
Print file on Printer.

File This will produce an ASCII file that you can send to people who don't have Ability

New-Page
who don't have Ability

New-Page
Position the paper to the top of the next page. This is done by sending a form-feed command to the printer. If the paper does not feed to the top of the next sheet, check that the form length is set properly by the printer DIP switches and that the printer was positioned at the top of the page when you turned it on. Adjust the paper manually if necessary.

Line Move paper up one line only.

Cpi Select character size menu.
    Pica   10 characters per inch
    Elite   12 characters per inch

`Condensed` condensed print size

Range
>   Pages or whole file menu

Shaded
>   Print shaded range.

All Print whole file

Paper
>   Select paper type
>   `Continuous` Continuous paper
>   `Single`   Single sheet paper

Sideways
>   Print file upright or sideways
>   `Sideways`   Print file sideways
>   `Upright`   Print file upright
>   Sideways printing is impossible with a daisywheel printer or impact printer which does not support graphics.

Quality
>   Quality Menu
>   `Final`   Best quality printer can do.
>   `Draft`   Print as fast as possible.

>   `Quality` only applies to dot-matrix printers with NLQ facilities. If the printer does not have NLQ, Ability may send the Double-Strike command to improve print quality.

File
[A+]
Load
>   Load a spreadsheet

Save
>   Save a spreadsheet

217

`Consolidate`
> This allows you to add, subtract, multiply or divide two spreadsheets. Each cell of spreadsheet one is compared with the cell at the same field address in spreadsheet 2. You will be asked to select `Add`, `Subtract`, `Multiply` or `Divide` followed by the names of the two spreadsheets.

`Quit`
> Exit spreadsheet without saving

[A] The Edit Command

On pressing the F4 key with the cursor on a cell you will see a menu of four options:

Edit
> Change the contents of the cell.

Format
> Change the Display format of the cell.

Width
> Change the width of the cell.

Name
> Change or remove the cell name.

Edit Cell

Displays the contents of the field on the edit line under the `Status` line. The cell can be edited using the usual editing keys.

Format

`Format` gives you further options. If you Shade an area you can define a `Format` for the whole area.

`Money`
> Select money format

`Standard`

eg, £1,234,567.89, Leading £ sign
Negative numbers in Brackets

`Leading-$-sign`
>   Use a leading currency symbol. This is a Yes/No option. In the
>   UK a £ is used in place of the $ sign which is always displayed in
>   the option title.

`Negative-sign`
>   Use accountancy standards for negative numbers ie, negative
>   numbers in brackets. This is a Yes/No option

`Commas`
>   Use commas to separate thousands: Yes/No option

`Fixed`
>   Fix the number of Decimal places (0-12)

`Variable`
>   Variable number of decimal places.

`Scientific`
>   Use Scientific notation. E indicates the exponent: 1,000,000 or 10^6
>   is shown as `1E6`

`Percent`
>   Show values as percentages

`Date`
>   Display the month, day and year
> | American | `06/05/88` |
> | European | `05-06-1988` |
> | Metric | `88-06-05` |
> | Long | `June 5, 1988` |

`Justify`
>   Right or left justify cell
>   `Left`

219

```
Right
```

Setting Column Width

Set the column width. There are three options:

```
Set   Type in the field width
      Increase-by-1
      Decrease-by-1
```

The latter two options allow you to set the field width using the cursor keys.

If you type a label, it will expand to cover as many unoccupied cells to the right as are needed. You can set the width of a range of columns simply by shading them.

Naming Cells

Name allows you to enter or change the name of a cell.

[A+]

On pressing the F4 key with the cursor on a cell in the spreadsheet you will see a menu of five options:

```
Edit            Change the contents of the cell.
Format          Change the Display format of the cell.
Width           Change the width of the cell.
Name            Change or remove the cell name.
Global-Format   Make this format global.
```

Edit Menu [A+]

The Ability Plus Edit Menu is obtained by pressing F4. Many of the F4 options have subsidiary menus. We will look at these in turn:

```
Edit   Allows you to edit the cell contents.
Format
```
        gives you eight further options. If you shade an area you can define a format for the whole area:
```
        Money           Select money format
```

```
Standard
```
        eg, £1,234,567.89,Leading £ sign

Negative numbers in Brackets

`Currency-sign`
Leading £

`User`
Display with user-defined symbol options 1-7.
Options are described on the hints line.

`Percent`
Show values as percentages

`Date`
Display the month, day and year in the style you set up in the
Library screen, eg,

Long	June 5, 1988
Short	05-06-88

`Reset`
Display without formatting symbols

`Number`
Punctuation and scaling menu

`Decimal`		
`Fixed`	Fixed number of decimal places	
`Variable`	Variable number of places	
`Scientific`	Displays numbers as a mantissa (a number) followed by an Exponent preceded by an E, eg, $1E6 = 1 \times 10^6 = 1,000,000$	
`Separator`	Use a separator to display thousands, eg, 1,000, (Yes/No)	
`Negative`	Use accountancy standards for negative numbers ie, negative numbers in brackets. (Yes/No)	
`Justify`	Right or left justify cell	
`Left`		
`Right`		

Width

> Set the cell width either by entering the number or selecting the
> width. A secondary menu is produced:

Set	Type in Field width.
Increase-by-1	Change width by 1 column
Decrease-by-1	Change width by 1 column

Name

> Name or change the name of the cell.

Global format

> Make a format global. This option produces the same secondary
> menu as Format. The Global format does not effect any local
> formats you may set subsequently or have set already.

15 : Advanced Spreadsheet

SPREADSHEET has a number of advanced features. You can import from, or export to Lotus 1-2-3, link spreadsheets and use spreadsheet fields in DATABASE and WRITE.

Importing from Lotus 1-2-3
[A+]
Ability Plus allows you to import files from Lotus 1-2-3 version 1.0a. To import, use F5 to Pick-up and F6 to Put-down the file in the SPREADSHEET column. Ability Plus will automatically convert the picked up file to Ability format.

Lotus Macros are not converted because the spreadsheet commands are different.

Some 1-2-3 formulae will be too long for Ability's 250 character formula limit. If this is the case, the formula will be translated as text which may then be edited in the usual way.

Some names may be changed, as will all references to that name. This will only be a problem if duplicate names are created. Warning messages are issued if a name is changed.

Ability spreadsheets tend to use more memory than those of Lotus 1-2-3, so large spreadsheets may not fit into the computer memory.

Some 1-2-3 functions do not have equivalents in Ability. These functions will not be translated.

If you use Lotus 1-2-3 version 2, you must convert it to version 1A format before attempting to translate it to Ability.

The WKS Program
Ability cannot import spreadsheet fields through the Library screen so a utility WKS.EXE is provided for the purpose.

To convert a file, move the cursor to WKS on the Programs menu. You will be asked for the rest of the command line. Enter the following information:

```
filename [drive] [>output]
```

Filename is the filename plus the `WKS` extension, drive is the optional drive and output is the optional destination to which any warning or error messages will be sent. This can be an MSDOS device or a filename.

Examples:

```
TEST.WKS
```
converts `TEST.WKS` to `TEST.XSS` (Ability format).
```
TEST.WKS C:
```
converts `TEST.WKS` to `TEST.XSS` on drive C:.
```
TEST.WKS >ERRORS.TXT
```
converts `TEST.WKS` to `TEST.XSS` and sends error messages to the file `errors.txt`.
```
TEST.WKS A: >CON:
```
converts `TEST.WKS` to `TEST.XSS` on drive A: and sends error messages to the screen. Other useful destinations are:
```
PRN:          Printer
COM1:         Serial Port
```

Lotus Macros are not converted because the spreadsheet commands are different.

Some 1-2-3 formulae will be too long for Ability's 250 character formula limit. If this is the case, the formula will be translated as text which may then be edited in the usual way.

Some names may be changed, as will all references to that name. This will only be a problem if duplicate names are created. Warning messages are issued if a name is changed.

Ability spreadsheets tend to use more memory than Lotus 1-2-3 ones, large spreadsheets may therefore not fit into the computer memory when converted.

Some 1-2-3 functions do not have equivalents in Ability. These functions will not be translated.

If you use Lotus 1-2-3 version 2, you must convert to version 1A before attempting to translate to Ability.

Exporting to Lotus 1-2-3

[A+]

Exporting files from Ability to Lotus 1-2-3 is simply the reverse of importing. Use F5 to Pick-up a spreadsheet from the SPREADSHEET column of the Library screen. F6 is then used to Put-down the file in the Files column.

The exported files are in Lotus 1-2-3 version 1.0a format. If you use version 2 you can use 1-2-3 to convert the file to and from version 1.0a.

Linking Cells

It is often useful to link cells in order to tie information in one cell to information in a second. If you change a value in one cell you will automatically change the value in the other. There are two possible types of link:

One Way Links

If you change the value in the original cell, the value in the linked cell also changes. However, if you change the value in the linked cell, the original cell remains unchanged. This also breaks the link between the cells.

To set up a one way link, move the cursor to the location where you want the link and type:

        +ORIG

where ORIG is the name of a spreadsheet cell.

Two Way Links

If you change the value in either cell, the value of the other also changes. Both cells in the link must be named, you cannot use cell addresses.

To create the two way link, move the cursor to the cell where you want to create the link and type:

        !ORIG

where ORIG is the name of the spreadsheet cell.

225

Linking Spreadsheets

You can also link two spreadsheets by defining the links preceded by the spreadsheet name and a backslash.

A one way link with a spreadsheet called SALES would be set up thus:

```
+SALES\ORIG
```

Not surprisingly, a two way link would be set up like this:

```
!SALES\ORIG
```

Creating links enables you to link values into other Ability applications. Spreadsheet values may be used in DATABASE, WRITE and GRAPH fields.

A Linked Spreadsheet

One major advantage of linking spreadsheets is that you can write several small spreadsheets in place of a single large one. The various spreadsheets could be completed by different people and subsequently linked together to give the complete picture.

Profit and Loss Spreadsheet

The first spreadsheet we will look at is a Profit and Loss spreadsheet. This is faster than waiting for an accountant and, if you are careful, at least as accurate. The spreadsheet can also be modified to give you sales targets and gross profit targets.

The purpose of this spreadsheet is to give a true picture of the trading state of a company. If you need to know the level of sales you need to break even, all you do is to adjust the sales figures to get a zero result in the nett profit column. If you keep the unit cost and sales volume constant you will get the gross profit margin you need. By keeping the gross profit constant you can see what sales you must achieve.

The Labels

We will start our spreadsheet design with the labels. We need a total of 14 columns, one for the headings, 12 for the months and one for the year to date summary. Months take up cells B3 to M3 starting with the first month of your financial year. I have started with January. Cell N3 contains the label Year to Date. Row 1 contains the name of the Company and the legend:

```
Profit and Loss Sheet Fiscal Year 1990-91
```

Shade cells B3 to M3 and copy to cell R1. Transpose the range to P1. Enter the numbers 1 to 12 in cells Q1 to Q12.

Move the cursor to M1 and type:

```
+LOOKUP (MONTH (TODAY ()) ,Q1..Q12,P1..P12)
```
and in N1 enter:

```
+YEAR (TODAY ())
```

Use F4,W to reduce the width of columns P and Q to 2.

With the cursor on A4 type:

```
*=
```

and replicate from B4 to N4 using the Copy command.

This completes the horizontal labels; we can now start on the vertical labels.

Increase the width of columns A to N to 15 and enter the following labels:

```
A5                  SALES
A6..N6              *-
A7                  STOCK
A8                  OPENING
A9                  CLOSING
A10..N10            *-
A11                 PURCHASES
A12..N12            *-
A13                 GROSS PROFIT
A14                 ^%
A15..N15            *=
```

The next section covers operating expenses. You can use the headings from your balance sheet, those shown below or can invent them. While it is not the function of this book to teach business management, remember that all items purchased for stock or sale are expenses. This does not include capital equipment or buildings, as these depreciate over a number of years. Depreciation is the loss in value in capital goods. For example, a computer might last 3 years and cost £3600.00. When you buy it it's worth £3600.00, a month later £3500.00, and so on. Thus we can say that this depreciation, £100 per month, is an expense.

The suggested headings are:

```
A17             EXPENSES
A18             *-
A19             Salaries
A20             Electricity
A21             Gas
A22             Water
A23             Insurance
A24             Rent
A25             Rates
A26             Motor Vehicles
A27             Travel
A28             Repayments
A29             Interest
A30             Bank Charges
A31             Plant
A32             Machinery
A33             Depreciation
A34             Advertising
A35             Promotions
A36             Exhibitions
A37             Stationery
A38..N38        *-
A39             TOTAL EXPENSE
A40..N40        *=
A41             Nett Profit
A42             ^%
A43..N43        *=
```

Having set up the labels we can now put in some formulae.

Formulae

Opening stock must be the same as the Closing stock for the previous month, so move to C8 and enter +B9. Use COPY to replicate this from D8 to M8. Enter the following formulae:

```
N5                  +TOTAL(B5..M5)
N8                  +B8
```

This formula gives the opening stock for the financial year. We now need the closing stock:

```
N9                  +LOOKUP(MONTH(TODAY()),Q1..Q12,B9..M9)
N11                 +TOTAL(B11..M11)
```

We now calculate the gross profit earned. The classic formula is:

```
SALES-(PURCHASES+Change in stock)
```

In the spreadsheet we use this formula, which amounts to the same thing:

```
B13                 +B5-B8+B9-B11
```

This should be replicated from C13 to N13.

It is useful to know the Gross Profit as a percentage of Sales. This formula can be replicated from C14 to N14:

```
B14                 +B13/B5
```

If we consider Expenses, we see that they fall into two classes: regular payments and occasional ones. The regular payments include Rent, Rates and Fuel. Stationery, Bank Charges and the like are occasional payments. We can use a formula to replicate regular payments and save a lot of time.

The thing to remember about expenses is that, no matter when they are paid, the indebtedness incurred is an expense. If you closed the business tomorrow, you would get a rebate on some advance payments and cease to pay others. Use this as a criteria for setting how you calculate expenses.

Spread Rates, Rent, Insurance, Depreciation and Repayments across twelve months. Move to the B23 and enter a figure, say £150.00. Make C23 a formula which only allows a figure when a positive sales figure occurs:

```
C22                +IF(C$5>0,B22,0)
```

Replicate this from D22 to M22, and from C to M on the following rows:

```
20,21,23,24,25,28,29,31,32,33
```

Gas and Electricity are paid quarterly, so we need only copy each entry twice:

Enter a zero in the following cells:

```
D20,D21,G20,G21,J20,J21,M20,M21
```

All you do is put an estimated value in the columns containing 0 and it will be copied to the next two months; any corrections can be made as the bills come in!

Finally, enter the following formula in cell N19:

```
+SUM(B19..M19)
```

Copy this to cells N20 to N37. Move to cell B39 and enter:

```
+SUM(B19..B36)
```

Copy from C39 to N39.

Move to cell B42 to enter the Nett Profit calculation:

```
+B13-B39
```

and the percentage in cell B43:

```
+B42/B5
```

which is copied across the range C43..N43.

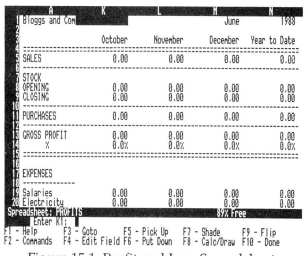

Figure 15.1. Profit and Loss Spreadsheet

[A+]

Set the `Global` format to `Money`.

[A]

Shade the whole spreadsheet and set to Money format.

Set rows 14 and 43 to `Percent`.

Set Format of N1 to fixed with 0 decimal places and no commas.

Naming ranges

Some of the expense entries are summations of what might be much more complex situations. A typical example is the salaries entry which would cover bonuses, commissions and Employers NI and pensions contributions. You can find this data by adding the total salary bill to the amount due to the Inland Revenue, or you might choose to have another spreadsheet listing all the salaries.

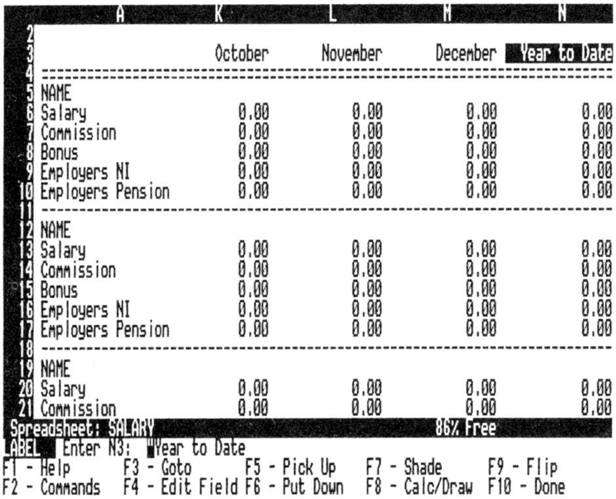

Figure 15.2. Salaries Spreadsheet

The bottom line of this spreadsheet could be the sum of all salary information. If we name the cells in this line JAN_SAL, FEB_SAL etc. we can call the data into our Profit and Loss spreadsheet.

Move to B19 and type:

```
+SALARY\JAN_SAL
```

This creates a one way link from the Salary spreadsheet to the Profit and Loss spreadsheet.

You will probably want to use this method on several expense entries in the Profit and Loss.

Data is simply typed in the month column, in the appropriate row. If the final figure is in brackets, then you have a loss, otherwise a profit.

Remember that spreadsheets cannot work miracles: if you do not enter all the information correctly, you will not get the correct result.

Using Spreadsheets in WRITE

Spreadsheets can be used in WRITE by using F9 to flip into the appropriate spreadsheet then picking up a shaded area using F5. Flip back into WRITE and use F6 to Put-down the spreadsheet at the appropriate place. This copies the spreadsheet as text. Changing the spreadsheet will not change the contents of the WRITE document.

You can also load a spreadsheet into a document. This will be updated as the original spreadsheet is updated. Conversely, if you update the part of the spreadsheet in the WRITE document, the original spreadsheet will be updated. To load all or part of a spreadsheet into WRITE press:

[A]   F2-S

[A+]   F2-IS

and enter the name of the spreadsheet to load. You are given a choice to include all or just a shaded part of the spreadsheet.

If you select the Shaded option, you will see the spreadsheet on the screen. Shade the area you wish to load and press F10 to load the shaded part into WRITE.

The spreadsheet will be centred on the page. To adjust the position, point the cursor at a spreadsheet field and select spreadsheet again:

[A]   F2-S

[A+]   F2-IS

This gives you a new menu:

Edit

> Selecting this returns you to the main spreadsheet so that you can edit it.

Adjust

> Use the cursor keys to move the spreadsheet left or right.

If you enter a spreadsheet name that does not exist, a blank spreadsheet is entered as for the shaded option. In this way you can design tables as part of the document. If you choose not to enter a name, Ability will select a name for you.

After completing the spreadsheet and pressing F10, you will be invited to include all or a shaded part of the spreadsheet.

The final method of entering spreadsheet data into a document is to establish a link between the spreadsheet and a field in the document. Use:

[A]   F2-F

[A+]   F2-IF

to set up a field. Enter the following in the field:

```
+Filename\fieldname
!Filename\fieldname
```

Where filename is the name of the spreadsheet, and the fieldname is the name of the spreadsheet field.

The first form, using a +, sets up a one way link. If you change the field contents in the document, the spreadsheet does not change and the link is broken. If you use a ! a two way link is set up. Changing the field contents in either application also changes the contents of the field in the other.

Using Spreadsheet in DATABASE

You can use a spreadsheet in DATABASE by setting up a master form with fields in the same order as in the spreadsheet. The database fields must be wide enough to contain the data in the spreadsheet. Shade the appropriate fields in the spreadsheet and press F5, enter the Browse screen and press F6.

You can include one way links to a spreadsheet within a master form. Two way links can be set up, but appear to blank the appropriate field in the spreadsheet.

16 : Example Spreadsheets

Spreadsheets are very easy to learn and to work with. There are a limited number of operations necessary to complete a spreadsheet and each is logical. The problem with spreadsheets is the initial planning to ensure that you get the information you want.

The previous chapter dealt with a profit and loss spreadsheet, this one will deal with three more basic spreadsheets, Price List, Cash Flow forecast and Moving Annual Total.

Price List

Pricing is often the most difficult part of any business planning operation. Pricing generates Gross Profit and it is surprising how often people get it wrong. We will base this spreadsheet on cost prices. If you are manufacturing, the cost price will be calculated as:

```
Cost of Materials + (Cost of Labour x Time)
```

This can obviously be further broken down into design, drawing, research and manufacturing costs if necessary.

If you are providing a service, such as building or plumbing, then you can break down the cost price as:

```
Cost of Materials + (Cost of Labour x Time)
```

Cost of Labour is also included in your profit and loss spreadsheet, but we are not, as you might think, using the same figure twice. In this case, the time taken affects the cost price, so it is valid to use it in cost calculations for pricing. You will notice that the gross profit on your profit and loss sheet will be higher than that on your price list, if you are in a labour intensive industry, as your purchases will simply be materials, labour being ignored.

If you are buying and selling, cost price is simply cost of materials.

The only complicated pricing problem is that of costing service contracts. In this case, you need to know the approximate lifetime of each module and the mean time between failures of the system. If you have mature products and you know that a motor has a mean service

life of five years, you can say that for each year there is a 20% chance
that you will have to replace that item. You therefore have to ensure
that your service contracts' costs include 20% of the cost of a new
motor. If the system has a mean time before failure of 4 months then
you also have to include the cost of 3 visits per year. In this case, the
cost of each visit is the time and travel plus 6.7% of the cost of a motor.
I do know a small engineering company who assume that each visit
will be the only one in a year and for service contracts multiply the
cost of an annual visit by the number of visits made in a year, thus
proving that the more the engineer visits the more unreliable the
product is! Not many service contracts are sold!

It is worth making a note of the purpose of the spreadsheet before you
start. In this case, the purpose of this spreadsheet is to calculate the
selling price and gross profit, given the cost price. Discount structures
for trade customers will also be calculated.

The Labels

Starting, as always, with the labels, move the cursor to A1. Start with
the name of the company and the issue date:

```
A1              Bloggs and Company - Price List
B2              +Today()
```

Format B2 for Long dates, ignore the fact that you get an overflow
error. Now set the width of column B to 30.

```
A3              Catalogue
B3              Description
C3              Retail
D3              Trade A
E3              Trade B
F3              Discount
G3              Discount
H3              Cost
I3              Mark-up
J3              Gross P.
K3              Gross P. %
L3              Gross P.
M3              Gross P. %
N3              Gross P.
```

O3	Gross P. %
A4	Number
C4	Price
D4	Price
E4	Price
F4	^A
G4	^B
H4	Price
I4	^%
J4	Retail
K4	Retail
L4	Trade A
M4	Trade A
N4	Trade B
O4	Trade B

Formulae

Now we can start entering the formulae:

Enter `100` as the cost price in H6 and 25% as the Mark-up in I6. I6 should show `0.25` at this stage. Now we have a cost price and a mark-up, we can calculate a selling price. Enter in C6:

```
+H6*(1+I6)
```

This provides a selling price of 125.

We now set up the Gross Profit cells:

J6	+C6−H6
K6	+J6/K6

In our case these give 25 and 0.2 respectively.

We have two groups of trade customers. Group B buy a great deal, so we give them a good discount to keep them loyal. Group A buy less so they get a smaller discount. Unless you are very lucky, your gross profit on goods will vary somewhat so you cannot allow a flat rate discount. It is a nuisance, to say the least, to have a large number of discount rates. To avoid this, we will restrict the discounts to steps of 5%. To calculate the discount on trade A terms we need this formula:

$$S * INTEGER(RGP*n*100/S)/100$$

S is the step size, in this case 5%

RGP retail gross profit %

n the percentage of the gross profit available for discount.

We will allow up to 50% of our Gross Profit for our top customers, and perhaps 25% for the normal trade customers. In this case, we can substitute in the equation above:

F6   5*INT(K6*.25*100/5)%

This simplifies to:

F6   5*INT(K6*5)%

and for the higher discount rates:

G6   5*INT(K6*10)

We can now calculate the prices for trade customers:

D6   (1-F6)*C6
E6   (1-G6)*C6

Finally, we enter the formulae for gross profit on the discounted prices:

```
            L6   +D6-H6
M6          +L6/D6
N6          +E6-H6
O6          +N6/E6
```

You can copy all the formulae from Row 6 to the bottom of the price list.

There may be a circumstance where you have a fixed selling price and discount. This spreadsheet allows you to handle this circumstance as well. The GP% Retail becomes the discount column. Enter the discount followed by a % sign in cell K7. You now need to change the Cost price, Mark-up and Retail price cells. The retail price cell contains the selling price. The following other changes must be made:

H7   (1-K7)*C7
I7   +J7/H7

Format Ranges

Format the whole spreadsheet from C6 to the end as money format. Format the following columns as Percent:

    F,G,I,K,M,O

Finally, fix the same columns with a fixed number of decimal points:

    F,G   0
    I,K,M,O   1

Entering Data

Enter data either into the Mark-up and Cost price columns or into the GP% Retail and Retail Price columns. Press F8 before saving to ensure that the spreadsheet is up to date. If the price list becomes long enough to be slowed by recalculation, turn automatic recalculation off and press F8 twice after entering all data.

Figure 16.1. Part of Price List

Cash Flow Forecast

This next spreadsheet is suitable for home and business use. The purpose of the cash flow forecast spreadsheet is to help you plan the use of your money, when to borrow and when to invest, when to buy that new computer and when to sell the car.

The Labels

The Labels are very similar to the profit and loss spreadsheet dealt with earlier. To make life easy, use the `Library` screen to copy from `PROFITS` to `CASH.XSS`. Move the cursor to `PROFITS` in the Spreadsheet column. Select `Copy` from the `F2` menu and enter the filename `CASH.XSS`.

Make the following changes:

F1	Cash Flow Forecast
H1	'1988-89
A5	INCOME
B5-N5	Blank (use <F2>B)

A6 to A9 contain the sources of income, we will use:

A6	SALARY
A7	INVESTMENTS
A8	ROYALTIES
A9	MISCELLANEOUS
A11	TOTAL
A43	CASH ON HAND
A45	Maximum Borrowing

`Shade` and `Remove` rows 13, 14, 15 and 40.

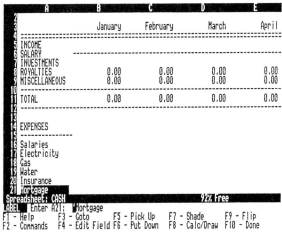

Figure 16.2. Income Section of Cash Flow

If you need a business cash flow forecast, it is identical except for the fact that your income would come from sales rather than salary.

If you are running a business spreadsheet, you will want to keep the expenses the same, so you can skip to the formula section of the spreadsheet.

Home users need to make a few more alterations, as follows:

A21	Mortgage or Rent
A22	Community Tax
A23	Maintenance
A24	Motor Vehicles
A25	Servicing
A26	Travel
A27	HP Repayments
A28	Credit Cards
A29	Telephone
A30	Bank Charges
A31	Food
A32	Clothing
A33	Holidays
A34	Subscriptions

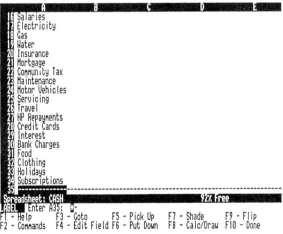

Figure 16.3. Expenses Section of Cash Flow

Note that we are retaining the salaries section of the expenses. I tend to put the children's pocket money in here: it is remarkable how a demonstration of deleting this expense gets the car cleaned!

Formulae

What we need are totals for Income and Expenses. Move the cursor to B11 and enter:

```
+SUM(B5..B9)
```

Copy this from C9 to N9.

Move to B36 and enter:

```
+SUM(B16..B34)
```

Copy into columns C to N. Next enter:

```
C5  +B39
```

Copy this from D5 to M5.

We now need to calculate the maximum we need to borrow:

```
C41              -Min(B39..M39)
```

The next collection of formulae all fall in column N. Enter this formula:

```
+TOTAL(B5..M5)    in cell N5
```

Copy to the following cells:

```
N6 to N9
N11
N16 to N34
N36
N39
```

Naming ranges

We will name columns B to M as follows:

```
Row 11          Income
Row 36          Expenses
Row 39          Cash_on_hand
```

Move to R11 and type:

```
INCOME=+B11..M11
```

Then to R12 and type:

```
EXPENSE=+B36..M36
```

Then in R13:

```
Cash_on_Hand=+B39..M39
```

Entering Data

We will assume you start the year with a total of £264.98 in the bank, put this in B5.

Next we will enter salary. Let's assume a salary of around £12000 p.a.

The government, in its wisdom, takes around a third of this in Tax (National Insurance is a tax!) so we will assume £670 clear each month until May, when you expect a 5% rise.

Enter the following:

```
C6              +B6
```

Copy this to D6..M6:

```
F6              E6*1.05
```

We'll also assume that you have some investments that bring in money three times a year, and your enlightened employer pays a month's Christmas Bonus, so we enter these:

```
E7              200
K7              200
M7              +M6
```

You get royalties on a record you made in your youth, not a lot, but it is paid every three months:

```
B8              189.60
E8              189.60
H8              189.60
K8              189.60
```

Finally, you do a few technical articles for an on-line database: this brings in around £50 every four months.

C9	50.00
F9	50.00
K9	50.00

Notice that these are all anticipatory, your best guess!

Now onto the expenses:

The following values are copied from, B to M in the following rows:

16	20
21	230
23	20
24	90
26	40
31	170

Now enter the following as data in individual cells:

D17	90
G17	50
J17	55
M17	70
F18	110
I18	70
L18	105
E19	250
E22	450
K22	450
D25	74
G25	92
J25	70
M25	65
D29	30
G29	30
J29	30
M29	30
D33	100
F33	400
C34	35
F34	60

```
I34           20
```

If we look at `N39`, we see that we still have a credit balance in December. From March to November we have to borrow money.

What can we do about it?

Community Tax can be spread over 10 months from April, so put `900/10` in each month from April to December. This has reduced the amount we have to borrow by £200, saving us at least ten pounds in interest!

What else can we do? We can spread out our insurance payments over the year, and do the same for Gas and Electricity bills. The insurance company wants another ten pounds for the privilege though. Enter `270/12` each month from January to December.

The Gas Company wants £40 a month to allow you instalment terms but they will repay you the £45 overpayment in December. Enter `40` from January to November and 40-45 in December. Enter `270/12` from January to December to cover Electricity.

That has made some improvement; perhaps there is more we can do. We can use a credit card to pay our holiday cost in May. If we choose the day right, we can pay this back in July so we move the contents of `F33` to `H33`. Now we are in credit until June! Pay for the car servicing in the same way and we are in the black until July.

What happens if you get the boss to give you a 10% rise? Edit `F6` to read `+E6*1.10`. If this is the case, we only need to borrow money from July to September and we have reduced our borrowing need by £400 or so.

Play with this spreadsheet after putting in your own figures then, if you still have some negative figures, go to see your bank manager with your spreadsheet!

Moving Annual Total

This is the last example spreadsheet we will construct. In some ways it is the most interesting. After this, if you are asked to budget sales you will be able to do it easily.

This spreadsheet produces a moving annual total (MAT), which is used to predict future trends. In this case, we will look at the sales of a fictitious company selling to Government establishments.

The Labels

We will use the usual identification labels:

```
A1              Bloggs and Company
A2              Moving Annual Total Analysis
```

A6 to A17 contain the months January to December

```
B4              1986
C4              1987
D4              Moving Annual Total
D5              Moving Average
A5..D5          *-
```

Formulae

D1 contains the current date:

```
+TODAY()
```

The following formulae are entered:

```
D6              +TOTAL(B7..B17)+C6
D7              +TOTAL(B8..B17)+TOTAL(C6..C7)
D8              +TOTAL(B9..B17)+TOTAL(C6..C8)
D9              +TOTAL(B10..B17)+TOTAL(C6..C9)
D10             +TOTAL(B11..B17)+TOTAL(C6..C10)
D11             +TOTAL(B12..B17)+TOTAL(C6..C11)
D12             +TOTAL(B13..B17)+TOTAL(C6..C12)
D13             +TOTAL(B14..B17)+TOTAL(C6..C13)
D14             +TOTAL(B15..B17)+TOTAL(C6..C14)
D15             +TOTAL(B16..B17)+TOTAL(C6..C15)
D16             +B17+TOTAL(C6..C16)
D17             +TOTAL(C6..C17)
```

We'll put in an additional column, the Moving Average which will help us with graph scaling.

```
E6              +D6/12
```

Replicate this from E7 to E17.

Naming Ranges

Name columns from rows 6 to 17 as follows:

```
B6..B17        Sales_1986
C6..C16        Sales_1987
D6..D17        MAT
E6..E17        MAV
```

Entering Data

The following items are entered:

```
B6              80926
B7             110987
B8             125654
B9             130987
B10             22876
B11             30670
B12             35345
B13             43598
B14             54989
B15             65876
B16             83798
B17             62125
C6              84972
C7             118756
C8             136963
C9             140596
C10             13079
C11             27790
C12             42061
C13             52754
C14             68186
C15             83663
C16            109775
C17             59765
```

If you look at the Moving Annual Total column, you will see that the numbers change much more smoothly whilst the sales figures vary wildly. This allows us to predict what is going to happen in the future. To see this more fully we need to move on to the next chapter.

17 : Graph

What is a Graph?

Graph is a way of showing the results of, say, a spreadsheet or other series of results in a highly visual way. A graph can show trends and relationships much more rapidly than a row of figures. Graph allows the use of all the function keys except F3 and F5.

Starting a new Graph

To start a new graph, move the cursor to NEW under the GRAPH option and press RETURN. Choose the filename GRAPH.A blank graph appears.

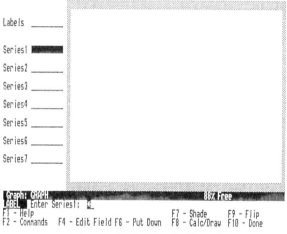

Figure 17.1. Blank Graph

The Graph area is bounded by the shaded area of the screen. As its name suggests, this is where your graph will appear. To the left of the Graph area is the labels field. This is where you enter information that will be displayed along the horizontal or X axis of the graph. Below this are the seven series fields, where you enter numbers you wish to use to draw the graph. You can have up to seven series on one graph. Below the status line is the command area. This has the same function in all Ability applications.

Moving Around Graph

The cursor keys are used to move between series fields, and from series fields to the label field. As usual, the contents of the field on which the cursor rests are displayed in the command area. All fields are initially set to *_

Entering a Series

To enter a series, move the cursor to the first vacant series field and type in a number or, more usually, a list,eg,

```
10,20,30,40,50
```

If you enter this list and press F8 a graph will be drawn.

The Series field now reads:

```
[Series 1]
```

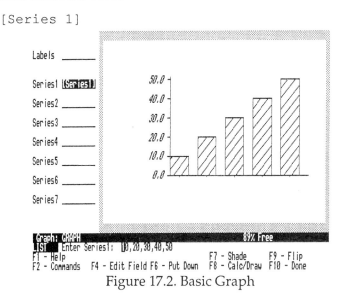

Figure 17.2. Basic Graph

Adding Series

To add series just enter data in another series. With the cursor on Series Field 1, enter the following formula:

```
+MAT\SALES_1986
```

This should result in an error N/A as the required spreadsheet is not in memory. Press F9 to Flip and select the MAT spreadsheet. Returning to Graph you should see that the field now reads:

```
[Series 1]
```

Move the cursor to the Series 2 field and type:

```
+MAT\SALES_1987
```

You will see a second set of bars appear on the graph.

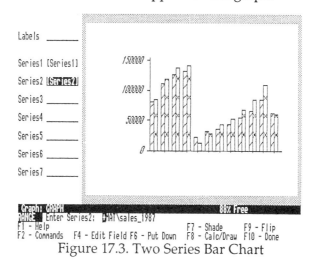

Figure 17.3. Two Series Bar Chart

Labelling

To label each bar in the graph, point to the Labels field and enter the data as a list. In this case try:

```
Jan,Feb,Mar,Apr,May,Jun,Jul,Aug,Sep,Oct,Nov,Dec
```

If you wish to leave a bar unlabelled, simply type two commas together. You can also use a link to enter a series of labels.

F2 Commands [A]

Pressing F2 prompts a menu of eight options.

Style	Line, Pie, Bar or stacked Bar
Design	Graph Design
Titles	Tile Axes and heading

`Blank`	Blank series
`Hard-Copy`	Print or Plot
`Redraw`	Auto or Manual redraw

Other provides two more options:

`File`	Load or Save a graph
`Quit`	Exit without saving

F2 Commands [A+]

Ability Plus commands are very similar to the Ability commands although the menus are a little different. Each command is listed below with a brief description and any sub-menu. If a name has changed, the Ability name is noted in brackets.

`Graph`	Erase redraw and titles options
	Erase (Blank)
	Redraw
	Titles
`Style`	Select Graph type
	Bar
	Stacked Bar
	Line
	Pie
	X-Y
`Design`	Graph Design Options
	Fill-pattern (11 options)
	Point-Marks
	Explode-Wedge
	Rotate
	Y-scale
	X-scale
`Hard-Copy`	Print Graph
	Print
	Start-plotting
	Colors
	Wait
	Quadrant

```
File            Load or Save file
                Save
                Load

Quit            Exit without saving
```

Titles on the Graph

You can add a main title, in large letters, a smaller sub-title, and titles for both X and Y axes. Selecting Title gives you four options:

Main-Title A large title at the top of the graph.
Sub-Title A smaller title beneath the main title.
X-Title   Title for the horizontal axis.
Y-Title   Title for the vertical axis.

Titles are automatically centred.

Changing the Style

The Style option defines the type of graph that is drawn, from:

```
        Bar
        Stacked Bar
        Line
        Pie
[A+]    X-Y
```

The style only applies to the series fields that are shaded either by the cursor or by F7. This means that it is possible to have bar and line graphs for different series.

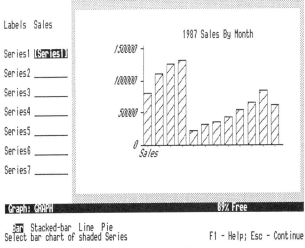

Figure 17.4. Bar Chart

Bar Charts

A bar chart is a graph in which the height of each bar is proportional to the value. This is useful for Maxima and Minima and for trends.

Stacked Bar Charts

A stacked bar chart is useful for examining relationships between the sum of groups of values. It is made up from a series of bar graphs with each bar being added to the corresponding bars in other series.

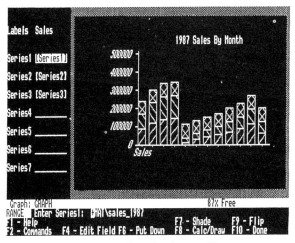

Figure 17.5. Stacked Bar Chart

Line Graph

Each point on the graph is joined to neighbouring points by a line. This results in a graph that looks like a hospital temperature chart. This type of graph is very useful for analysing trends.

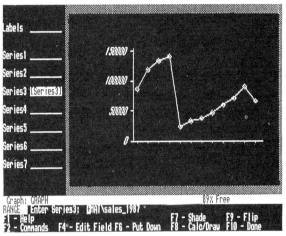

Figure 17.6. Line Graph

Pie Chart

A Pie Chart is a very useful way of assessing the overall contribution of each factor making up the total. By presenting the relevant values as areas of a circle, your eye can easily analyse the differences. You can choose to show some wedges pulled out of the pie. This is called Exploding Wedges.

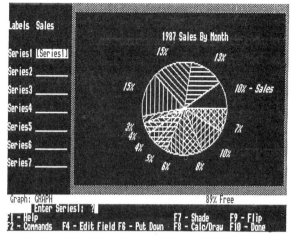

Figure 17.7. Pie Chart

X-Y Graph [A+]

Ability Plus also allows you to graph one series against another. This can provide non-linear scales if you wish.

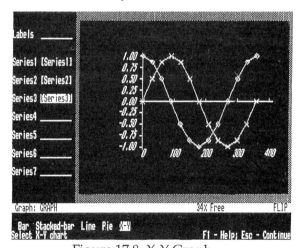

Figure 17.8. X-Y Graph

When to use Styles

You will find that the various graph styles suit various applications. You can see trends best on a line graph. A pie chart is best for illustrating proportions.

The secret is to look at the graph in various styles to see which conveys the information the best.

Using Two Styles

Style options, with the exception of the Pie chart, operate on only those fields pointed to by the cursor or shaded by F7.

To have more than one graph type on screen, simply select the appropriate style for the correct fields.

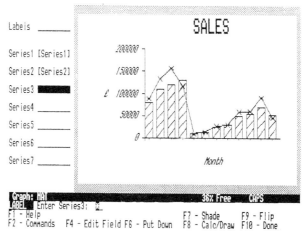

Figure 17.9. Two styles on a Graph

Graph Design

The design option allows you to select various parameters for the graphs, as follows:

Fill Pattern

The pattern that is used to fill each bar. Ten patterns are available for Ability and eleven for Ability Plus.

Each is selected using the cursor key and the RETURN key.

[A]

A	Blank
B	Solid
C	Right Diagonal Lines
D	Wide Right Diagonal Lines

E	Right Pin-stripe
F	Left Diagonal Lines
G	Wide Left Diagonal Lines
H	Left Pin-stripe
I	Narrow Cross-hatch
J	Wide Cross-hatch

[A+]

A	Blank
B	Right Diagonal Lines
C	Left Diagonal Lines
D	Narrow Cross-hatch
E	Right Pin-stripe
F	Left Pin-stripe
G	Wide Right Diagonal Lines
H	Wide Left Diagonal Lines
I	Wide Cross-hatch
J	Horizontal Lines
K	Solid

Point-Marks

The `Point-Marks` option allows you to choose whether to mark each data point on a line graph, and to choose the marking symbol. Eight options are available.

A	No marking
B	Box
C	X
D	Diamond
E	Circle
F	Triangle
G	Dagger
H	Pyramid

Explode Wedge

Ability will draw one Pie segment pushed out from the others. This is called an exploded wedge. You can elect to explode any number of wedges or none at all.

A second menu is produced:

> `All`　　Explode all wedges
> `None`　Explode no wedges
> `Single` Explode or unexplode one wedge

The single option can be repeated to explode additional wedges. To explode or unexplode a wedge, specify it by number. Wedges are numbered anticlockwise from the three o'clock position.

Rotate

Draws the graph either upright or on its side. In effect the graph is rotated by ninety degrees. Repeat selection toggles between the two orientations.

Y-Axis

Allows you to select the graph scaling to be automatic or manual. You may also select the number of figures to print after the decimal point. A menu is produced on selection:

`Automatic`
> Scale graph automatically.

`Manual`
> Manually scale graph

`Number-Format`
> Select the number of digits after the decimal point. You can select any number from 0 to 9, or allow Ability to select automatically.

X-Axis
[A+]
This is identical to the Y-Axis option except it applies to the data or X (horizontal) axis.

Blank

Blank allows you to remove one or more series from the graph. There appears to be no way to unblank so you have to re-enter the contents of a series if you change your mind, unless you have saved the original before you try this.

If you want to blank more than one field, use `F7` to `Shade` appropriate fields. `Blank` allows you a `Yes` or `No` option.

Hard-Copy

`Hard-Copy` allows five options:

```
Print
Start-Plotting
Colors
Wait
Quadrant
```

Printing

`Print` produces a new menu:

Go   Print now

To-file   Print to file or Printer. If you print to a file you
               will be asked for a filename. The file can be
               printed using the MSDOS `PRINT` command.

Sideways   Print the graph sideways or upright. Sideways
               print produces a larger graph which is turned
               through ninety degrees. If you print a rotated
               graph it will be upside-down.

Plotting

The following options only apply to plotter systems:

`Start-Plotting`
   The start plotting option sends the graph to the plotter.

`Colours`
   The `Colors` (sic) option gives you a choice of seven areas of the
   graph. You can choose a pen number from one to eight for each
   area.

   The areas are:

   `Outline`   Set the outline for the shaded series.
   `Fill`   Set the fill colour for the shaded series.

`Axes`	Set the colour of the Axes.
`Titles`	Set the colour of the titles.
`X-Labels`	Set the colour of the X labels.
`Y-Labels`	Set the colour of the Y labels.
`Wedges`	Set the colour of wedges for a pie chart: you can set all or just one wedge colour. Wedges are numbered anti-clockwise from the three o'clock position.

Wait

Makes the plotter pause so that you can change pens as it plots the graph.

Quadrant

Plot the graph either on the whole page or in just one corner or quadrant. Quadrants are numbered left to right from the top-left corner.

Quadrant	Position
1	Top-Left
2	Top-Right
3	Bottom-Left
4	Bottom-Right

Using Spreadsheet Data

You can use spreadsheet data from a named range. If the cells are next to each other, you can define a range thus:

```
RANGE=A1..Z1
```

If the cells are separated, you can still define a series but in this case you must use a list:

```
RANGE=A1,B3,C5..F5,S9..Z9
```

Set up a link to the spreadsheet in the usual way:

```
+FILENAME\RANGE
```

Note that you must load the spreadsheet to memory before attempting to graph it. To do this, use F9 to Flip the screen and load the spreadsheet by selecting it in the usual way.

You can plot all three ranges of the MAT spreadsheet on the same graph. If you do this, you will notice that the MAT range is nearly a straight line, whilst the sales figures include seasonal swings. If you draw a line through the MAT graph and extend it, you will be able to predict the MAT for the next twelve months if conditions remain the same. Any changes must therefore be due to other factors, such as new products, increased competition, new salesmen etc. You can use these figures in your cash flow forecast by simply adding the mean growth rate, (which is the percentage difference in MAT between this year and next) to this year's sales figures. Useful, isn't it?

Redrawing the Graph

Ability will normally redraw the graph every time that a change is made. This may be inconvenient at times. By selecting Redraw, you can choose whether or not to re-draw the graph every time there is a change.

You can force the graph to be redrawn by pressing F8 at any time.

Editing the Graph

Positioning the cursor over a series field and pressing F4 enables you to edit the field in the normal way.

Using Database Data

In order to use data from a database you must first export it to a spreadsheet using F5 and F6. Position the cursor over a field and use F5 to pick up the data from the database, then open a spreadsheet, position the cursor and press F6 to put down the fields. Note that all the fields in all the forms are transferred.

18 : Communicate

COMMUNICATE is the Ability application that facilitates the exchange of files, data and information between computers. You can communicate locally, over a cable or at long distance over the telephone lines. COMMUNICATE allows your computer to act as a terminal to another computer and, incidentally, allows the other computer to act as a terminal to yours.

If you connect to a local computer, that is by direct link, you will need a null modem cable. This is simply a RS232 cable with internal cross connections. RS232 is a standard connection for transferring data between computer components using just a pair of wires for the data. The data is split into single bits and each bit is sent one after the other down the pair of wires. This is called serial transmission. In practice, a minimum of five wires is needed for a two-way serial link:

Function	Abbreviation
Receive	RXD
Transmit	TXD
Common	Ground
Clear to Send	CTS
Data Terminal Ready	DTR

There are a number of other connections available on RS232 but these are the most commonly used.

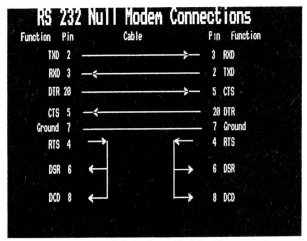

Figure 18.1. Null Modem Cable Connections

Modems

If you send data over the telephone lines, you will need a device to encode the serial information onto a carrier tone that can be handled by the telephone network. To receive data, you need a device that will decode serial information from a received carrier. Encoding a carrier is called modulation, so to send and receive you need a Modulator /Demodulator, more usually called a *modem*.

With a modem you can communicate with computers all over the world, send telexes, data and electronic mail. With the right equipment you can even send facsimiles.

In the UK there are a number of databases you can contact using your computer. There are also a number of electronic mail services that also provide telex. British Telecom runs one called Telecom Gold. A second British Telecom service, Prestel, also provides database, message and telex facilities, albeit a little more limited.

At the time of writing, Prestel cannot be accessed using Ability but improvements to Prestel are expected to change this soon.

The COMMUNICATE Screen

To start COMMUNICATE, either select a current file or select NEW in the `Communicate` column. If using a new file, you will have to enter filename. The COMMUNICATE screen will appear.

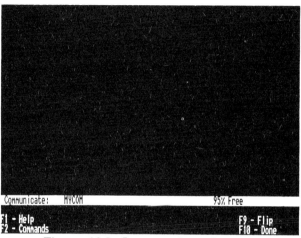

Figure 18.2. Communicate Screen

The COMMUNICATE screen allows the use of just four function keys:

F1	Context sensitive help
F2	Commands
F9	Flip
F10	Exit

F2 has a sub menu of seven options

List	List a file to the port
Capture	Start or stop saving the communication session on disc.
Port	Port parameters
Terminal	Terminal and Modem settings
Modem	Modem operations:

> Call
>
> Hangup

267

```
                    Answer
                    Noanswer

        Send        Send files
                    Single
                    Many

        Receive     Receive files
                    Single
                    Many
```

Modem allows you to select one of four options:

`Call`   Call the telephone number entered in the Terminal settings screen. This produces a message:

> CONNECT

at the top of the screen when the other computer answers. You can then start sending and receiving data.

`Hangup`   Used to end a communications session by freeing the telephone line. If using a commercial service, make sure you follow the log-off instructions first, otherwise the other computer may hold the line open.

`Answer`   Tells the modem to answer the phone.

`Noanswer`   Tells the modem not to answer the phone.

We will deal with the other options later in the chapter.

Port and Terminal Settings

If we have started a new `Communicate` file, we must first set the port and terminal parameters for our session file. Once these are set, they will be saved with the file so you will only need to do it once. You need to either agree these settings with another computer user or, if using a commercial service, get the protocol from the system operator.

Obviously if you access a number of sources with different protocol you will need a file for each.

Many of the fields for the parameters allow a limited number of choices. Where you can type in data F4 becomes available to allow you editing facilities.

If using an existing file, we can just proceed with sending and receiving data.

Sending Data

There are four basic ways of exchanging data with another computer:

```
List
Send
Receive
Capture
```

List allows you to send a file to the other computer by listing it to the communications port.

Press:

```
F2-L
```

and enter the filename. If it is a Write file just enter the filename; for any other file you must include the extension.

The listed file must be on the current drive and directory.

Send allows you to send a file or group of files to another computer. You can only send files that are on the current directory and drive.

Press:

```
F2-S
```

You can take a file from another computer by selecting receive:

```
F2-R
```

The file must be on the current drive and directory. If the other computer's modem has been set to Answer, the other computer need not be attended.

Finally, you can use `capture` to capture all or part of a session.

```
F2-C
```

prompts for the name of a file in which the data is to be stored. Ability will store everything that appears on the screen in a file that can be loaded into `Write` for review and editing.

Pressing `F2-C` a second time causes Ability to stop capturing data. A third use of the Capture command starts capturing data to the same file once again. In this way you can save several parts of the session to a single file.

Ending a Session

A `Communicate` session can be ended in one of two ways, either press `F10` from the communicate screen or press:

```
F2-H
```

to 'Hang up' the phone. Ensure that you have followed all the required log-off procedures first or you could find a nasty surprise from the telephone company!

Login Files

If you frequently communicate with the same computer, it is worth writing a special 'Login' file to speed the process of logging-on to the system.

Login files cause Ability to run a sequence of commands when you call another computer. For example, if you use Telecom Gold you may wish to include your user id in the file. It is not a good idea to put your password in an auto login file, especially if you allow access to the computer by other people.

You create a Login file using `Write` and enter its filename in the `Terminal` and `Modem` screen. The file can contain three different commands:

```
SEND
WAIT
TIMEOUT
```

SEND

> The Send command tells Ability to send the one or more characters you type on the same line as the command to the other computer. If you simply type SEND on a line, Ability just sends a Carriage Return.
>
> If you want to send a control character, precede the character with a caret (^). Thus:
>
> ```
> ^M  =13     =CR
> ^J  =10     =LF
> ```
>
> and so on. If you actually want to send a caret, type ^@.

WAIT

> The Wait command tells Ability to wait until it receives one or more specified characters from the keyboard before running the next login command.

TIMEOUT

> Ability normally waits two seconds after each SEND or WAIT command before sending the next command. This period is called the TIMEOUT. You can change this by using the TIMEOUT command as the first line of your login file. The period may be from one second to two minutes, and must be entered in seconds. To set the timeout period to one minute ten seconds type:
>
> ```
> TIMEOUT 70
> ```

Port Settings

Pressing:

```
F2-P
```

produces the port setting screen. This should be edited in accordance with the settings required by the other computer.

Communication Port

The communication port is where the cable or modem is plugged in. Pressing RETURN selects either COM1 or COM2. The serial port is usually COM1.

Parity

Set this to suit the other computer. Parity checking is a way of looking for errors. An extra bit is added to the data-stream after each character. The value of this bit is selected to ensure that total number of ones in the word is either odd or even.

Many systems now do not check parity. The correct setting for these systems is None.

Parity settings available are as follows:

```
Odd
Even
None
Space
Mark
```

Baud Rate

Baud rate is the number of signals per second that the two machines use to communicate. Conventionally, it's also taken to indicate the data rate in bits per second, though this may not be true at higher speeds. Ability allows speeds (in bits per second) of:

```
 110
 300
 600
1200
2400
4800
9600
```

Some systems, for example many Viewdata type services, use two baud rates: 75 for your transmission and 1200 for you to receive. Ability, in common with virtually all PC communications programs, cannot cope with this, although some modems will perform a 'translation' for you and convert the signal to 1200 baud both ways, which can be dealt with.

Duplex

This is a mode of communication, duplex meaning simultaneous two way transmission, and this determines whether or not Ability displays the characters you type. Full duplex allows the characters you type to be printed on the screen after being received and retransmitted by the other computer. Half Duplex cannot receive when sending, so Ability prints the characters you type on the screen and sends them to the other computer. Local prints the characters you type but does not send them to the other machine.

You will usually use Half duplex for communicating with another personal computer, and Full duplex for commercial systems.

Character Size

Characters are transmitted either as seven or eight bit characters. The protocol is usually determined by the other computer.

Stop Bits

Stop bits mark the end of a character; Ability allows either one or two. The protocol is usually determined by the other computer.

Local Linefeed

Ability can generate a linefeed when you press RETURN. If the remote computer generates linefeeds and you have a full duplex system, choose No.

Remote Linefeed

If the remote computer generates a linefeed after receiving a carriage return, set this field to Yes.

Local Flow Control

Flow control refers to the method the two computers use to tell each other to start or stop sending data. This is sometimes implemented by the computer itself, in which case you can select None. Local Flow

Control determines which, if any, characters Ability sends to the remote computer. Protocols available are:

```
None
EIA
XON/XOFF
```

Remote Flow Control

This determines which, if any, control codes Ability expects the other computer to send.

Protocols available are:

```
None
EIA
XON/XOFF
```

Send Break

The `Send Break` field determines whether Ability sends a break character to the remote computer when you press `CTRL-Break`. If the remote computer cannot handle breaks, choose `No`.

Break Character

The `Break` character determines the value of the character that is sent to the other computer when you press `CTRL-Break`. The default is the hexadecimal FFh.

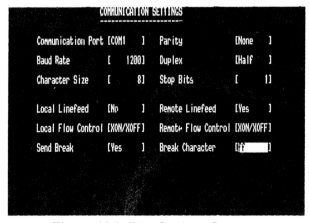

Figure 18.3. Port Settings Screen

Terminal Settings

Having got our communicate screen, we must first set the modem and terminal parameters for our session file. Once these are set they will be saved with the file so, if you need to access several different services, simply make a file for each.

Press

```
F2-T
```

from the communicate screen to reach the Terminal and Modem Settings screen.

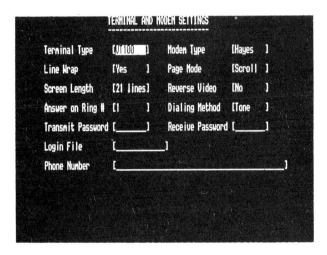

Figure 18.4. Terminal and Modem Settings Screen

Phone Number

The first thing to do is to enter the telephone number of the service you wish to access. Move the cursor to the Phone number field and type in exactly what you would dial to access the service. If you would dial 9 to get an outside line, include this in the number.

Pause

Your telephone system may need a pause at various places in the dialling sequence, for example, to pick up an outside line or access the international STD system. When you need a pause in the dialling, simply add commas in the correct place in the sequence. Each comma causes Ability to pause for two seconds.

Terminal Type

Now we can set various options. Move the cursor to `Terminal Type` and press `RETURN` a number of times until the correct terminal type is shown. The choices are:

```
VT100
Dumb
Trans
VT52
```

`Trans` is only used for testing a system as it allows you to see all characters, including control characters, sent by the other computer.

`VT100` an `VT52` are probably most useful for computer to computer communications, and dumb for dial up services. The System operator (SYSOP) of the service will advise you.

Modem

Move the cursor to `Modem Type` and press `RETURN` until the correct Modem type is shown.

The choices are:

Hayes	Hayes compatible modem
Migent	Migent Pocket Modem
Generic	Any other Modem
None	Null-Modem cable

Line Wrap

Move the cursor to `Line Wrap`. Press `RETURN` to select either automatic word-wrap at the end of a line, or stop and overwrite at the end of a line.

The choices are:

```
Yes
No
```

Page Mode

Move the cursor to Page Mode and press RETURN to select either a scrolling terminal, in which when text reaches the bottom of the screen it scrolls up one line, or Page in which the page is erased and the next characters start at the top of a new page.

The choices are:

```
Page
Scroll
```

Prestel uses a Page terminal, Telecom Gold a scrolling terminal.

Screen Length

Move the cursor to Screen Length and press RETURN to select either a 21 or 24 line terminal. The 24 line terminal uses the command area in addition to the screen area.

Reverse Video

Reverse video shows dark characters on a light background. The choices are Yes or No. If you choose Yes you will not see reverse video until you start the communication session.

Answer on Ring

The Answer on Ring field allows you to select how many times Ability will let the telephone ring before answering it.

Ability only answers the phone if you have selected Answer from the modem menu.

Dialling Method

The Dialling Method field is used to select Pulse dialling or tone dialling. If you can play tunes on your telephone, select tone dialling.

Transfer Protocol

You can choose either the Ability or the Xmodem transfer protocol. Use Xmodem except when communicating with another Ability user.

Passwords

Enter Send and Receive passwords in the password fields. Passwords are dealt with in more detail later in this Chapter.

Login File

You can make a file that automatically logs into another computer sending your user identity and password. The name of the file can be entered into the appropriate field.

When you have completed the screen, press F10 to return to the Communicate screen.

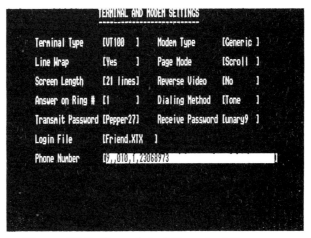

Figure 18.5. Completed Terminal Screen

Generic Modems

If you use a modem that does not follow either the Hayes or Migent modem protocols, Ability will not be able to send the the commands to cause your modem to call, hangup, dial or answer. You can type the commands for the modem or follow the log-on instructions for the particular modem you are using.

Send

Send allows you to send a file to another user. You can only send files that are on the current drive and directory.

Receive

The Receive command is used to receive files from another user. You do not need to select Receive if the other user selects Send. You can select to receive one or many files in the same way as you can select to send one or many files.

If the other user has selected Answer on his PC, you can dial and receive files from the active drive and directory of his or her machine even if it is unattended.

Exchanging Files

You can exchange either a single file or a group of files with another computer. After selecting Send or Receive, you will be presented with a choice of exchanging a single or many files. If you select a single file, you will be asked the filename. If you select Many, you will be asked for the name of the file containing the list of files you want to send. The list file is simply a Write file containing the filenames and extensions of the files you wish to send.

The following extensions are used by Ability files:

XTX	Write Documents
XSS	Spreadsheets
XDB	Databases
XRP	Database reports
XPF	Database Master Forms
XGR	Graphs
SNA	Snapshots

Remember that you must send XDB and XPF files to define a database.

After you enter the filename you will see the transmission statistics on the screen. These include:

1. The estimated time required to complete the transmission.
2. The number of corrected errors that occurred during transmission.
3. The number of files being sent and received.
4. The number of bytes sent or received so far.
5. The file number being sent or received.

6.   The name of the file being sent or received.

Interrupting a Transmission

You can interrupt a transmission by pressing CTRL-Break. This stops transmission immediately.

Passwords

For security, you can choose passwords for both Send and Receive. Your Send password must match the recipient's Receive password and vice-versa. Passwords should be chosen with care and changed frequently. It is surprising how often a spouse or child's name is used as a password! Other favourites are birthdates and other anniversaries. One large corporation recently used the password 0000 for access to a supposedly secure system!

If you don't mind people dialling your computer and reading your mail, fine; if you do, be careful!

Ability allows you to set two passwords: one for send and one for receive.

Problems

Although basically a simple technique, a number of problems can occur when trying to communicate between computers.

If you do not succeed at first, be patient and think logically.

Nothing Sent or Received

*   Make sure all cables are intact and correctly connected.
*   Is the modem (if used) switched on?
*   Check the baud rate is correct for both computers.
*   Are Parity and Stop bit fields are correctly set on both computers.
*   Ensure that you have not chosen Local in the Duplex field

You can see what the other computer types, but not your typing

*   Set Half in the Duplex field.

Random characters are missing from text sent by the other computer

- Select XON/XOFF
- If this does not cure the problem, try a lower baud rate.

Incoming Text is garbled

- Check the baud rate is correct for both computers.
- Are Parity and Stop bit fields are correctly set on both computers.

Doubling of characters you type

- Select Full in the Duplex field.

ERR seen throughout the incoming text

- Check the baud rate is correct for both computers.
- Are Parity and Stop bit fields are correctly set on both computers.
- Check the Character Size is correct on both computers.

Incoming text overwrites end of line

- Set the Line Wrap field on the Terminal and Modem setting to Yes.

Incoming lines are double spaced

- Set the Remote Linefeed field to Yes.

Outgoing lines are double spaced

- Set the Local Linefeed field to No.

Text overwrites the same line

- If incoming text overwrites line, set Remote Linefeed to No.
- If outgoing text overwrites line, set Local Linefeed to Yes.

Escape Sequences and Control Codes

Ability recognises several terminal types. You can select the terminal you wish to use on the Terminal and Modem Settings screen.

The escape sequences and control codes that are recognised for each of the terminals are listed for the more technically minded reader.

Dumb Terminal

The Dumb Terminal only recognises the following codes:

CHAR	MEANING
CTRL-H	BACKSPACE, move the cursor left one column.
CTRL-I	TAB, move the cursor to the next tab stop. Tab stops are automatically set every eight columns
CTRL-J	LINEFEED, move the cursor down one line and scroll if necessary.
CTRL-M	CARRIAGE RETURN, move the cursor to column 0 of the current line.
CTRL-L	CLS, Clear Screen.

Trans Terminal Type

The Trans terminal does not accept any cursor escape sequences. It simply displays all received characters as visible characters according to the following table:

CHARACTER	SHOWN AS
CTRL-A to CTRL-Z	^A to ^Z.
CTRL-[	^[(Escape)
CTRL-\	^\ (FS)
CTRL-]	^] (GS)
CTRL-^	^^ (RS)
CTRL-_	^_ (US)

VT52 and VT100 Terminals

The VT52 and VT100 terminal types interpret the same set of control codes. These codes are shown in the following table:

CHAR	MEANING
CTRL-H	Move the cursor left one column (Backspace)
CTRL-I	Move the cursor to the next tab stop (Horizontal tab).
CTRL-J	Move the cursor down one line and scroll if necessary (linefeed).

CTRL-L   Same as CTRL-J (Form feed).
CTRL-K   Same as CTRL-J (Vertical Tab).
CTRL-M   Move the cursor to column 0 of the current line (Carriage return).
CTRL-X   Cancel the current escape sequence (CAN).
CTRL-Z   Same as CTRL-X (SUB).

VT52 Escape Sequences

The VT52 terminal type interprets the following codes whenever one of these sequences of characters is typed in half duplex mode or received by a communication session that has been set to the VT52 terminal type:

CODE	MEANING
Esc A	Move the cursor up one line.
Esc B	Move the cursor down one line.
Esc C	Move the cursor right one character.
Esc D	Move the cursor left one character
Esc H	Move the cursor to row 0, column 0.
Esc I	Scroll up one line.
Esc J	Erase to the end of the screen.
Esc K	Erase to the end of the line.
Esc Y y x	Move the cursor to row y, column x.

where y is the row number and x is the column number, position 0,0 being the top left-hand point of the displayed screen.

x and y are 32 (20 Hex) plus the row or column being moved to. This offset of 32 makes the values of x and y into printable ASCII characters. See Appendix K for a table of ASCII Characters

For example, to move to row 4 column 8 send:

Esc Y 48	Move to row 4, column 8
Esc /	Ignored
Esc <	Begin VT100 mode.

VT100 Escape Sequences

The VT100 terminal type interprets codes shown in the following table whenever one of the sequences of characters is typed in half duplex mode or received by a communication session that has been set to the VT100 terminal type.

In the table, P1,PX1,PY1,PO, and Pb stand for 0, 1, or 2 digit numbers which are used by the escape sequences. Where a number is given as part of the name, that number is the default value used if you don't enter a number.

CODE	MEANING
Esc D	Scroll down.
Esc E	Return and scroll down.
Esc M	Scroll up.
Esc H	Set tab at current column.
Esc 7	Save attributes (cursor position)
Esc 8	Restore attributes (cursor position)
Esc /	Ignored
Esc C	Reset the terminal and refresh the screen.
Esc [P1 A	Move cursor up P1 lines.
Esc [P1 B	Move cursor down P1 lines.
Esc [P1 C	Move cursor right P1 columns.
Esc [P1 D	Move cursor left P1 columns.
Esc [PX1;PY1 H	Move the cursor to column PX1, Row PY1. Where PY1 is the row number and PX1 is the hand point of the displayed screen.
Esc [PX1;PY1	Move the cursor to position PX1,PY1 same as above.
Esc [PO]	Erase screen according to the value of PO;
	0 Erase from cursor to end of screen.
	1 Erase from home to cursor.
	2 Erase entire screen.
Esc [PO	Erase line according to the value of PO;
	0 Erase from cursor to end of line.
	1 Erase from beginning of line to cursor.

	2 Erase entire line.
Esc [PO	Clear tab stops according to PO:
	0 Clear the tab stop at cursor position.
	3 Clear all the tab stops.
Esc [PL1; PL24	Change the scrolling region to line PL1 to line PL24 inclusive. Lines are numbered from 1 at the top of the screen to 24 at the bottom of the screen.
Esc [? Pb	Set terminal features on according to the value of Pb:
	20 Set local linefeed on
	7 Set autowrap on.
	6 Set relative addressing on.
	5 Set reverse video on.
	2 Set VT52 mode on.
	There is no default value for Pb.
Esc [? Pl	Set terminal features off according to the value of Pl:
	20 Set local linefeed off.
	7 Set autowrap off.
	6 Set relative addressing off.
	5 Set reverse video off.
	2 Set VT52 mode off.
	There is no default value for Pl.

19 : Presentation

PRESENTATION will only run on a machine fitted with a CGA or composite graphics card. If you are running Ability Plus on a 350 line EGA machine, PRESENTATION does not work. Amstrad machines allow you to put the following command in the ABILITY.BAT file:

```
DISPLAY=CGA
```

If you type this command and the screen changes from a 43 to a 25 line display, you can run PRESENTATION.

What is PRESENTATION?

PRESENTATION is the Ability application which allows you to prepare whole screen displays from other Ability applications.

These displays can be arranged into 'slide shows' useful for illustrating lectures and presentations. If you have a screen dump facility, you can present the screens on paper. This is the way many of the illustrations for this book were prepared.

PRESENTATION is in two parts, the snapshot acquisition system which is part of the main Ability program, and the display and editing module which forms a program in its own right.

Creating a Snapshot Library

If you have a floppy disc system, ensure that the Presentation Disc is in Drive B.

Enter the Library screen and press:

[A]   F2-OS

[A+]   F2-S

Now enter the name of the file you wish to store the snapshots in. You will see the file appear in the Other Files [A] or Files [A+] column.

When you have the required display on the screen, simply press the snapshot key. This is the long key marked + on the extreme right of the keyboard.

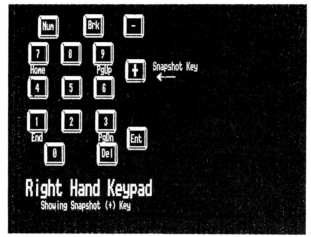

Figure 19.1. Snapshot Key

Open a snapshot file called Snaps. Now select one of the graphs and display it. Press the snapshot key. Change the graph by editing one or more of the series or styles and make another snapshot. Do this three more times so that you have five snapshots stored.

Starting PRESENTATION

Before starting PRESENTATION, ensure that your snapshot library is on the current drive and directory.

You can start PRESENTATION from either the Library screen or from the MSDOS prompt.

From Ability

Move the cursor to Present in the Other Programs [A] or Programs [A+] screen and press RETURN. You will see a message asking you to type the rest of the command line. In this case, type Snaps. The Presentation Logo will appear on the screen and pressing the space bar will take you to the display creation screen. If you do not supply a snapshot library filename, the command line will ask you for one. Entering an unknown filename will allow you to start a new snapshot file if you wish.

From MS-DOS

Simply type either:

```
PRESENT filename
```

or:

```
PRESENT
```

where filename is the name of your snapshot library, in our case SNAPS. If you omit the name of the library file, a command line message will ask for one.

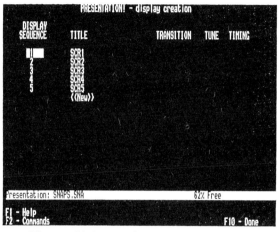

Figure 19.2. Display Creation Screen

Each column on the display creation screen controls a different aspect of your presentation. The first column, display sequence, controls the order in which the snapshots appear when you view a presentation. At first they appear in the order in which you captured them but, by changing the numbers, you can change the sequence in which the snapshots appear.

Changing the Name of the Snapshot

The next column contains the titles of the individual snapshots. Ability gives them names SCR1 SCR2 and so on, to change these simply overtype them. Try rewriting the names of your spreadsheet snapshots.

Transitions

You can choose a style for the transition from one snapshot to the next. For example, if you choose LR the new snapshot overwrites the previous one from left to right. Press:

    F2-T

to select transition and choose the style you desire. The choices are:

LR	Left to right
RL	Right to left
TB	Top to bottom
BT	Bottom to top
SQ	Shrinking square
V4	Four vertical blinds
H4	Four horizontal blinds
D4	Four diagonal blinds in four quadrants

If you don't choose a specific transition, one snapshot will immediately follow the last without any gradual transition.

Tunes

You can make PRESENTATION play a tune, within the (rather severe) limits of your PC's sound system, on transitions.

To do this, move the cursor to the snapshot you require and press:

    F2-M

This selects the Music Menu. You can choose from approximately 25 different tunes under the sub headings, Happy, Sad, Familiar and Other.

If you leave a tune field blank, the transition will be silent.

Timing

Timing selects how long the snapshot will remain on the screen. Point to the column and enter the time in seconds. If you leave a timing field blank, PRESENTATION will display a menu on the bottom line of the spreadsheet. You can return to the Display creation screen by pressing F10 or move to either the next or previous snapshot by using the cursor up or down keys.

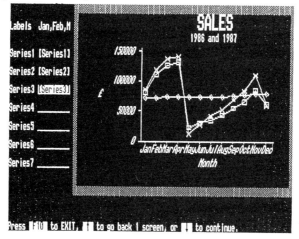

Figure 19.3. Snapshot Without Timing

Viewing

Now we have completed the display creation screen, we can move on to viewing the snapshots.

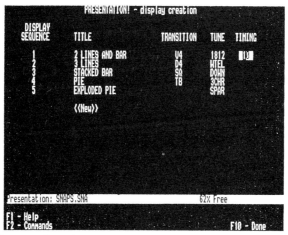

Figure 19.4. Completed Display Creation Screen

Point to the first snapshot in the sequence and press:

F2-V

to select the View option. PRESENTATION will display the sequence of snapshots in the order you selected with both transitions and tunes if you requested them.

You may not wish to see the whole presentation: perhaps you need only to try out an effect on one snapshot. To see just one snapshot, point the cursor at the appropriate snapshot and press:

```
F2-B
```

This selects the `Browse` option.

Editing a Presentation

We can edit one or more of the snapshots by adding a wide variety of lines, symbols and text to the screen. To do this, point to the snapshot you wish to edit and press `F2-A` for the `Add` option. To demonstrate the `Add text` option, we will add the words 'The Bad News' to our first snapshot. Press:

```
F2-AT
```

to select Text from the menu and type:

```
The Bad News
```

You will then be asked to select a text size from one to seven. In this case enter 2. Next you have to choose a slant: in this case select 0 for no slant. Finally select if you want shadowed text. This is text printed twice with one partially superimposed on the other. This produces emphasised text. The final press of RETURN puts the text at the top left of the snapshot. The following keys will move the text to the position you require.

↓→↑←	Move a small distance in the direction of the arrow.
Ctrl→	Move left in large steps.
Ctrl←	Move right in large steps.
Home	Left side of screen.
End	Right side of screen.
PgUp	Move up in large steps.
PgDn	Move down in large steps.
Ctrl-PgUp	Move to top of screen.

Ctrl-PgDn   Move to bottom of screen.
Ctrl-Home   Move to top left of screen.
Ctrl-End   Move to bottom right of screen.

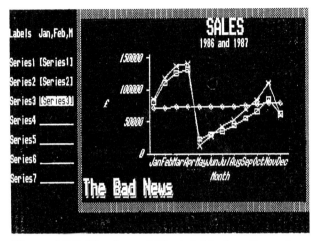

Figure 19.5. Shadowed Text Added to Snapshot

You can also add symbols. Press:

```
F2-AS
```

to select the symbol menu. You have a choice of:

Arrows	Left, Right, Up, Down
Bullets	Box, Circle, Diamond, Keycap, Star
Lines	Short, Medium, Long etc
Punctuation	in large format
Icons	Lightning bolts etc.
Other	Cloud, face, Sun, Pills, Bells, Heart

Once selected, symbols can be moved in the same way as text.

If you need to erase a symbol or text, select a second time and position the new copy exactly over the old. Both copies will disappear.

If you partially cover a symbol with another, only the places where they overlap will be erased.

Changing the Sequence

If you change the numbers in the `Display Sequence` column, the order of display will remain the same until you ask PRESENTATION to sort the snapshots. This is done using the `Reorder` option.

Press:

```
F2-R
```

If you wish to remove any snapshots from the display, point to the snapshot and use the `Delete` option:

```
F2-D
```

The snapshot will not be included in the `View` presentation and will be deleted when you exit from PRESENTATION. If you wish to restore the snapshot, simply type in a new title over the `DELETE` marker in the `Title` column.

If you wish to temporarily delete a snapshot, just type an X alongside the sequence number.

By-passing the Display Creation Screen

If you wish to bypass the display creation screen, change the starting PRESENTATION command to include the word VIEW.

For example:

```
C>PRESENT VIEW SNAPS
```

If you start presentation from the `Library` screen, answer the 'rest of the command line' question with:

```
VIEW FILENAME
```

Loading and Saving Snapshots

The Library command:

```
F2-L
```

allows you to load a new snapshot library to replace the one you are currently working on. Before loading, the new `Library` Presentation ensures that any changes in the old `Library` file are saved.

Press:

    F2-F

The `Files` command allows you to load or save one or a group of snapshots. The `Files` command gives you a menu of three options:

Load	Load a single snapshot
Save	Save a single snapshot
Group Save	Save a group of snapshots

PRESENTATION will only load snapshot files with a `BLD` extension. The loaded snapshot will be added to the bottom of the list in the current display creation screen. The `Save` command saves the snapshot pointed to by the cursor to its own file. You will be asked to provide a filename.

The `Group Save` command saves a group of snapshots to individual files. Point the cursor at the first snapshot to save and select:

    F2-FG

Press `RETURN` for the current drive or enter the Drive number for the saved images.

Ability will display each of the snapshots in the sequence, together with the filename to which it is to be saved. If the filename already exists, PRESENTATION asks you if you wish to overwrite the old file. If you choose not to overwrite the file, the snapshot will not be saved. Change the name, and use `Reorder` to move it to the bottom of the file before trying to save it again.

A : Your Computer

If you are new to computing, this appendix should help you get started with Ability.

First set up the equipment in accordance with the manufacturer's instruction manual. You should have the following:

> Computer (sometimes called a CPU or processor)
> Keyboard
> Monitor (sometimes called a VDU)
> Mouse (optional)
> Printer (parallel or centronics interface)
> Printer Cables (Power and interface)
> Plotter (optional)
> Plotter Cables (optional)
> Modem (optional)
> Cable (for modem or Serial Cable)

The plotter and its cables are optional. If you want to use COMMUNICATE you will need either a modem or a serial cable. The serial cable will usually have to be the null modem type. This is just a cable with two pairs of leads reversed on one plug.

Booting

With all connected up correctly, turn on the machine. What happens next depends on which machine and model you have.

Starting a machine is called booting, because the initial loader program is called a bootstrap loader, derived from the notion of pulling itself up by the bootlaces. Switching on a machine is called a cold boot. Many PC type machines reboot if you press Ctrl, Alt and Del simultaneously. This is called a warm boot.

In either case, if you have a hard disc machine with MS-DOS installed on the hard disc, you will see either a message to enter the date and time, or a C> prompt if you have a battery-backed clock. If the former, you should enter the date. You will probably be prompted on how to enter it, but don't forget the dashes to separate the day, month and year. Press RETURN. You may then be asked to enter the time. Doing this will produce the C> prompt.

If you have a floppy disc machine you may be asked to put a system disc (or disk) in drive A:. This is normally the slot on the left of the CPU box. Insert your MS-DOS system disc in this drive and close the door. The computer can then load MS-DOS from the disc.

Floppy discs are inserted with the label uppermost, the label towards you and the square write protect cut-out on the left of the disc as you look at it.

If you have 5.25" discs and you wish to prevent the computer writing on the disc, cover the notch with a small label. If you have 3.5" discs you will find a small plastic tab on the underside of the disc. Move this to uncover the hole in order to protect the disc against writing.

Some machines start with an internal application such as BASIC. Reboot using Ctrl-Alt-Del and put an MS-DOS disc in drive A:

Whichever way you achieve it, you should finish with a letter on the left of the screen followed by a prompt >. Normally, the prompt is A> for a floppy disc system and C> for a hard disc machine.

Turning off the machine is simply a matter of removing the discs, leaving the drive doors open and turning off the power. If you have a hard disc machine you must park the hard disc first. This is detailed in your instruction manual. Parking is vital to protect the disc against damage when you turn the machine on again. Don't forget to do this. Hard disc drives are expensive and it takes a long time to recover the data you can lose.

With the system prompt (>) on the screen you can start to operate the machine. MS-DOS has a number of built in functions like, DIR, TYPE and COPY. These are part of MS-DOS. There are a number of other MS-DOS utilities supplied as programs on disc and of course there are commercial software programs like Ability.

Programs are started by typing their filename alone, other files need the extension to be added, eg,

    FRED

runs a program called FRED.EXE, FRED.COM or FRED.BAT

```
TYPE FRED.TXT
```

types the file on the screen

Filenames

Computer programs, documents, letters, spreadsheets, databases and graphs are all stored on disc. To identify each item it is given a name, called a filename. Items that you save on disc will also need a name, so we should lay down a few ground rules.

A filename can be from one to eight characters in length and can contain any combination of letters, and numbers. In addition the characters:

```
$ # & @ ! % ( )  -  _  ^  ~  '
```

can be used. Ability is a little more fussy with filename characters. MS-DOS has a few reserved words like PRN COM and CON, which are names of MS-DOS devices like printers etc., that cannot be used.

A filename should be chosen that reflects the contents of the file. A letter to the Bank could be called BANK etc.

In addition to the filename, MS-DOS allows a three letter extension. This is preceded by a dot when you type it. The extension usually indicates the type of file. You can choose these at will, but here are a few suggestions:

TXT	Text file
LTR	Letter
DOC	Document
MEM	Memorandum
DAT	Data file
ASC	ASCII file
HLP	Help Files
BAS	Basic Language Program

A letter to the bank might, therefore, be called:

```
BANK.LTR
```

You must avoid three extensions unless you are a machine code programmer:

COM   Short program file
EXE   Long program File
OVL   Program overlay

A program extension you should avoid for routine use is BAT. This is used for user programs in BATCH mode. We deal with Batch files in Appendix B.

The extension SYS is used for system files so you would be wise to avoid it, the exception being the text file CONFIG.SYS which is used to set up the machine when you boot it.

Programs with the extensions BAT, COM or EXE can be run simply by typing in the file name.

Ability also reserves the following extensions for its own use:

XCO   Communicate file
XTM   Communicate Terminal file
XAB   Parameter file
XDB   Database
XPF   Database Master form
XRP   Database Report
XSS   Spreadsheet
XTX   Document
GRP   Graph
SNA   Snapshot Library

Although the computer also recognises a three character extension to the filename, Ability hides its own extensions from you in every column but the `FILES` column. The combination of Filename and Extension is called a file specification (FSP) and the two parts of the FSP are written with a full stop separating them, eg:

```
COMMAND.COM
filename.EXT
```

Some utilities let you use a wildcard to specify a group of files. In this case the file specification becomes ambiguous and is known as an ambiguous file specification (afsp), eg:

```
DIR *.EXE
```

displays all files with the extension EXE in the current directory.

Files can be larger than the machine's memory. In this case only part of the file is read in. If more is needed part of the file in memory is either discarded or, more usually, written back to disc. The process can best be imagined as the file being a book. You, the computer memory, only sees part, the rest remains in the book and becomes available only as you need to see it. The process of getting into a file, like getting into a book, is called opening and putting away a file is known as closing the file.

Drive Names

MS-DOS allows disc drives to be numbered from A to P. Drives A and B are generally floppy discs and drive C a hard disc. If you have a RAM disc (a memory based logical drive) it is generally given the letter D or, if there is no hard disc, C.

To select a disc drive from the prompt simply type the drive name followed by a colon (:). Thus, to select drive B type:

```
B:
```

If you select a drive you are said to be logged on that drive.

You can use any drive name as part of a filename. In this case we have a file specification:

```
C:FILENAME.EXT
```

Hard discs and some floppy discs are split into logical segments called directories. These directories are named by the user using the command MD (Make Directory):

```
MD ABILITY
```

The first directory on a disc is the ROOT directory. You do not create this. This can contain both files and other directories, which are called sub-directories, of the root directory. Directories are signified by a backslash (\) in file specifications.

For example:

```
TYPE C:\ABILITY\README.TXT
```

means type on the screen the file found on Drive C (C:) in the root directory (C:\) sub directory ABILITY (C:\ABILITY\) named README.TXT.

If you wish to log onto a directory, use the command:

```
CD directory
```

CD means Change Directory.

If you happen to be using the correct drive and directory for the command you wish to use, you do not need to type them in the command. For example

```
DIR
```
is equivalent to:

```
DIR A:
```

when you are 'logged' onto drive A:

In the rest of this appendix I will use the symbol:

```
d:
```

to indicate where a drive and directory may be inserted in commands.

Formatting Discs

As with so many things, the computer industry has a great deal of difficulty in standardising on floppy disc formats. For this reason, you have to set up blank floppy discs specifically for your machine.

First buy the correct disc type:

Number of sides	one or two (SS or DS)
TPI	48 for 40 track

	96 for 80 track
Density	Double

Most IBM PC type machines use:

DSDD 48tpi discs

BBC type machines use:

DSDD 96tpi discs

To format a disc for your machine ensure you have your MS-DOS utilities either on your hard disc or on floppy disc in drive A: Type:

```
FORMAT d:
```

where d: is the drive to format (you cannot format only part of a disc).

When you see the message:

```
Place a blank disc in drive d: and press RETURN
```

Formatting irrevocably destroys any data already on a disc, so be careful!

While the discs are formatting, copy the label contents from your Ability discs onto blank labels. Remember you should never write on a label that is fixed to a disc unless it is absolutely necessary. If you do have to, use a fibre tip or other soft pen and be very gentle.

System Files

We mentioned putting a system disc into the machine when you switch the power on or press Ctrl-Alt-Del. You can make your own system discs by modifying the Format command:

```
FORMAT d: /S
```

This formats a floppy disc and puts MS-DOS onto it. You can then add whatever programs or files you wish to the disc. You will have slightly less storage space than on non-system discs.

Making Backups

Before using any program disc, you must make a backup. The ways to do this will be described in detail later in the chapter, for now we need to establish a pattern for disc backups to protect vital information. The relationship grandfather, father, son is often used to illustrate this process.

The disc you are using is called the work disc. After you have finished for the day, back up the disc onto a new one. The new one becomes the son, and the one that generated it the father. This goes in your fire safe. At the end of the next day you generate a new son disc. The other two discs move up a generation and the new father disc goes into the fire safe. The grandfather disc goes home with you. In this way, whatever the disaster, the most you can lose is two days work.

It is probably not worth doing this for letters but vital for accounts, contracts and the like.

REN

If you wish to change the name of a file all you need to do is to type:

```
REN filename newname
```

Where `filename` and `newname` are the old and new names respectively.

DIR

You can always find out what is on a disc by typing:

```
DIR
```

This gives you the a listing similar to this:

```
Volume in drive C is HARDDISK
Directory of C:\MSDOSUTL
CRC       COM     2689     5-02-88    24:07
COMPARE   COM     1793     5-02-88    24:13
CHKDSK    EXE     9680    31-03-87    02:04
COMP      EXE    14560    31-03-87    02:05
4 File(s)     39804992 bytes free
```

Volume is simply a label you give the disc, you can use the

```
LABEL d:name
```

command to do this, in this instance

```
LABEL C:HARDDISK
```

The listing is in five columns, reading from the left they are:

```
Filename, Extension, Length, Date Written, Time
Written
```

You can read the directory from any drive or directory:

```
DIR d:\directory
```

If you want to copy a directory or any other screened text to a file, use the pointer > to point to the destination.

```
DIR d:\directory >LIST.TEM
```

copies the directory listing to a file called LIST.TEM

Wildcards

MS-DOS lets you use two wildcards in filenames:

*	replaces one or more characters
?	replaces just one character

eg,   `DIR *.COM`

Displays all files with the extension COM.

DEL

If you wish to permanently delete a file, use:

```
DEL d:filename
```

You may use wildcards in filenames.

```
DEL *.*
```

removes all files from the currently logged directory.

COPY

You may need to copy files from disc to disc, or directory to directory.

```
COPY d:filename d:{filename}
```

The filename in brackets may be omitted if the filenames are the same. Wildcards may be used.

DISKCOPY

DISKCOPY is used to make a copy of floppy discs. It can be used for making backups. Whilst it is faster than using COPY *.*, it does copy any errors or bad sectors from disc to disc.

When you use discs, MS-DOS allocates space in the best way it can. You might find that a file gets spread over several non-contiguous areas of the disc, ie, the file is not necessarily stored in consecutive sectors on the disc. This causes the reading and writing mechanism to move around to find the bits of file, and hence slows down disc operations.

COPY *.* writes each file back in a contiguous format. DISKCOPY copies the organisation of the original disc.

To use DISKCOPY, ensure that the utility DISKCOPY.EXE is on the current directory and type:

```
DISKCOPY d: d:
```

Where d: indicates drive letters. If you diskcopy from one drive to the same drive you will be prompted to insert the source and target discs.

If necessary, DISKCOPY will format target discs.

Function Keys

Three function keys are used in editing commands:

F1   Copy a letter from the last command to the corresponding position in a new command.

F2   Does nothing until you type a character that is in the last command. All characters in the last command up to, but not including, the typed character are entered in a new command.

F3   Copy the whole of the last command to a new command.

Two other keys are used for editing command lines:

DEL   Delete NEXT character in the command line.

INS   Insert character at this point.

B : Installing Ability

Before installing Ability, format the necessary number of blank discs and label them with the names of the Ability original discs. Put the originals in a safe place.

Hard Disc

To install Ability on a hard disc, first set up a directory for Ability. You can, if you wish, use the root directory but it is good practice to restrict this to system files, batch files and directories. To create a directory, boot the computer to get the C> prompt. Now type after the C> prompt:

```
C>MD ABILITY
C>CD ABILITY
```

Don't forget to press RETURN after each entry.

We have now created and logged onto the new directory, so put the Ability System disc into drive A: and type:

```
C>COPY A:*.* C:\ABILITY
```

When the copying is complete, put disc 2 in drive A: and press:

```
F3 RETURN
```

to repeat the operation. Continue until all the discs have been copied. Now we can get rid of our CONFIG.SYS file which we won't need.

```
C>DEL CONFIG.SYS
C>CD\
```

We are now back in the root directory. We need to set the machine up for Ability. Use EDLIN, RPED or any other text editor to modify the CONFIG.SYS file. If you prefer, you can type directly into a file by typing:

```
C>COPY CON: CONFIG.SYS
```

Whichever way you choose, you should finish with a file like this:

```
files=12
```

```
buffers=20
country=044
stacks=20,128
```

If you use COPY remember to finish with a CTRL-Z.

The stacks line is only really necessary for Amstrad Computers.

The next thing we need to do is to create a new AUTOEXEC.BAT file. You should not attempt to make a new file: just add a few lines.

```
ECHO OFF
PATH C:\;C:\MSDOS;C:\ABILITY
prompt $p $g
KEYBUK
GRAFTABL
DATE
TIME
```

If you are uncertain of the use of EDLIN or RPED, type a new file called ABILITY.BAT which includes the following lines. These are the first few lines, the rest of the file will be dealt with later, so type nothing yet!

```
ECHO OFF
PATH C:\;C:\MSDOS;C:\ABILITY
prompt $p $g
KEYBUK
GRAFTABL
```

A few points to note:

The Path command links three directories MSDOS, ABILITY and ROOT. I tend to keep linked items in separate directories, so most of my MS-DOS system disc programs are in a directory called MSDOS. You can ignore this part of the path command if you do not have this directory.

Ensure that you have KEYBUK.EXE and GRAFTABL.EXE on the current or a linked directory. (Mine are on \MSDOS.)

The prompt line is simply a way to help you find your way around the hard disc. Instead of the unhelpful C> prompt, the computer will now display the current directory followed by the prompt >.

Machines such as the Amstrad PC series, which have built in clocks, do not need the date and time commands. If you have such a machine, ignore those lines.

Finally, we need one more file on the root directory ABILITY.BAT. This file contains:

```
ECHO OFF
DISPLAY=CGA
cd \ABILITY
ABILITY
```

If you have a multistandard video system like that of the Amstrad PC1640, line two is needed to set CGA standard for Ability. If you have Ability Plus, you can replace this with a line reading:

```
DISPLAY=EGA
```

provided you have an EGA Monitor. This will give you an extra 18 lines per screen.

To start Ability from the Root directory simply type:

```
ABILITY
```

Floppy Disc

Installing Ability on a floppy disc is simply a matter of copying System disc 1 onto a blank disc that has been formatted with the /S option. Copy KEYBUK.EXE, GRAFTABL.EXE and AUTOEXEC.BAT onto the disc.

Now copy the rest of the discs onto blank, formatted discs without MS-DOS.

Modify the CONFIG.SYS file on the system disc to read thus:

```
files=12
buffers=20
country=044
stacks=20,128
```

Modify the AUTOEXEC.BAT file to include these lines:

```
ECHO OFF
```

```
KEYBUK
GRAFTABL
DISPLAY CGA
ABILITY
```

If you have a multistandard video system like that of the Amstrad PC1640, line four is needed to set CGA standard for Ability. If you have Ability Plus you can replace this with a line reading:

```
DISPLAY=EGA
```

provided you have an EGA Monitor. This will give you an extra 18 lines per screen.

The Ability Plus system disc is almost full. If you find you cannot fit all of the additional files on the copy disc, just copy the Ability files onto a non MS-DOS system disc. Format a new MS-DOS system disc then type in a new AUTOEXEC.BAT:

```
echo off
keybuk
graftabl
CLS
ECHO PLACE ABILITY SYSTEM DISC IN DRIVE A
PAUSE
```

To start Ability reboot the system with the Ability system disc or the new boot disc in drive A:.

C : Online Help Tips

Ability has an excellent help system. Unfortunately, if you are using a floppy disc based computer, it is a little cumbersome. To avoid the need to change discs when we need help we can employ a couple of useful tricks.

First make backup copies of all your Ability discs and put the originals somewhere safe. Label the backups and work on these only. Copy the System disc or System Disc 1 by formatting using the /S option to copy the system. Copy by putting the newly formatted disc in drive B (If you only have one drive put the disc to copy from in drive A: when you see the prompt to put the a disc in drive B:, remove the disc in A: and replace with the new disc). Type:

```
COPY A:*.* B:
```

If you get a message that there is not enough room, use:

```
DEL b:*.*
```

to clean up the disc. Proceed with:

```
COPY A:COMMAND.COM B:
COPY A:*.HLP B:
```

to get the relevant files onto the new BOOT disc. Format a new disc without using the S option and copy the system disc onto it by putting the new disc in B: and:

```
COPY A:*.* B:
```

Remove the unwanted help files by:

```
DEL B:*.hlp
```

and proceed as for option 2.

We will start with the assumption that the Ability system disc contains the MS-DOS system, so you can boot the computer from it, the Ability or Ability Plus system files from System disc 1, and approximately 20000 bytes of free space. If this applies to your machine carry on; if not you need to use an extra BOOT disc as described in option 2.

Your machine must have 512k of user RAM or more. If you have less RAM, you cannot use this method without upgrading.

RAMDRIVE.SYS

Finally, you must have three files called RAMDRIVE.SYS or perhaps RAMDISK.SYS, KEYBUK.EXE and GRAFTABL.EXE available. If you have RAMDISK.SYS, simply type this where you see RAMDRIVE.SYS.

The first step is to copy RAMDRIVE.SYS KEYBUK.EXE and GRAFTABL.EXE from your MS-DOS disc to the Ability boot disc.

CONFIG.SYS

Use RPED or EDLIN to produce a new version of CONFIG.SYS. If you prefer, you can use:

```
COPY CON: CONFIG.SYS
```

and type it in at the keyboard. In this case you have to finish with a CTRL-Z.

There are different files for Ability and Ability Plus:

[A]

```
files=12
device=ramdrive.sys 66
buffers=20
country=044
stacks=20,128
```

[A+]

```
files=12
device=ramdrive.sys 80
buffers=20
country=044
stacks=20,128
```

Notice that the only difference is in the size of the RAMDRIVE parameter. This reflects the difference in ABILITY.HLP help files.

When you boot the Ability disc, this sets up a new logical disc drive in memory. This will hold the help files.

AUTOEXEC.BAT

The AUTOEXEC.BAT program is run when you boot the system. Use the same technique that you did for writing the CONFIG.SYS file to create it, containing:

```
echo off
keybuk
graftabl
copy a:*.hlp c:
path C:\;A:
ability
```

Option 2

Format a new MS-DOS system disc or use the BOOT disc prepared above. Copy ABILITY.HLP from your Ability System disc to the new disc and delete it from your system disc. Carry out all the instructions from the heading RAMDRIVE.SYS to the heading AUTOEXEC.BAT then type in a new AUTOEXEC.BAT:

```
echo off
keybuk
graftabl
copy a:*.hlp c:
path C:\;A:
CLS
ECHO PLACE ABILITY SYSTEM DISC IN DRIVE A
PAUSE
```

Help will now be read from the Ramdisk.

D : Customising Ability

Ability positively invites you to customise it to suit your own temperament. You can change the screen colours, set up a printer, a modem or a plotter. Modem set-up has already been dealt with in the Chapter on COMMUNICATE, so in this appendix we will concentrate on printers, plotters and the screen.

To set up Ability screen colours, printer or plotter first press F2 commands and select OTHER followed by DEVICES. You should now see the screen in Figure D.1

[A+]
If you are using Ability Plus the 'OTHER' command has been replaced by the 'ABILITY' command.

```
                    Printer, Plotter and Screen Color
                    --------------------------------

   Printer [None    ]    Printer Port        [LPT1]   Printer Flow Control [XON/XOFF
                         Printer Baud Rate   [1200]
                         Page Width          [8.5 ]
                         Page Depth          [11  ]

   Plotter [None    ]    Plotter Port        [COM1]   Plotter Flow Control [XON/XOFF]
                         Plotter Baud Rate   [9600]

   Country [UK      ]

   Normal Screen color [Green    ]

   "Flip" Screen color [Cyan     ]

         Screen mode   [Text     ]


      View or change printer, plotter or screen color       95% Free

   F1 - Help
                                                         F10 - Done
```

Figure D.1. The Ability Devices Screen

Printer Type

There are unfortunately no standard commands for driving printers, although many of the popular makes are compatible with each other. In order for Ability to make the printer do clever things, like underlining, boldfacing and printing sideways, it has to know what commands the printer uses for these functions. These commands are stored in a Printer Driver. Ability has a number of these. All you have to do is select the right one. The same is true of plotters, and Ability also has a store of plotter drivers from which you can select.

Point the cursor at the `Printer` box and press return or the left-hand mouse button until your printer is shown. If your own printer is not in the list, try `DIABLO_630` for a daisywheel printer, and `EPSON_MX` or `IBM_STD` for a dot-matrix printer. If these don't work, you may have to use the `GENERIC` printers. These have severe limitations, however, so only use this if you have to.

If your printer always generates a line feed with a carriage return use `GENERIC 1` or `GENERIC 2` if you don't want all your document to appear on one line!

If your printer can `BACKSPACE` choose `GENERIC 2` or `GENERIC 4`.

If your printer is an unlisted dot-matrix type you can experiment with the effects of other drivers. If you have a daisywheel printer driver that works, stick to it. If you have a laser printer that doesn't appear in the list, buy Ability Plus!

Printer Port

This is where your computer expects to find the printer. If your printer has a 'Centronics' parallel interface you should select `LPT1`. If it has a serial interface choose `COM1` or `COM2` (if fitted). If you use a `COM` port ensure that your printer's protocols are set up for eight bits, no parity, one stop bit.

Printer Flow Control

Your computer can send information to the printer far faster than it can possibly be printed. Some means must be provided to ensure that the computer only sends data when the printer needs it, if we are to avoid losing data. This process is called flow control. Flow control is sometimes effected by special signal connections between computer and printer, known as hardware flow control. Alternatively, special characters may be passed between the two machines along the data lines in order to effect flow control. This is software flow control. ETX/ACK and XON/XOFF are the two most common software protocols.

Select the flow control you wish to use by pointing the cursor at the `Flow Control` box and pressing `RETURN` until the appropriate control is seen. Use `NONE` if your printer is a parallel type or has hardware flow control. The flow control methods available on your printer will be shown in the printer handbook.

Printer Baud Rate

Basically, the higher the baud rate, the faster data will be transferred to the printer. If you have a printer buffer, either built into the printer or as a separate interface, try 9600 baud. Make sure both your printer and Ability are set to the same baud rate. The Printer's baud rate and protocol selections are usually made by dip switches. If you need to change any of these, remember to switch the printer off first as the printer usually only reads the dip switch settings when you turn it on. Turning printers off and immediately on again to re-read the dip switches is a sure recipe for large repair bills!

Page Size

The next two entries define the size of the printer page. Point the cursor at the appropriate box and type in the size of paper you are using. Standard continuous paper is 11 inches per page.

Plotter

If you have a graphics plotter, set it up in exactly the same way as a printer, but use the plotter boxes to select the correct driver and protocols.

Country

Point the cursor at the COUNTRY box and press RETURN or left hand mouse button until the appropriate country is shown.

[A+]
On some versions of Ability Plus the COUNTRY selection has been moved to a separate menu.

Screen Colours

Set both 'Normal' and 'Flip' screen colours by pointing the cursor at the appropriate box and selecting the appropriate colour with the RETURN key or left-hand mouse button. Don't worry if at this stage the screen is still white on black, all you need to do is to select the GRAPHIC screen mode to get colour.

[A]

If you are using an EGA screen with 350 lines, you may not get colour with Ability. In this case, either select TEXT mode and work with white on black or set the monitor to CGA mode using the command applicable to your machine.

If you are using an Amstrad PC1640, the following command could be inserted immediately after 'ECHO OFF' in the ABILITY.BAT file:

```
DISPLAY CGA
```

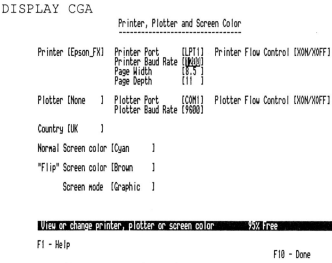

Figure D.2. Completed Devices screen

Leaving the Devices screen

Pressing F10 will save all the changes you have made and will return you to the Library screen.

E : Advanced Installation for Ability+

Ability Plus users have a separate configuration program called `DEVICES.EXE`. This can be used to extend the installation to printers and plotters which are not listed in the standard `Devices` screen. Unfortunately, in order to use it you have to have some knowledge of your printer or plotters control codes. You will find these in the device manual.

Bytes and Bits

This is a good point to introduce some new technical terms. We will need them to carry out the installation.

A byte is a character. All characters are stored inside the computer or on disc as a hexadecimal number which translate to decimal values of 0 to 255. These 256 possible numbers (0 is a number!) can be expressed as 2 to the power 8, or 2^8 or:

$$2 \times 2 \times 2 \times 2 \times 2 \times 2 \times 2 \times 2$$

The word byte is actually contraction of 'BY EIGHT'. The highest number possible is 255 or:

$$2^7 + 2^6 + 2^5 + 2^4 + 2^3 + 2^2 + 2^1 + 2^0$$

Inside a computer or printer, the value of each power of 2 is carried as an on-off signal on separate wires which are arranged in groups of eight (bus is another word for a group of associated wires). So to represent the number 11, wires 0,1 and 3 would carry an on signal (or a 1 signal as it is often called) all the others carry an off or 0:

$$11 = (1 \times 2^3) + (1 \times 2^1) + (1 \times 2^0) = 8 + 2 + 1$$

We can represent the signal wires with ones and zeros:

value	0 0 0 0 1 0 1 1
wire number (bit)	7 6 5 4 3 2 1 0

Each digit is called a Binary Digit as it can only have two values 0 and 1. Binary Digit has been shortened to BIT. The most significant bit is on the left and in a byte is equal to 128 (2^7) if on.

Hexadecimal and Octal

It is a little inconvenient to think and work in lumps of 256. Computer people, being basically lazy, like us lesser mortals, soon found ways to make things easier.

The only reason for the difficulty is that we count in tens. We happen to have ten fingers, so we have ten numbers, 0-9. When we need the number nine plus one we have one 'full set' of numbers and no remainder. We call this 10. Let's forget our thumbs now we only have eight digits. We are now only using the numbers 0-7 so eight becomes 10 octal (one full set of numbers and none over) and 256 becomes 400 octal. A much easier number to work with!

If we allow 16 numbers, 256 becomes 100 hexadecimal: this is even easier as each byte can be represented by two digits only and the number of bytes are represented by the most significant digits. We have one problem: we lack any digits for the numbers ten to fifteen. We can either invent some or we can use some alphabetical letters. As the latter was the easiest course, the letters A-F were chosen to represent the higher hexadecimal digits.

A programmer's note here: if we use hexadecimal, two digits define one byte. One digit defines a number in the range 0 - 15, which is a four bit number. A four bit number is half a byte and is called a nybble (honest!).

It is fairly easy to remember 16 bit patterns, so by using hexadecimal any quantity can be speedily converted into bit patterns in the programmer's head.

The following table shows the relationship between Hex, Decimal, Binary, and ASCII for the first few ASCII Codes:

Decimal	Symbol	Binary	Hex	Octal
0	NUL	00000000	00	000
1	SOH	00000001	01	001
2	STX	00000010	02	002
3	ETX	00000011	03	003
4	EOT	00000100	04	004
5	ENQ	00000101	05	005
6	ACK	00000110	06	006
7	BEL	00000111	07	007
8	BS	00001000	08	010
9	HT	00001001	09	011
10	LF	00001010	0A	012
11	VT	00001011	0B	013
12	FF	00001100	0C	014
13	CR	00001101	0D	015
14	SO	00001110	0E	016
15	SI	00001111	0F	017
16	DLE	00010000	10	020

N.B Protocol codes   Codes 3 and 4 are used for ETX/ACK
Code 17, DC1, is used for XON
Code 19, DC3, is used for XOFF

Table E.1. Codes with Equivalents

Appendix K contains a complete ASCII Table.

DRIVERS.EXE
[A+]
To use this program either type from DOS or select from the Library screen:

    DRIVERS

You should see the following menu:

```
Öáááááááááááááááááááááááááááááááááááááááááááááááááááááááááááááááááááááááááááñ
   ·                    Printer\Plotter Drivers Version 2.0                    ¤
   ·                                                                           ¤
   · PRINTERS        PLOTTERS       PRINTER FILES  PLOTTER FILES  LIBRARY FILES ¤
   · <<New>>         <<New>>        <<New>>        <<New>>          <<New>>     ¤
   · ADCP2000        HP2PEN                                       COUNTRY.XAB   ¤
   · AN9625B         HP6PEN                                       DRIVERS.XAB   ¤
   · BRO_HR15        SWEETP                                                     ¤
   · BRO_HR25                                                                   ¤
   · CI_8510                                                                    ¤
   · CI_F10                                                                     ¤
   · DIABL630                                                                   ¤
   · EPSON_FX                                                                   ¤
   · EPSON_LQ                                                                   ¤
   · EPSON_MX                                                                   ¤
   · EPSON_RX                                                                   ¤
   · FUDL2400                                                                   ¤
   · GEMINI10                                                                   ¤
   · GENERIC1                                                                   ¤
   · GENERIC2                                                                   ¤
   · GENERIC3                                                                   ¤
   áëëëëëëëëëëëëëëëëëëëëëëëëëëëëëëëëëëëëëëëëëëëëëëëëëëëëëëëëëëëëëëëëëëëëëëëëëëëëëëë¥
    Point to a file name and press Enter

    Current library: drivers.xab                         F10-Done
```

Figure E.1. The Drivers Menu

There are two ways of installing a new printer driver: either by making a completely new driver or by modifying an existing one. The first option is used in the unlikely event that you cannot find a printer driver to work with your printer. The second option is used when your particular printer fails to work in the way you want on only some functions.

If you choose the first option, point the cursor at the New area under Printers and press RETURN. You will be asked for the name of the printer. After entering the name, you will see the Printer Text Parameters Menu:

Printer Text Parameters Menu

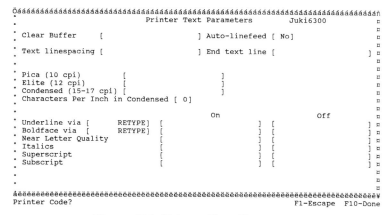

Figure E.2. Printer Text Parameters

We will fill this in for the Juki 6300, (an unlisted printer). To do this, we need the printer manual in which you will find a list of 'Escape Codes'. Escape is a character sent to the printer to indicate that the following characters form a command to execute a function. We will look at this menu in detail. Enter characters by pressing keys or typing decimal numbers preceded by a hash (#) and followed by RETURN. A useful tip is that the CTRL key will cause a letter key to enter a number equal to its position in the alphabet. CTRL-@=0 CTRL-A=1 etc.

Clear Buffer
This just means reset the printer. The Juki requires ESC SUB I, in English (27)(26)"I". We enter this by pressing ESCAPE, CTRL-Z, I

Auto Linefeed
Set this to NO

Text Linespacing
The code needed to set linefeeds to 1/6 inch. Usually (ESC) (30) (9)

End Text Line
Usually (13)(10) Carriage return, Line feed.

Pica
Set the Horizontal Motion Index to 1/10 inch.

Elite
Set the Horizontal Motion Index to 1/12 inch.

Condensed
Set the Horizontal Motion Index to 1/15 inch.

CPI in Condensed
15 in the case of the Juki 6300.

The next two sections ask whether you underline or boldface by:

- a carriage return and RETYPING the appropriate text.

- BACKSPACING and retyping the character.

- issuing CONTROL CODES

The Juki uses control codes for both these functions.

This completes the Text Handling menu.

```
Öáááááááááááááááááááááááááááááááááááááááááááááááááááááááááááááááááááááááááááááááñ
                        Printer Text Parameters          Juki6300          ¤
                                                                           ¤
  Clear Buffer      [(ESC)(26)I         ] Auto-linefeed [ No]              ¤
                                                                           ¤
  Text linespacing [(ESC)(30)(9)        ] End text line [(13)(10)       ]  ¤
                                                                           ¤
  Pica (10 cpi)           [(ESC)(31)(13)      ]                            ¤
  Elite (12 cpi)          [(ESC)(31)(11)      ]                            ¤
  Condensed (15-17 cpi)  [(ESC)(31)(9)        ]                            ¤
  Characters Per Inch in Condensed [15]                                    ¤
                                                                           ¤
                                  On                    Off                ¤
  Underline via [   CTRL-CODE]  [(ESC)E           ]  [(ESC)R         ]  ¤
  Boldface via  [   CTRL-CODE]  [(ESC)W           ]  [(ESC)&         ]  ¤
  Near Letter Quality          [                 ]  [               ]  ¤
  Italics                      [                 ]  [               ]  ¤
  Superscript                  [(ESC)D           ]  [(ESC)U         ]  ¤
  Subscript                    [(ESC)U           ]  [(ESC)D         ]  ¤
                                                                           ¤
                                                                           ¤
àëëëëëëëëëëëëëëëëëëëëëëëëëëëëëëëëëëëëëëëëëëëëëëëëëëëëëëëëëëëëëëëëëëëëëëëëëëëëëëëëëëë¥
Press the Enter key to change the field                   F1-Escape  F10-Done
```

Figure E.3. Completed Text Parameter Menu

Graphics Parameter Menu
Press F10 to get to the Graphics Menu.

```
Öáááááááááááááááááááááááááááááááááááááááááááááááááááááááááááááááááááñ
  ·                        Printer Graphics Parameters     Juki6300          ¤
  ·                                                                          ¤
  · Dots Per Print Head Pass    [1]          Ordering of bits      [M]       ¤
  ·                                                                          ¤
  · Horizontal Dots Per Inch   [ 60]         Vertical Dots Per Inch [ 48]    ¤
  ·                                                                          ¤
  · Graph Linespacing [(ESC)(30)(2)             ]                           ¤
  ·                                                                          ¤
  ·                      Start                        End                    ¤
  · Graph              [                   ]    [                   ]        ¤
  ·                                                                          ¤
  · Graph Line       [(ESC)(31)(3)         ]    [(13)(10)           ]        ¤
  ·                                                                          ¤
  · Byte Count in Start Graphics Line [ No]   Graphic Control Character [  0] ¤
  · Number of bytes in Byte Count      [2]                                   ¤
  · Byte Count byte order              [L]                                   ¤
  ·                                                                          ¤
  ·                                                                          ¤
  ·                                                                          ¤
  ·                                                                          ¤
  ·                                                                          ¤
áëëëëëëëëëëëëëëëëëëëëëëëëëëëëëëëëëëëëëëëëëëëëëëëëëëëëëëëëëëëëëëëëëëëëëë¥
Dots Per Print Head Pass?                            F1-Escape  F10-Done
```

Figure E.4. Completed Graphics Parameters Menu

Dots per Head Pass
The number of dots that can be vertically printed for each head pass.

Ordering of Bits
M indicates that the most significant bit of each byte is at the top of the column of dots.

L indicates that the most significant bit of each byte is at the bottom of the column of dots.

H indicates that the most significant bit is printed on the left.

R indicates that the most significant bit is printed on the right.

Vertical DPI
The number of vertical dots in an inch

Graph Linespacing
Set equal to the 'height' of one dot: in our example 1/48 inch.

Graph Line Start
The code required to put printer into graphics mode for one line.

Graph Line End
The code required to put printer out of graphics mode.

Byte count
Some printers need a count of the number of graphics bytes to be printed. This box is either Yes or No.

Number of bytes in byte count

This is usually 2. If your printer requires an ASCII string then enter 0.

(See printer graphics information).

Byte count byte order

Normally L (low) byte first.

When you have finished filling this menu press F10 to get to the next menu.

Character translation

```
Öáááááááááááááááááááááááááááááááááááááááááááááááááááááááááááááááááááááááááñ
.                    Printer Character Translations    Juki6300           ¤
.                                                                          ¤
.   []->[#        .      ]  [ ]->[        ]  [ ]->[        ]  [ ]->[      ] ¤
.   [^]->[(ESC)Y    ]  [ ]->[        ]  [ ]->[        ]  [ ]->[      ] ¤
.   [|]->[(ESC)Z    ]  [ ]->[        ]  [ ]->[        ]  [ ]->[      ] ¤
.   [ ]->[          ]  [ ]->[        ]  [ ]->[        ]  [ ]->[      ] ¤
.   [ ]->[          ]  [ ]->[        ]  [ ]->[        ]  [ ]->[      ] ¤
.   [ ]->[          ]  [ ]->[        ]  [ ]->[        ]  [ ]->[      ] ¤
.   [ ]->[          ]  [ ]->[        ]  [ ]->[        ]  [ ]->[      ] ¤
.   [ ]->[          ]  [ ]->[        ]  [ ]->[        ]  [ ]->[      ] ¤
.   [ ]->[          ]  [ ]->[        ]  [ ]->[        ]  [ ]->[      ] ¤
.   [ ]->[          ]  [ ]->[        ]  [ ]->[        ]  [ ]->[      ] ¤
.   [ ]->[          ]  [ ]->[        ]  [ ]->[        ]  [ ]->[      ] ¤
.   [ ]->[          ]  [ ]->[        ]  [ ]->[        ]  [ ]->[      ] ¤
.   [ ]->[          ]  [ ]->[        ]  [ ]->[        ]  [ ]->[      ] ¤
.   [ ]->[          ]  [ ]->[        ]  [ ]->[        ]  [ ]->[      ] ¤
.   [ ]->[          ]  [ ]->[        ]  [ ]->[        ]  [ ]->[      ] ¤
.   [ ]->[          ]  [ ]->[        ]  [ ]->[        ]  [ ]->[      ] ¤
.   [ ]->[          ]  [ ]->[        ]  [ ]->[        ]  [ ]->[      ] ¤
äëëëëëëëëëëëëëëëëëëëëëëëëëëëëëëëëëëëëëëëëëëëëëëëëëëëëëëëëëëëëëëëëëëëëëëëëëëëëÑ
Translated into?                          PgDn-More  F1-Escape  F10-Done
```

Figure E.5. Character Translation Menu

This is your chance to set up your printer to match the keyboard characters. In particular you will want to translate the hash sign to the pound sign. To do this all you need to is to insert the keyboard character in the first of a pair of boxes. In the other box type the characters the printer needs to print what you want. On the Juki 6300 the hash sign prints as a pound on English daisywheels, so fill in the screen as shown in the illustration. Many daisywheels have two additional characters called 'Phantom Space' and 'Phantom Rubout': these are often useful and can be accessed on the Juki 6300 by using ESC Y and ESC Z. You can of course assign any keyboard character to these. In the illustration I have assigned two little used characters ^ and | to these.

Editing a Printer Driver

That completes installation of a new printer driver. If you want to modify an existing printer driver simply point the cursor at a file name and press RETURN. Then select Copy, either from the menu to make a copy of the driver at the bottom of the printers column or EXTRACT to make a copy of the driver as a new printer file. Whichever method you choose you can then point the cursor at the new file, press RETURN then select TEXT from the menu and use the mouse or cursor keys to scroll through the parameters changing them as you require. This process can be repeated for the GRAPHICS and XLATE (translate), options by pressing F10 followed by RETURN and selecting the menu option you need.

After installing a new printer driver, you should test it by selecting the driver from the Devices screen and printing the file PRNTEST from the WRITE Menu.

Installing a Plotter

Plotter installation is very similar to printer installation. From the devices screen, select a plotter driver to modify or select NEW for a new driver. Select the Setup function from the Plotter menu.

```
Öáááááááááááááááááááááááááááááááááááááááááááááááááááááááááááááááááááñ
                        Plotter Parameters       HP2PEN            ¤
                                                                  ¤
  Number of pens   [     2]              First pen      [    49]  ¤
                                                                  ¤
                    Minimum    Maximum                            ¤
  X-coordinate     [     0]   [ 32767]  Order of coordinates  [ (X,Y)]  ¤
  Y-coordinate     [     0]   [ 32767]                         ¤
                                                                  ¤
  Character Height [   525]             Lower Left X-coordinate [    0]  ¤
  Character Width  [  1400]             Lower Left Y-coordinate [  -400]  ¤
                                                                  ¤
  Initialize plot  [       IN;SC0,32767,0,32767;\033.N;19:\033.I81;;17:]  ¤
  Terminate plot   [                           SP;PU0,32767;]  ¤
  Select pen       [                             PU;SP%c;]  ¤
  Draw to (x, y)   [                             PD%d,%d;]  ¤
  Move to (x, y)   [                             PU%d,%d;]  ¤
  Italics on       [                               SL0.5;]  ¤
  Italics off      [                                 SL0;]  ¤
  Normal text      [                   SI0.14,0.27;LB%s\003;]  ¤
  Large text       [                   SI0.28,0.54;LB%s\003;]  ¤
  Huge text        [                   SI0.56,1.08;LB%s\003;]  ¤
                                                                  ¤
àëëëëëëëëëëëëëëëëëëëëëëëëëëëëëëëëëëëëëëëëëëëëëëëëëëëëëëëëëëëëëëëëëëëë¥
Number of pens?                               F1-Escape   F10-Done
```

Figure E.6. Plotter Parameter Table

In general you should type characters into the appropriate box exactly as needed. If you need to use an unprintable code such as ESCAPE, enter a backslash (\) followed by the ASCII value in OCTAL.

- If a text string is needed, use %s

- If a decimal number is to be sent, use %d

- If a single number is to be sent, use %c

Most of the field boxes are quite straightforward: the information you need will be in the plotter's manual.

Number of Pens
The number of pens

First Pen
This requires the value that must be sent to identify the first pen. Be aware that "1" may mean ASCII 1 or 49 decimal.

X-coordinate
The maximum and minimum values of the 'horizontal' or X coordinate.

Y-coordinate
The maximum and minimum values of the 'vertical'.

Order of coordinates
Either X before Y or vice-versa.

Character Height
The height of a character in plotter units.

Character Width
The width of a character in plotter units.

Lower Left X Lower Left Y
Plotters define a character position in one of two ways. The position is either the bottom left or the centre of the character. These two entries define the offset from the entered position to the lower left corner of the character.

Initialisation plot

This is the string used to reset the plotter. The pen(s) are positioned and paper loaded.

Terminate plot
The string needed to unload the paper and park the pen(s).

Select Pen
The string needed to select a particular pen.

Draw to (x, y)
String to draw to x,y.

Move to (x, y)
String to move pen to x,y without drawing.

Italics on
String to turn italics on.

Italics off
String to turn italics off.

Normal text
String to select 'normal' size text.

Large text
String to select text twice 'normal' size.

Huge text
String to select text four times 'normal' size.

Once you have finished with the plotter installation press F10 to exit.

When you have completed the installation of a new plotter driver, test it by selecting the driver at the Devices menu and plotting the PRTEST GRAPH. You should try different colours to ensure all pens are activated correctly.

Library Installation [A+]

Version 1.0 of Ability Plus has a separate installation screen for the Library. This is available by typing:

```
F2-AL
```

The `Library` installation screen allows you to change the title that appears at the top of the `Ability Plus Library` screen. This can be edited using F4 in the usual way or overtyped.

The next three lines on the screen deal with importing and exporting files from the main applications. In all cases, Ability Plus automatically defines the format of the file it is going to import and changes it to the appropriate Ability format, so you need do nothing to the format. Ability can cope with the following file types:

```
             Library Screen and Country Settings

  ============================================================

  Library Screen Title [((((     Ability Plus v1.0    ))))      ]

  Database import    [Automatic ]   Database export   [Comma-Sep ]
  Write import       [Automatic ]   Write export      [ASCII     ]
  Spreadsheet import [Automatic ]   Spreadsheet export [1-2-3 v1A ]

  Country Setting    [UK        ]   Long date format  [20 December 1987  ]
  Numeric punctuation [1,234,567.89]  Short date format [dd-mm-yy ]
  Argument separator [,]            Date deliniters   [-] [-]

  Currency symbol    [£  ][Leading ]  4th user symbol  [cm ][Trailing]
  1st user symbol    [$  ][Leading ]  5th user symbol  [m  ][Trailing]
  2nd user symbol    [DM ][Leading ]  6th user symbol  [lbs][Trailing]
  3rd user symbol    [FF ][Leading ]  7th user symbol  [kg ][Trailing]

  ============================================================
  View or change Library Screen settings          42% Free
  Enter :
  F1 - Help
                F4 - Edit Field                    F10 - Done
```

Figure E.7. Library Installation Screen

ASCII files (including Wordstar non-document files)
PeachTree document files
Multimate document files
Lotus 1-2-3 (v.1A) WKS files
dBASEII, dBASEIII and dBASEIII PLUS .DBF files
Enable database files
PFS data and form files

Ability Plus unfortunately cannot read minds, so you have to specify what type of file you wish to export to. If your software is not listed, try `ASCII` for documents and `Comma-sep` for databases, as your software may be able to translate these formats.

Ability Database files may be translated into the following formats:

Comma-sep

dBASE II
dBASE III

Simply move the cursor to the format box and press RETURN until the appropriate format is shown.

Ability WRITE files may be translated into the following formats:

ASCII
PeachText
Multimate

As before, move the cursor to the format box and press RETURN until the appropriate format is shown.

Ability SPREADSHEET files may only be translated into Lotus 1-2-3 version 1A files.

The next line is the country setting: by placing the cursor over the COUNTRY box you can select:

UK
USA
GERMANY
FRANCE
HOLLAND

This affects things like the money format.

The following field deals with number punctuation for decimal points and thousands. Select the correct one using the RETURN key. The ARGUMENT SEPARATOR field is set automatically.

There are three date format fields. These set the format of the long and short dates and the date delimiters. Once again, select the field and press RETURN until the required option is displayed.

You can select the currency symbol you wish to use in financial calculations and then select leading or trailing presentation.

The remaining 14 fields are for you to install the user symbols. You simply type the symbol in and then move the cursor right and select whether it is to be a leading or a trailing symbol. Use RETURN for this.

When you have finished with the installation, press F10 to return to the Library screen.

F : WRITE Functions

WRITE is a very versatile wordprocessing system, with a large number of features and functions. This appendix contains a reference list of these functions. Further details are in the text.

Block operations

Use F7 and the cursor keys to shade the text for copy, delete, move, print enhancements, linespace etc.

Boilerplate paragraphs

Use F5 Pick-up to move blocks of text from one document to another using F9 to Flip between the two.

[A+]
The two documents may be on screen at the same time.

Use Load F2-FL to include whole documents in your text.

Boldface

Use to emphasise shaded text:

    F2-TB

Bottom Margin

[A+]
Set the white space margin at the bottom of the page in lines. One line is 1/6 inch:

[A+]
    F2-WMB

Centring

Centre the line the cursor is on:

[A]   F2-C
[A+]   F2-AC

Copying

Press:

    F5

to Pick-up shaded text. Move the cursor to where the copy is to be placed then press:

    F6

This technique can be used in conjunction with Flip:

    F9

to copy text between documents.

Cursor

The cursor points to the position in which the next typed character is to be placed. It can be moved with the nine 'number' keys on the right hand keypad and with TAB and RETURN.

Date

Can be included in headers and footers either from the menu in the following formats:

-American	M/D/Y (eg, 4/27/88)
-European	D-M-Y (eg, 27-4-88)
-Metric	Y-M-D (eg, 88-4-27)
-Long	eg, April 27, 1988

or by including the appropriate code in text.

Month

#mm	Month shown as a two digit number
#mmm	Month shown as a three letter abbreviation, eg, Apr
#mmmm	Month spelt out it full eg, April

Day

#dd	Day shown as a two digit number

| #ddd | Day shown as a three letter abbreviation, eg, Fri |
| #dddd | Day spelt out it full eg, Friday |

Year

| #yy | Year shown as a two digit number eg, 88 |
| #yyyy | Year in full eg, 1988. |

Day and Date:
| #dddd | #dd |

Delete

| DEL | delete the character under the cursor |
| DEL LEFT | delete the character to the left of the cursor |

If you have shaded a block DEL will delete the shaded block.

Find Page

To find a page press:

    F3-P

and enter the page number required.

Find

Find a pattern of characters in the document.

To find a pattern:

    F3-FS

and type in the pattern which may contain wildcards followed by RETURN. Press N to search forward and P to search backwards.

Flip

Switch between two screens or windows:

    F9

Footers

[A]   F2-OPF

[A+] F2-WF

Delete either by selecting text and pressing RETURN to give an empty entry or, if you have Ability Plus, using the Remove option on the Footer menu.

Headers

[A]   F2-OPH

[A+] F2-WH

Delete either by selecting text and pressing RETURN to give an empty entry or, if you have Ability Plus, using the Remove option on the Header menu.

Importing

Data can be imported using Load for ASCII files or copying or moving text from Write files via F9.

Spreadsheet data can be imported using:

[A]   F2-S

[A+] F2-IS

Database data is imported by using the Mail-merge facility.

Indent

Position the cursor to the point where you want the indenting to start. Ability indents to the next carriage return in the text.

[A]   F2-I

[A+] F2-AI

Inserting

Press Ins key with cursor at the place you want the insert to start. Any cursor movement key or a second press of Ins will end inserting and close up text.

Italics

Use to italicise shaded text:

```
F2-TI
```

Justifying
Set ragged or straight right margin:

[A]   `F2-OPJ`

[A+] `F2-AJ`

Left margin
Set the white space margin on the left of the page in character widths:

[A]   `F2-OPL`

[A+] `F2-WML`

Linespace
[A+]

Set the spacing of lines of shaded text. Text may be spaced at 6, 3 or 2 lines per inch (Single, double or triple spacing):

[A+] `F2-AL`

Load
Include other documents in your text

```
F2-FL
```

Mail-merge
Include Database fields in your text so that the text can be obtained from a database file. This enables you to mail form-letters to several people automatically.

[A]   `F2-F`

[A+] `F2-IF`

Margins

Set dimension and position of text on a page. See Left and Right Margins, Top and Bottom margins and Page Length.

[A]   F2-OP

[A+]   F2-W

Moving

Shade the block of text you wish to move and press:

    DEL

This will delete the shaded block.

Move the cursor to the new site for the block and press:

    F6

to undelete the block in its new position. This technique can be used in conjunction with flip:

    F9

to move text between documents.

Overtype

This is the normal mode for Write. Text typed will overwrite text already present.

Page breaks

Use the cursor movement keys to move to a new page when required or if the automatic page break is in the wrong place.

[A+]   F2-AB

Page length

Set the number of lines of text printed on a page and hence the white space margin at the top and bottom of the page in lines. One line is 1/6 inch:

[A]   `F2-OPP`

[A+] `F2-WMP`

Page number

Page numbers may be automatically included in `Footers` and `Headers` either from the Page-number menu in a defined format:

```
-Alone      4
-Hyphens   -4-
-Page   Page 4
```

or you can define your own page number format from the text menu by including:

```
#pp
```

in the text at the appropriate point.

Print Options

Options are to `Print` on paper or to a file. Printing to a file produces an ASCII file.

[A]   `F2-OP`

[A+] `F2-P`

Printing

From the print option menu a number of options can be obtained. Select G for Go when you are ready to print.

Remove Print Enhancements

Use to remove all typestyle changes from shaded text.

```
F2-TP
```

Replacing

Search for a pattern of characters in the document and, when found, replace with a new pattern. To search for a pattern:

```
F3-FR
```

and type in the pattern which may contain wildcards followed by
RETURN. When the pattern is found, select:

F   To replace this occurrence only
S   To miss this occurrence and go on to the next. [A]
N   To miss this occurrence and go on to the next. [A+]
R   Change this and all other occurrences after this

Reshading
Reshade the last block

```
F7-F7
```

Right margin
Set the white space margin on the right of the page in character
widths:

[A]   F2-OPR

[A+] F2-WMR

Save
Save a document to a file

```
F2-FS
```

[A+]

A shaded block may be saved to a File

```
F2-FB
```

Search
Search for a pattern of characters in the document. To search for a
pattern:

```
F3-FS
```

and type in the pattern which may contain wildcards followed by
RETURN. Press N to search forward and P to search backwards.

To find a page press:

```
F3-P
```

and enter the page number required.

Shading

Use F7 and the cursor keys to shade the text for copy, delete, move, print enhancements, linespace etc.

Spelling
[A+]

Check the spelling of each word in a document against the built in dictionary. Move the cursor to the beginning of the area you wish to check:

[A+] F2-SC

Superscript
[A+]

Print shaded text above the line, eg, X^2

```
F2-TR
```

Subscript
[A+]

Print shaded text below the line, eg, H_2O

```
F2-TR
```

Tabs

Use TAB to move to the next Tab stop or SHIFT-TAB to move to the previous one.

[A+]

Decimal Tabs will shift typed numbers left until a decimal point is typed. This enables columns of figures to be easily aligned.

Set Tabs using the Tab Ruler and the C,D,E and S keys.

      C   Clears all Tabs

      E   Erases the tab at the cursor

      S   Set one Tab

[A+] D   Set Decimal Tab

To set up Tabs:

[A]   F2-OPT

[A+]   F2-WT

Top Margin
[A+]

Set the white space margin at the top of the page in lines (1 line = 1/6 inch):

Typefaces
Set various print enhancements via the typefaces menu:

Undelete
Press:

      F6   to undelete.

Underlining
Use to emphasise shaded text:

      F2-TS   to underline words and spaces

      F2-TW   to underline words only

Wildcards
Use in search operations

      *   replaces any number of characters

      ?   replaces a single character only

Windows

[A+]

Select two files using the flip command:

    F9

then press:

    F2-WW

Select from the following:

H   for a horizontal split between windows
V   for a vertical split between windows
S   Synchronise windows
U   Unsynchronise windows
C   Clear windows (return to one window)

Use the cursor keys after V or H to define the window size and press RETURN.

G : Database Facilities

A brief review of the facilities available in DATABASE.

Add

The add forms screen is available after pressing F10 from the master form screen, or by pressing:

[A]   F2-A

[A+]   F2-DA

Backup

Back-up a database and remove any deleted forms:

[A]   F2-OB

[A+]   F2-FB

Brackets

Brackets are used to change the order in which formulae are calculated.

Browse

The Browse screen is the centre point of the DATABASE. Browse allows you to sort or search the database, amend fields, and delete forms.

Built-in Functions

Ability has a range of built-in Functions. See Chapter 12 for details.

Calculated fields

Calculated fields contain formulae. The formulae are calculated and the result displayed. Formulae start with either + or -, eg,

```
+3-acct
```

Change master form

Master forms can only be amended by writing a new database containing all the old information in a new file.

[A]   F2-C

[A+]   F2-DC

Commands

F2 displays the Commands menu

Consolidate

Produce a summary report containing totals of numeric fields.

F2-S

to enter the Sort screen. Add c to the sort number.

Dates

Dates are calculated as the number of days since 31st December 1899. They can be displayed as dates in long or short format.

Deleting

In Browse press Del to delete a whole form.

In other screens:

F2-C

Edit field

Retype when in Browse or master form. Type F4 to move a field entry to the edit line.

Errors

Ability has a number of error expressions when fields will not calculate. There are seven error messages.

Error   Explanation

<N/A>   Either the formula refers to a field that doesn't exist or it attempts to use a label field in a calculation.

<CIRC>   The formula contains a circular reference - that is, it refers to its own value. Circular references usually occur when a formula refers to a field that in turn refers to the field in which you enter the formula. Only one of these two fields shows <CIRC>. Normally, circular references are created accidentally but you can use them to solve certain types of problems that involve iterative calculations.

<FUNC>   The formula contains an error in the built-in function. For example, the built in function may have:
- Too many or too few arguments, eg, DATE (May, 1985)
- Incorrect arguments, eg, DATE (1984, OCT10)
- Invalid arguments, eg, SQRT (-1)
- Improper use of exponentiation, eg, 1^.5
- Illegal date codes which you try to format, eg, -1

<DIV 0>   The formula attempts to divide by zero.

<ERROR>   The formula refers to a field that previously contained a value or formula but the field has changed to a range, or a list, making the formula invalid.

OVER   The formula calculates a number that is too large or too small for Ability. This results in an overflow or underflow. The largest number possible is approximately 1×10^{308}.

UNDER   The formula calculates a number that is too large or too small for Ability to handle, resulting in an overflow or underflow. The smallest possible number is approximately 1×10^{-308}

Exporting

[A+]

In Library, move cursor to file to export and press:

    F5

to Pick-up file. Move cursor to Files column and press:

    F6

to Put-down the file on any available Directory or Drive. Set export file type using `Library Settings` screen.

Field identifiers

Plain text entered on master form to identify field contents.

Field names

Field names can be up to 13 characters long. The first three must be letters or underscores. Spaces must not be used in fieldnames. Names should be selected to indicate the field contents.

Fields

A field is a space of defined length that contains data. Data may be numbers, text or formulae.

File

A database of forms is stored in a file.

Form

A complete set of fields is a form.

Forms

Search for a form by number:

```
F3-F
```

Hash

[A+]

A hash signifies a relationship between two databases as the start of a relational expression.

Importing

[A+]

In `Library`, move cursor to file to import and press:

```
F5
```

to `Pick-up` file. Move cursor to Database column and press:

    F6

to `Put-down` and translate the file.

Joined master form

It is possible to join two databases to make a third containing information from both.

[A]   `F2-C` and select name then;
       `F2-J` and name database to join to

[A+]   `F2-DC` and select name then;
       `F2-J` and name database to join to

Select join field

A joined Master form is produced which may be edited to produce the new database.

Join field

A Field common to both databases that you wish to join. Joins will occur where fields contain identical information.

Link expression

The contents of a field in one database that points to a field in a second conditionally joined database. Entered as:

    +FILENAME\FIELDNAME

Logical Functions

There are two logical functions available:

IF(x,true,false)

The IF function calculates x and evaluates it. If x is true (not zero), the true value is displayed. If x is false (zero), the false value is displayed.

ISERR(list)

The ISERR function checks the list and counts the number of fields that contain error messages. The list can be field addresses, ranges or field names. To check the entire spreadsheet for errors, enter list as the range of fields in the whole spreadsheet.

You can combine the IF function and the ISERR function to check for errors and return an error message if something is incorrect.

Logical Operators

Logical operators can be used in searches for information in Ability files or in the IF function. The logical operators are listed in their natural order of evaluation. If you combine either AND or OR with relational operators in an expression Ability evaluates the relational operators before evaluation the AND or OR.

```
OPERATOR       LOGIC          TRUE IF         EXAMPLE

&              AND            A AND B         A=B AND A=C
|              OR             A OR B          A=B OR A=C
~              NOT            A NOT B         A <> B
```

Mail-merge

A merger of fields from a database with a document created using WRITE. This is a rapid way of sending form-letters or addressing envelopes.

Make-subset

A subset is a part of a larger database selected by criteria similar to those used in the search function.

```
F2-M
```

Master form

The blank form that is used to design and position fields for the completed database. Select a new database from the Library screen or use the Change option from F2 Commands menu.

Mathematical Operators

The following mathematical operators are used in formulae which are built into fields. The operators are listed in their order of priority from the highest (calculated first) to lowest (calculated last). You can use brackets to control the order of calculation and to group information.

Operator	Meaning
-	Negation/Change Sign. Changes the sign of a number, for example -A9 or -INCOME.
%	Percent. The percent sign divides the value to its left by 100. For example, 5% is the same as 0.05.
^	Exponentiation. The exponentiation sign (called a caret) raises the number to its left to the power on its right. For example: 3^2 is 3^2 or 9
*	Multiplication
/	Division N.B. * and / have equal priority.
+	Addition
-	Subtraction N.B. + and - have equal priority

Money format

A defined format for fields containing numbers. The Money field adds a currency symbol and allows two decimal places.

Moving around

Use the normal cursor movement keys.

Pick-up

Pick-up a file.

    F5

Print

Print a form, or a report. Ability often displays the print menu when necessary. Otherwise press:

    F2-P

Put-down

Put-down a picked up file.

    F6

Records

A completed form is a record.

Recover

Ability keeps a copy of deleted forms. To recover a form:

    [A]   F2-OR

    [A+]   F2-FR

Use search or PgUp and PgDn to find form then press INS.

Relational expression

[A+]

Relates a field in one database to the field in another. Used as a fieldname of the form:

    #Filename\fieldname

The hash # indicates it is a relational expression.

Relational Operators

You can search for forms where the value in a numerical field is not precisely known. To do this you use relational operators.

Operator	Meaning
<	Less than
>	Greater than
=	Equal to
<=	Less than or equal to (or, not greater than)
>=	Greater than or equal to (or, not less than)
<>	Not equal to
~=	Not equal to

Report

A printed or screen report of the information in a database. You can print the report as a series of forms or as a Summary report. You may also merge fields with a document created using WRITE to produce a mail-merge. This is a rapid way of sending form-letters or addressing envelopes.

    F2-R

Report grouping

Adding a b after the sort number in a Summary report field will present the report grouped into sets which contain identical information in that field. Adding a t to any numerical field then produces a total of all the figures in the field for all records displayed on the report. A sub total is also generated for each group.

    F2-RS

Search

Search for form by search criteria:

    F3-S

and enter the search criteria followed by F10.

Sort

Sort the database by fields. A blank Master form is displayed and numbers entered into fields. Sort priority is given by the value of the number.

    F2-S

Sorted file

After setting the sort criteria press F10 and enter a filename to which the sort file will be saved. The sort file is not a complete database: it only contains pointers to the main database.

    F2-S

Subsets

A subset is a part of a larger database selected by criteria similar to those used in the search function.

```
F2-M
```

Summary

A summary report shows data in columns. You can select fields and add column headings, groupings and totals.

```
F2-RS
```

produces a master form copy which can be used to select the names and order of fields in the report in the same way as Sort. The sort number can be followed by a comma and the text for a heading. A backslash inserts a new line in the heading.

Summary totals

Adding a t after the sort number will total the values of fields in a column of numeric fields. Adding a b to the sort number in a field groups the report into sets with the same contents in that field.

Typestyle

The typestyle command allows you to select underline, italics or boldface etc. for a field or field identifier.

Validate

Validate allows you to update the calculations throughout the whole database. F8 updates the calculations on the current form

Virtual joining

[A+]

Use a relational expression to link and relate fields from one database to another without creating a third database.

Wildcards

Wildcards can be used where you wish to use only partial information to search or make subsets. For example, MI* would find MIKE, MINE and MIND etc.

     *   Replace any characters

     ?   Replace any one character

Write subset

The subset you select can be saved by using the Write command.

[A]   F2-W

[A+]   F2-FW

H : Spreadsheet Facilities

There are two rules to remember when compiling a spreadsheet:

1. Keep it simple
2. Plan it thoroughly

If the spreadsheet becomes large, consider splitting it into several small sheets and using two way links.

Cursor Keys

The following keys are used for moving around the spreadsheet:

`Arrow keys`
　　　　One cell in appropriate direction
`Ctrl-End` To the last column in the last row that contains information.
`Ctrl-Home` To cell A1.
`Ctrl-PgDn` To the last cell in the current column that contains information.
`Ctrl-PgUp` To the first cell in the current column.
`End` To the last column, in the current row, that contains data.
`Home` To the first cell in the current row.
`PgUp` To the top of the screen if the cursor is not at the top of the screen already. If it is, then scroll up 20 rows at a time.
`PgDn` To the bottom of the screen if the cursor is not at the bottom of the screen already. If it is, then scroll down 20 rows at a time.
`Shift-Tab` To the left one cell.
`Tab` To the right one field.

Function Keys

`F1` Context sensitive help
`F2` Commands Menu
`F3` Search and Goto a cell

```
F4    Edit cell contents
F5    Pick-up cell contents as text
F6    Put down cell contents as text
F7    Mark area for subsequent operation
F8    Recalculate spreadsheet
F9    Flip screen
F10   Save and exit
```

Absolute addresses

When moving or copying cells, all addresses in the moved cell are changed unless they are declared absolute addresses. Use $ to indicate an absolute column or row address:

```
A1    Non-absolute address.
A$1   Absolute column, non-absolute row.
A1$   Non-absolute column, absolute row.
A$1$  Absolute address
```

Adjust

To adjust the position of a spreadsheet in WRITE, point to any field in the spreadsheet and press F2, select Adjust and move the spreadsheet to the desired position using the horizontal arrow keys.

```
F2-A
```

Blank

You can blank any single or range of cells. To blank a range use F7 to shade the appropriate cells.

[A]   F2-B

[A+] F2-RE

Brackets

Brackets are used to change the order in which formulae are calculated.

Built-in Functions

Ability has a range of Built-in Functions. See Chapter 12 for details.

Calculated cells

Calculated cells contain formulae. The formulae are calculated and the result displayed. Formulae start with either + or -, eg,

```
+3-sales
```

Cells

Spreadsheet fields are often called cells. A cell may contain:

> A numerical value
> A formula
> A label

Columns

Cells are arranged in Rows and Columns. Ability columns are 'numbered' A to ZZ.

Commas

Commas are only used as list separators: they must not be used when entering numbers.

Copying

To copy a range Shade it using F7 then press F2 and select Copy. Use the cursor keys and/or F7 to define where the copy is to be placed. All non-absolute addresses are amended by copying.

```
F2-C
```

Dates

Dates are calculated as the number of days since 31st December 1899. They can be displayed as dates in long or short format.

Editing a Cell

Press F4 to edit the cell under the cursor.

Errors

Ability has a seven error expressions which appear when cells will not calculate.

Error	Explanation
<N/A>	Either the formula refers to a field that doesn't exist or it attempts to use a label field in a calculation.
<CIRC>	The formula contains a circular reference - that is, it refers to its own value. Circular references usually occur when a formula refers to a field that in turn refers to the field in which you enter the formula. Only one of these two fields shows <CIRC>. Normally, circular references are created accidentally but you can use them to solve certain types of problems that involve iterative calculations.
<FUNC>	The formula contains an error in the built-in function. For example, the built in function may have: - Too many or too few arguments, eg, DATE(May, 1985) - Incorrect arguments, eg, DATE(1984,OCT10) - Invalid arguments, eg, SQRT(-1) - Improper use of exponentiation, eg, 1^.5 - Illegal date codes which you try to format, eg, -1
<DIV 0>	The formula attempts to divide by zero.
<ERROR>	The formula refers to a field that previously contained a value or formula but the field has changed to a range, or a list, making the formula invalid.
OVER	The formula calculates a number that is too large or too small for Ability. This results in an overflow or underflow. The largest number possible is approximately 1×10^{308}.
UNDER	The formula calculates a number that is too large or too small for Ability to handle, resulting in an overflow or underflow. The smallest possible number is approximately 1×10^{-308}

Exporting

Files can be exported to Lotus 1-2-3, using F5 and F6 from the Library screen.

[A+]

In Library move cursor to file to export and press:

    F5

to Pick-up file. Move cursor to Files column and press:

    F6

to Put-down the file on any available Directory or Drive. Set export file type using Library Settings screen.

Field names

Field names can be up to 13 characters long. The first three must be letters or underscores. Spaces must not be used in fieldnames. Names should be selected to indicate the field contents.

Formulae

The formula is at the heart of a spreadsheet. Ability formulae can contain any mixture of:

Values
Arithmetic operators
Ranges
Numerical data
Cell addresses
Built-in functions

Forward references

If a cell refers to the contents of a cell with higher row and column addresses, it is said to be forward referenced. The information in the forward cell will be used before it is updated. Ability copes well with forward references but it is good practice to update twice before printing the spreadsheet.

Freezing Titles

Freezing Titles allows you to display horizontal and vertical information permanently on screen. In this way your column and row titles can remain visible wherever you are in the spreadsheet. Move the cursor to a position immediately below the last row you wish to freeze and immediately right of the last column to freeze.

```
F2-TF
```

Insert

Insert a row or column. Move the cursor to the place at which the insert is to be made and press:

[A]   F2-I

[A+]   F2-SI

then select row or column

Importing

[A+]

In Library move cursor to file to import and press:

```
F5
```

to Pick-up Lotus 1-2-3 file. Move cursor to Spreadsheet column and press:

```
F6
```

to Put-down the file and translate it.

[A]

Use the WKS program to import Lotus 1-2-3 files.

Iteration

You can use a circular reference to calculate a result when a number of calculations are required, each refining the answer more. The F2 Recalculate option allows you to specify a set number of recalculations or to recalculate until the contents of a specified field becomes 0.

Label Formatting

Labels can be right, left or centre justified. A label is indicated by one of the following characters:

' Left Justify
"   Right Justify
^   Centre
*   Fill cell

A label starting with * will fill the cell with a row of the following character. This is a useful way of underlining.

Labels

Ability assumes that an entry is a label unless it starts with:

A number
A bracket
+
-

Linking

Two types of links can be set up:

A one way link simply reads the data from the referred cell:

+A6   Value of cell A6
+SHEET\A6   Value of cell A6 on spreadsheet SHEET

Changing data in the linked cell destroys the link.

Two way links allow data to be changed in either cell in the link:

!A6   Link to cell A6
!SHEET\A6   Link to cell A6 on spreadsheet SHEET

List

A list of items can be named or used in a built in function. Data items in a list are separated by commas.

eg,   `+A6,C7,I9,Q11..Q27`

Lock

You can lock cells to prevent overwriting using the `Lock` option from the `F2` menu. Shade the cells you wish to lock using `F7`.

[A]   F2-OLL

[A+] F2-RLL

Logical Functions

There are two logical functions available:

IF(x,true,false)

The IF function calculates x and evaluates it. If x is true (not zero), the true value is displayed. If x is false (zero), the false value is displayed.

ISERR(list)

The ISERR function checks the list and counts the number of fields that contain error messages. The list can be field addresses, ranges or field names. To check the entire spreadsheet for errors, enter list as the range of fields in the whole spreadsheet.

You can combine the IF function and the ISERR function to check for errors and return an error message if something is incorrect.

Logical Operators

Logical operators can be used in searches for information in Ability files or in the IF function. The logical operators are listed in their natural order of evaluation. If you combine either AND or OR with relational operators in an expression, Ability evaluates the relational operators before evaluation the AND or OR.

OPERATOR	LOGIC	TRUE IF	EXAMPLE
&	AND	A AND B	A=B AND A=C
|	OR	A OR B	A=B OR A=C
~	NOT	A NOT B	A <> B

Mathematical Operators

The following mathematical operators are used in formulae which are built into fields. The operators are listed in their order of priority from the highest (calculated first) to lowest (calculated last). You can use brackets to control the order of calculation and to group information.

Operator	Meaning
-	Negation/Change Sign. Changes the sign of a number, for example -A9 or -INCOME.
%	Percent. The percent sign divides the value to its left by 100. For example, 5% is the same as 0.05.
^	Exponentiation. The exponentiation sign (called a caret) raises the number to its left to the power on its right. For example: 3^2 is 3^2 or 9
*	Multiplication
/	Division N.B. * and / have equal priority.
+	Addition
-	Subtraction N.B. + and - have equal priority

Money format

A defined format for fields containing numbers. The Money field adds a currency symbol and allows two decimal places.

```
F4-FM
```

Moving

To move a cell or range of cells shade if necessary using F7. Press F2 and select Move. Point cursor at new location.

```
F2-M
```

Naming Cells

A cell can be named by using F4 Name or by entering the name as part of the formula:

```
FRED=+A6/C6
```

Naming Ranges

A contiguous range of cells can be named by moving to a cell outside the spreadsheet and entering:

```
FRED=+A6..Z6
```

A non contiguous set of cells can be named in much the same way using a list:

```
FRED=+A6..Z6,B10,C15,D25,E1..E15
```

You can use up to 250 characters in the formula.

Pointing

When entering data, you can use the cursor keys to point to the cell whose address you wish to use in a formula. If you type a +,(,),.,comma or number the cursor will return to the cell you are editing and the address of the cell you were pointing to is entered in the formula.

Print

Print a spreadsheet report. Press:

```
F2-P
```

Range Intersections

You can define the intersection of two named ranges using, for example:

```
FRED=JIM;BERT
```

Recalculation

Ability normally recalculates the spreadsheet every time a change is made. If the spreadsheet becomes large, the time taken for recalculation becomes significant. F2 recalculate allows you to select manual or automatic recalculation. You can also choose to recalculate a set number of times or until a specified cell is equal to 0.

Relational Operators

Ability allows three relational operators which may be used in formulae:

```
~     NOT   IF(A is NOT=B)
&     AND   IF(A=0 AND B=0)
|     OR    IF(A=0 OR B=0)
```

Removing

Columns and rows can be removed by positioning the cursor on the row or column and pressing:

[A]   F2-R

[A+]   F2-SD

Rows

Ability has 9999 horizontal rows in its spreadsheet. The row address is the second part of the cell address.

Search

Use F3 Search to find specified labels.

Wildcards * and ? can be used in the usual way.

Sort

You can sort by row or column. If you sort by column, rows are rearranged and vice-versa.

[A]   F2-OS

[A+]   F2-DS

Spreadsheet in DATABASE

DATABASE can use spreadsheet links in the usual way.

You can also put spreadsheets into a database provided that the database and spreadsheet have the same fields in the same order. Use F5 to Pick-up the spreadsheet cells and F6 to Put-down in the Browse screen.

Spreadsheet in Wordprocessing

You can transfer all or part of a spreadsheet into WRITE. Linked fields may also be used.

Part of a spreadsheet can be copied as text using F5 and F6.

Unfreeze

To unfreeze titles press CTRL-Home followed by F2-TF.

Unlock

You can unlock cells to allow overwriting using the Lock option from the F2 menu. Shade the cells you wish to unlock using F7.

[A]   F2-OLU

[A+]   F2-RLU

I : Graph Facilities

Key Summary

F2   The command key, gives a menu of facilities.

F4   The Edit Key. Use to edit the contents of a graph field.

F7   Shade two or more series in preparation for further action.

F8   Redraw the graph. Ability will normally automatically redraw a graph each time a change is made. Some graphs, pie charts especially, take a long time to draw. In this case select Manual redraw and press F8 to redraw after making all the changes.

F10 Save and exit Graph.

Bar Chart

A graph where the height of a bar is proportional to the value of an item in the series.

Blank

Delete a series from the Graph:

[A]   F2-B

[A+]   F2-GE

Ability plus substitutes Erase for Blank.

Colours

Spelt in the American form, colors, by Ability. This option allows you to specify the colour of various areas of the graph.

    F2-HC

Database

You can only graph database data by exporting it to a spreadsheet first.

Design

Use the design option to select the way you want your graph to look on screen and on paper.

```
F2-D
```

Editing

F4 allows you to edit a series. Titles must be retyped.

Explode Wedge

Draw one or more wedges of a pie chart 'pulled out' from the pie.

```
F2-DE
```

Fill Patterns

Select a fill pattern for the shaded series.

```
F2-DF
```

Hard Copy

Print or Plot the graph; a menu of choices is presented:

```
F2-H
```

Labels

The Labels field can be filled by a list or series. It provides a label or series of labels along the X-Axis identifying the point, bar or wedge.

Line Graph

All the values in the series are plotted as points. Lines are drawn between these points.

Links

A series may comprise a link to one or more named ranges or lists in a spreadsheet. The link must take the form:

```
+SHEET\range
```

where SHEET is the filename of the spreadsheet and range is the named range.

Pie Chart

A graph based on a circle. Segments are drawn whose areas are proportional to the value of the corresponding item in the series.

Plotting

Output the graph to an X-Y plotter.

Point-Marks

All points on the graph are invisible but may be surrounded by a marker to show their position. The `Point-Marks` option allows you to specify these markers.

Printing

Print the graph on paper using a printer. You cannot print graphs on a daisy-wheel printer: use a dot-matrix machine.

```
F2-HP
```

Quadrant

When plotting a graph you can choose to draw the graph over the whole page or just in one of the four corners, or quadrants, of the paper.

```
F2-HQ
```

Redrawing

Use F8 to redraw the graph at any time. If you wish not to redraw the graph automatically, use the redraw option.

[A]   `F2-R`

[A+]   `F2-GR`

Rotate

The graph can be drawn upright or on its side (rotated). Select using the Rotate option.

```
F2-DR
```

Series

A series is a list of values that will be used to draw the graph. It may be a simple list or a spreadsheet range or list. Ability allows up to seven series on one graph.

Sideways Print

Instead of the usual printing orientation, the graph is printed sideways on the paper. This results in a larger graph on most printers.

    F2-HPS

Stacked Bar Chart

A bar chart for two or more series. In this case, the bar chart for each item in a series is drawn on the bar for the corresponding item in the previous series. A useful graph for comparing proportions.

Styles

The Styles option allows you to choose the style for the graph you wish to draw. Choices are:

[A]   Line, Bar, Stacked bar, Pie

[A+]   Line, Bar, Stacked bar, Pie, X-Y

The X-Y option can be used to produce non-linear scales.

    F2-S

Titles

The Titles option allows you to produce a large main title for the graph, a smaller subtitle and titles for both X and Y axes.

[A]   F2-T

[A+]   F2-GT

Wait

If you have a single pen plotter you can still produce multi-colour graphs. The Wait option causes the plotter to pause for you to change pens.

```
F2-HW
```

X-Axis

The horizontal axis of the graph. Ability Plus allows you to choose a scale for this if you wish.

X-Y

A type of graph in which the contents of one series are plotted against the contents of another. Useful if you need non-linear scales or to determine a trend from regularly fluctuating data.

Y-axis

The vertical axis of a graph. The scale of this axis may be changed by the user.

J : Communicate Facilities

A brief review of the facilities in COMMUNICATE:

Function Keys

F1	Help
F2	Commands
F4	Edit on Terminal and Port Fields only
F9	Flip
F10	Done

Answer

Set up the modem to answer the telephone.

    F2-MA

Automatic log-on

Set up a log-on file using WRITE and put the filename in the Terminal screen:

    F2-T

Baud rate

The rate at which data is transferred between the computers. Set the baud rate on the `Port Settings` screen.

    F2-P

Break

Pressing `CTRL-Break` stops transmission and sends the break character to remote computer.

You can define the break character, and whether to send it, via the `Port Setting` screen.

    F2-P

Capture

You can save all or part of the communicate session by selecting `Capture` and defining a filename. Selecting `Capture` again stops the process. Further selections toggle the `Capture` function.

    F2-C

Character size

Either seven or eight bits. Select via the `Port Setting` screen.

    F2-P

Dialling

The dialling method can be selected for tone or pulse dialling. A telephone number can be sent automatically. Settings are via the `Terminal` screen.

    F2-T

Dumb Terminal

The Dumb Terminal is a very limited terminal used for some computer services.

    F2-T

Duplex

This defines how characters you type are echoed to the screen.

Full	Characters echoed back from remote computer
Half	Characters not echoed back from remote computer but taken from typed input.
Local	Characters typed on screen but not sent to remote computer

Set via `Port Settings` screen.

    F2-P

Electronic mail

Mail transmitted and retrieved solely by electronic means. The computer analogue of a telephone conversation.

Flow control

The way computers tell each other when to start and stop sending data. Choices are XMODEM, EIA and None. Set via `Port Settings` screen:

    F2-P

Line Wrap

Wrap characters at the end of line or overtype characters at end of line. Set via `Terminal` screen.

    F2-T

Linefeed

Set remote and local linefeeds. Linefeeds can be added when a return is issued or received. Set via `Port Settings` screen:

    F2-P

List

A file can be listed to the remote computer. If the file was not produced by WRITE, include the extension in the filename.

    F2-L

Modem

A MOdulator/DEModulator device for converting RS232 output to audible tones and vice versa. Tones can be transmitted over the normal telephone lines.

Null Modem

An RS232 cable with internal connections between pins 4,6 and 8 at each end and pins (2 and 3) and (5 and 20) cross connected.

Page mode

When the text reaches the bottom of the screen, clear it and start at the top left again. Set via the `Terminal` screen:

```
F2-T
```

Parity

A bit which is either 1 or 0 is added after each data word to check for transmission errors. The bit can make an odd or an even number of 1s, giving rise to odd or even parity.

Passwords

Passwords can be added for Transmit or Receive. If passwords are used, the local Transmit password must match the remote Receive password and vice versa.

```
F2-T
```

Pause

A pause can be injected into the auto-dial sequence by including a comma in the telephone number. Each comma injects a pause of 2 seconds.

```
F2-T
```

Phone Number

The Phone number for Autodialling can be included in the `Terminal` screen.

```
F2-T
```

Port Settings

The main communications port setting menu of COMMUNICATE.

```
F2-P
```

Prestel

An on line database run by British Telecom.

Receive

Using `Receive` you can copy files from the remote computer even if it is unattended. The files must be on the current directory and passwords, if set, must match.

    F2-R

Reverse Video

Dark text on light background colour.

    F2-T

Screen length

Normally 21 lines, but can be extended to 24 lines for services needing a larger screen. Screen length is set via the `Terminal Settings` screen.

    F2-T

Send

Using `Send` you can send files to a remote computer. The files must be on the current directory, and passwords, if set, must match.

    F2-S

Stop Bits

There can be one or two stop bits. The choice is set via the `Port Settings` screen.

    F2-P

Sysop

SYStem OPerator. One who operates a dial-up service.

Telecom Gold

A dial-up electronic mail system operated by British Telecom.

Telex

A text transmission service using special lines and exchanges coupled to teleprinters. Computers work much better in this application.

Timeout

Timeout is the delay between command lines in activating a login file. Timeout can be set by making the first line of the login file:

```
TIMEOUT n
```

where n is the timeout in seconds.

Trans Terminal

A test terminal that prints all received characters on the screen. This is only used for testing communications systems.

Transfer Protocol

The combination of stop bits, parity, baud rate and flow control that defines the way data is exchanged between computers.

```
F2-P
```

VT100 Terminal

An intelligent terminal selected via the `Terminal Settings` screen.

```
F2-T
```

VT52 Terminal

A semi-intelligent terminal selected via the `Terminal Settings` screen.

```
F2-T
```

Wait

Wait, when used in a login file, causes Ability to pause until a specified character or group of characters is received from the keyboard.

K : ASCII Table

ASCII is an acronym for 'American Standard Code for Information Interchange'. This is simply a standard where numbers between 0 and 127 (seven bit numbers) are used to represent all the characters on a keyboard. Thus, if a computing device receives the number 65 from another machine, it knows that this is a capital letter A. As we are dealing in bytes we have eight bits available so the numbers between 128 and 255 are often used for graphic shapes, italics etc. As far as the author is aware, there is no standard for these characters.

The following is an ASCII table for IBM type terminals.

The first 32 characters are the Control Characters. They are used for a number of functions by software and hardware. The names given reflect their usage on mainframe computers and teleprinters. Do not rely on their use to produce the results suggested by the code name. For example, ETX acts more like CAN in CP/M and MS-DOS, SUB is usually taken to mean the end of text and so on. DC1 and DC3 are sometimes called X-ON and X-OFF as they are used in some control protocols.

The control codes are:

0	NUL	No value character
1	SOH	Start of Heading
2	STX	Start of Text
3	ETX	End of Text
4	EOT	End of transmission
5	ENQ	Enquiry
6	ACK	Acknowledge
7	BEL	Bell
8	BS	BackSpace
9	HT	Horizontal TAB
10	LF	Line Feed
11	VT	Vertical TAB
12	FF	Form Feed
13	CR	Carriage Return

14	SO	Shift Out
15	SI	Shift In
16	DLE	Device Link Escape
17	DC1	Device Control one (X-ON)
18	DC2	Device Control two
19	DC3	Device Control three (X-OFF)
20	DC4	Device Control four
21	NAK	Negative Acknowledgement
22	SYN	Synchronous Idle
23	ETB	End of Transmission Block
24	CAN	Cancel
25	EM	End of Medium
26	SUB	Substitute
27	ESC	Escape
28	FS	File Separator
29	GS	Group Separator
30	RS	Record Separator
31	US	Unit Separator

The next set of characters are called the printable characters. You will recognise them:

32	<SPACE>	33	!	34	"	35	#
36	$	37	%	38	&	39	'
40	(	41	)	42	*	43	+
44	,	45	-	46	.	47	/
48	0	49	1	50	2	51	3
52	4	53	5	54	6	55	7
56	8	57	9	58	:	59	;
60	<	61	=	62	>	63	?
64	@	65	A	66	B	67	C
68	D	69	E	70	F	71	G
72	H	73	I	74	J	75	K
76	L	77	M	78	N	79	O
80	P	81	Q	82	R	83	S
84	T	85	U	86	V	87	W
88	X	89	Y	90	Z	91	[
92	\	93	]	94	^	95	_

96	£	97	a	98	b	99	c
100	d	101	e	102	f	103	g
104	h	105	i	106	j	107	k
108	l	109	m	110	n	111	o
112	p	113	q	114	r	115	s
116	t	117	u	118	v	119	w
120	x	121	y	122	z	123	{
124			125	}	126	~		

One more control character:

127   DEL   Delete character at cursor.

Characters between 128 and 255 vary somewhat. Look in your printer and computer manual for details applicable to your machine. You may see control codes represented in hexadecimal or in Binary as well as in Decimal. The following table should help:

Decimal	Symbol	Binary	Hex	Octal
0	NUL	00000000	00	000
1	SOH	00000001	01	001
2	STX	00000010	02	002
3	ETX	00000011	03	003
4	EOT	00000100	04	004
5	ENQ	00000101	05	005
6	ACK	00000110	06	006
7	BEL	00000111	07	007
8	BS	00001000	08	010
9	HT	00001001	09	011
10	LF	00001010	0A	012
11	VT	00001011	0B	013
12	FF	00001100	0C	014
13	CR	00001101	0D	015
14	SO	00001110	0E	016
15	SI	00001111	0F	017
16	DLE	00010000	10	020
17	DC1	00010001	11	021
18	DC2	00010010	12	022

19	DC3	00010011	13	023
20	DC4	00010100	14	024
21	NAK	00010101	15	025
22	SYN	00010110	16	026
23	ETB	00010111	17	027
24	CAN	00011000	18	030
25	EM	00011001	19	031
26	SUB	00011010	1A	032
27	ESC	00011011	1B	033
28	FS	00011100	1C	034
29	GS	00011101	1D	035
30	RS	00011110	1E	036
31	US	00011111	1F	037
32 - 126	Printable characters			
127	DEL	01111111	7F	177
255		11111111	FF	400

N.B Protocol codes

Codes 3 and 4 are used for ETX/ACK

Code 17, DC1, is used for X-ON

Code 19, DC3, is used for X-OFF

Table K.2. ASCII Codes with Equivalents

L : Other Dabs Press Products

Dabs Press publishes a wide range of books on computer topics. There follows a list of some of our recent and forthcoming titles.

If you are interested in any of these books, details of how to obtain them are given at the end of the list.

IBM PC Compatibles

BASIC on the PC: A Dabhand Guide by Geoff Cox

Price £16.95. Available NOW.

In this book, Geoff Cox provides a comprehensive tutorial and reference to the programming language provided free with most IBM-compatible machines. As well as a friendly and helpful tutorial in BASIC programming, the book contains a complete command reference, detailing every command in GW-BASIC with examples of its use. The book is also suitable for programming with Microsoft QuickBASIC and Borland TurboBASIC.

WordStar 1512: A Dabhand Guide by Bruce Smith

ISBN 1-870336-17-8. Price £14.95. Available NOW.

This is the most comprehensive tutorial and reference guide ever written about the WordStar 1512 and WordStar Express wordprocessors on the IBM/Amstrad PC and compatibles.

Both beginner and advanced user will find the book to be a valuable companion whether merely writing a simple letter or undertaking a thesis.

Amstrad PCW

The Amstrad PCW Series: A Dabhand Guide by F. John Atherton

ISBN 1-870336-50-X. Price £15.95. Available NOW.

The Amstrad PCW9512 personal computer word processor and its accompanying software, the LocoScript 2 system has revolutionised low-cost wordprocessing and introduced a whole generation of people to computer-based word processing for the first time.

In this easy-to-follow guide, John explains how to use the program starting from first principles, with no prior knowledge assumed, either of the Amstrad PCW system, the LocoScript program or even computers in general.

You are shown in practical detail how to set the system up to your own preferences and how to produce neatly laid out letters, reports, essays and so on.

Difficult subjects are not avoided: instead they are introduced in a painless and straightforward way. After you have read this book, you will without knowing it, become a perceptive and sagacious word processor user!

Acorn Archimedes

Archimedes First Steps: A Dabhand Guide by Anne Rooney

ISBN 1-870336-73-9. Price £9.95. Available NOW.

This book is the ideal starting point for first-time users of the Archimedes, taking you through the first few days and months of owning and using the machine.

There is an abundance of software provided with the Archimedes and Anne goes through the programs, telling you how to get them started and how to get the most out of them.

Budget DTP for the Acorn Archimedes & A3000: A Dabhand Guide by Roger Amos

ISBN 1-870336-11-1. Price £12.95. Available Now.

Every Archimedes and BBC A3000 owner receives copies of the !Draw, !Paint and !Edit software, along with the RISC OS operating software. This book shows how these applications can be used to produce high-quality documents without the need for an expensive desktop publishing package.

The book includes detailed descriptions of the various applications and helpful tips are given on how to get special effects such as drop shadows and pie charts. There are also sections on fonts, clip art and page layout as well as printers and reproduction of your finished work.

Archimedes Assembly Language: A Dabhand Guide by Mike Ginns

ISBN 1-870336-20-8. Price £14.95. Programs Disc £9.95. Available NOW.

Learn how to get the most from the remarkable Archimedes micro by programming directly in the machine's own language, ARM machine code. This is the only book that covers all aspects of machine code/assembler programming specifically for the entire Archimedes range.

Archimedes Operating System: A Dabhand Guide
by Alex & Nic Van Someren

ISBN 1-870336-48-8. Price £14.95. Programs disc £9.95 inc.VAT. Available NOW.

For Archimedes users who take their computing seriously, this guide to the Operating System gives you a real insight into the micro's inner workings. This book is applicable to any model of Archimedes.

The Relocatable Module system is one of the many areas covered. Its format is explained and the information necessary for you to write your own modules and applications is provided. This tutorial approach is a common theme running throughout the book.

BASIC V: A Dabhand MiniGuide by Mike Williams

ISBN 1-870336-75-5. Price £9.95. Available NOW.

This is a practical guide to programming in BASIC V on the Acorn Archimedes. Assuming a familiarity with the BBC BASIC language in general, it describes the many new commands offered by BASIC V, already acclaimed as one of the best and most structured versions of the language on any micro.

The book is illustrated with a wealth of easy-to-follow examples.

BBC Micro & Master
Master 512: A Dabhand Guide by Chris Snee

ISBN 1-870336-14-3. Price £9.95. Programs Disc £7.95 inc.VAT. Available NOW.

This is a comprehensive reference guide for all users of the Master 512, Acorn's PC-compatible add-on for the Master 128 and BBC Micros, and the companion Volume to this book.

Highly practical in approach, the book provides detailed information on all DOS Plus commands and explains how they differ from MS-DOS. It shows 'step-by-step' how to install and run PC applications on the Master 512, including useful techniques such as the creation of batch files.

Master 512: A Dabhand Technical Guide by Robin Burton

ISBN 1-870336-80-1. Price £14.95. Program Disc £7.95 inc. VAT. Available now

This second volume on the Acorn Master 512 covers the more technical issues associated with the system and provides useful information on technical utilities provided with the system, such as EDBIN, the binary file editor.

Also included in the book are some custom hardware expansion projects, including a design to allow an additional 512k of RAM to be added to the Master 512.

Master Operating System: A Dabhand Guide by David Atherton

ISBN 1-870336-01-1. 272pp. Price £12.95. Program Disc £7.95 inc. VAT. Available NOW.

Now in its second edition, this is the definitive reference work for programmers of the BBC Model B+, Master 128, and Master Compact computers. It also contains much material of interest to BBC Model B and Electron users.

Mini Office II: A Dabhand Guide by Bruce Smith and Robin Burton

ISBN 1-870336-55-0. Price £9.95. Program Disc £7.95 inc.VAT. Available NOW.

Bruce Smith and Robin Burton have joined forces to write this official tutorial and reference guide to the award-winning and revolutionary Mini Office II software. This book covers the BBC Micro and Master versions of the program.

VIEW: A Dabhand Guide by Bruce Smith

ISBN 1-870336-00-3. Price £12.95. Program Disc £7.95 inc.VAT. Available NOW.

Now in its second edition, this is the most comprehensive tutorial and reference guide ever written about the Acornsoft VIEW wordprocessor, for the BBC Micro, and issued as standard (but without a manual!) on the BBC Master 128 and Compact computers.

Commodore Amiga
AmigaBASIC : A Dabhand Guide by Paul Fellows

ISBN 1-870336-87-9. Price £15.95. Available NOW.

This book provides a fully structured tutorial to using AmigaBASIC on the Amiga500. Practical application is one of the many themes running through the pages and as such the many varied programs contained in its pages are both informative, in terms of programming technique, and useful.

The reader is assumed to have a base understanding of the way in which his or her Amiga works but no prior knowledge of BASIC itself.

AmigaDOS: A Dabhand Guide by Mark Burgess

ISBN 1-870336-47-X. Price £14.95. Available NOW.

This is a comprehensive guide to the Commodore Amiga and its disc operating system, covering releases 1.2 and 1.3 of AmigaDOS/ Workbench. It provides a unique perspective on this powerful system in a way which will be welcomed by the beginner and experienced user alike.

Psion Organiser
Psion Organiser LZ: A Dabhand Guide by Ian Sinclair

ISBN 1-870336-92-5. Price £14.95. Available NOW

In this exciting book, Ian Sinclair, the UK's premier computer author delves into the new LZ Organiser from Psion, explaining how to use the various utilities and the built-in programming language.

Ian Sinclair has written over a hundred books on computers and other technology-related subjects.

General

C: A Dabhand Guide by Mark Burgess

ISBN 1-870336-16-X. Price £14.95. Discs £7.95-£9.95 inc. VAT. Available NOW.

This is the most comprehensive introductory guide to C yet written, giving clear, comprehensive explanations of this important programming language.

The book is packed with example programs, making use of all C's facilities. Unique diagrams and illustrations help you visualise programs and to think in C.

Obtaining Dabs Press Books and Software

You can obtain Dabs Press books and software from any good bookshop or computer dealer, or in case of difficulty directly from us, post free.

Orders can be sent by post and payment can be made by cheque (drawn on a UK bank), postal order, credit card (quote number and expiry date) or official order (education/public sector/PLCs only).

Telephone or fax orders can be made with a credit card — this is the simplest and most popular method.

Our address, telephone number and fax number are on page 2 of this book.

Index